THE AMERICAN MIDDLE CLASS

The middle class is often viewed as the heart of American society, the key to the country's democracy and prosperity. Most Americans believe they belong to this group, and few politicians can hope to be elected without promising to serve the middle class. Yet today the American middle class is increasingly seen as under threat. In *The American Middle Class: A Cultural History*, Lawrence R. Samuel charts the rise and fall of this most definitive American population, from its triumphant emergence in the post-World War II years to the struggles of the present day.

Between the 1920s and the 1950s, powerful economic, social, and political factors worked together in the United States to forge what many historians consider to be the first genuine mass middle class in history. But from the cultural convulsions of the 1960s, to the 'stagflation' of the 1970s, to Reaganomics in the 1980s, this segment of the population has been under severe stress. Drawing on a rich array of voices from the past half-century, *The American Middle Class* explores how the middle class, and ideas about it, has changed over time, including the distinct story of the black middle class. Placing the current crisis of the middle class in historical perspective, Samuel shows how the roots of middle-class troubles reach back to the cultural upheaval of the 1960s.

The American Middle Class takes a long look at how the middle class has been winnowed away and reveals how, even in the face of this erosion, the image of the enduring middle class remains the heart and soul of the United States.

Lawrence R. Samuel is the founder of Culture Planning, LLC, a consulting company offering cultural insight to Fortune 500 companies. He holds a Ph.D. in American Studies from the University of Minnesota, and was a Smithsonian Institution Fellow.

THE AMERICAN MIDDLE CLASS

A Cultural History

Lawrence R. Samuel

Routledge
Taylor & Francis Group

NEW YORK AND LONDON

First published 2014
by Routledge
711 Third Avenue, New York, NY 10017

Simultaneously published in the UK
by Routledge
2 Park Square, Milton Park, Abingdon, Oxon OX14 4RN

Routledge is an imprint of the Taylor & Francis Group, an informa business

© 2014 Taylor & Francis

Library of Congress Cataloging in Publication Data
Samuel, Lawrence R.
The American middle class : a cultural history / Lawrence R. Samuel.
pages cm.
Includes bibliographical references and index.
1. Middle class--United States--History.
2. Middle class--Political activity--United States. 3. United States--Economic conditions--1945- 4. United States--Social conditions--1945- I. Title.
HT690.U6S26 2013
305.5'50973--dc23
2012049732

ISBN: 978-0-415-83186-4 (hbk)
ISBN: 978-0-415-83187-1 (pbk)
ISBN: 978-0-203-48166-0 (ebk)

Typeset in Bembo
by Taylor and Francis Books

Printed and bound in the United States of America by Publishers Graphics, LLC on sustainably sourced paper.

"Of the three classes, it is the middle that saves the country."

Euripides, c.420 B.C.

"The most valuable class in any community is the middle class."

Walt Whitman, 1858

CONTENTS

INTRODUCTION

At the end of World War II, when another generation of heroes returned home from combat, they built the strongest economy and middle class the world has ever known ... They understood they were part of something larger; that they were contributing to a story of success that every American had a chance to share—the basic American promise that if you worked hard, you could do well enough to raise a family, own a home, send your kids to college, and put a little away for retirement. The defining issue of our time is how to keep that promise alive. No challenge is more urgent. No debate is more important. We can either settle for a country where a shrinking number of people do really well, while a growing number of Americans barely get by. Or we can restore an economy where everyone gets a fair shot, everyone does their fair share, and everyone plays by the same set of rules. What's at stake are not Democratic values or Republican values, but American values. We have to reclaim them.

Excerpt from President Obama's 2012 State of the Union Address

It is not an exaggeration to say that most Americans, including the President of the United States, are thinking and talking a lot about the middle class these days. Indeed, the plight of the American middle class—its dwindling numbers and loss of economic, social, and political power—is in fact one of the biggest stories of our time and place, but few people know how and why we got here. *The American Middle Class* places the current crisis of the middle class in much needed historical perspective, adding valuable context to what is arguably the most important issue in the national conversation. Knowing the backstory is essential for anyone claiming to be fluent in areas ranging from contemporary affairs to politics to economics. Tracing the cultural history of the *idea* of the American middle class over the last half-century—its values, attitudes, and behavior, and role within society at a given time—also adds an important chapter to our understanding of the United States and its people, especially regarding the intersection between class and race.

A cultural history of the American middle class also plainly reveals that countless scholars, pundits, and journalists have weighed in on the subject over the decades, a fair reflection of its central role within the national discourse. Because the fate of the middle class carries such political weight in America, what these observers and advocates have said matters. Depending on how the "middle class" was defined, its fortunes were seen as rising or falling, the group seen as either unified or hopelessly divided. By focusing on rhetorical and ideological shifts in the arc of the American middle class rather than simply tracking relevant socio-economic developments, the main story becomes quite clear. A long view of the middle class reveals the long, painful slide of the group as the cultural tide began turning against it in the 1960s, a process showing few signs of reversing.

True to form, a cultural history of the American middle class leads us directly to important findings that challenge current thinking. The consensus among historians is that it was 1970s "stagflation" and 1980s "Reaganomics" that marked the dismantling of the American middle class, with tax policies favoring the rich creating a "haves" vs. "have nots" society. The plump economic mid-section became much skinnier in these decades, this thinking goes, as members of the middle class became either upwardly mobile (the "haves") or downwardly mobile ("the have nots"). While this indeed took place, the roots of the shrinkage of the American middle class can be located a decade earlier. The fragmentation of the middle class was part of the larger splintering of American culture that began in the 1960s, I argue, an important idea that makes us rethink the causes of what was perhaps the beginning of the end of our global dominance. More powerful forces than simply the economy and politics were thus instrumental in triggering this major shift, in other words, factors that other (usually partisan) writers have ignored.

Despite the centrality of the American middle class and its prominent role within the nation's history, defining the term and designating who belongs to the group (and who does not) is difficult, if not impossible. "Many scholars agree that the middle class for the last three centuries has been elusive to investigation and slippery to define," observed Burton J. Bledstein in his introduction to *The Middling Sorts: Explorations in the History of the American Middle Class*, with many possible criteria from which to choose when determining membership.[1] When it came to defining the middle class, "we have made little headway toward anatomical precision," conceded Peter N. Stearns in 1979, the very subject "fraught with ideological overtones."[2] Little progress has been made in recent decades. "Defining who is middle class is tricky," Bill Wolpin of *American City and County*, a magazine about state and local government, wrote in 2010, listing having a college education, health care, and a home as the three most relevant criteria.[3] "Searching for the American middle class is a little like looking for air," echoed Loren Baritz in his *The Good Life: The Meaning of Success for the American Middle*

Class, the group "everywhere, invisible, and taken for granted."[4] Determining membership in the black middle class has proved to be particularly difficult, with some even arguing that African Americans have had (and perhaps continue to have) a distinct class system separate from or parallel to the one dominated by whites.

Although challenging, any attempt to characterize the American middle class is worth the effort. "America's spirit and tone, its historical mythology and official aspirations, political bent, educational arrangements, the centrality of business enterprise, as well as the dreams of the vast majority of its people, derive from the psychology of the great imperial middle," Baritz proposed.[5] A good argument could be made that there is no bigger story in 20th century American history than the economic and social ascent of the middle class. "The chief historical event of the past century has been the expansion of the middle class," Nathan Keyfitz plainly put it in *Society* in 1992, the entry of people like clerks, assembly line workers, and even managers of fast food restaurants into the group nothing short of extraordinary.[6]

The evolution of the African American middle class is a particularly compelling story, its telling shedding new light on racial dynamics in this country and the role of class within the civil rights movement. The predicament of the black middle class is a topic not often enough discussed in general surveys and one that has considerable potential to move us toward a more comprehensive understanding of how class is lived in America. As badly as the current (post-2008) recession has impacted the general population, it has particularly devastated African American wealth accumulation, additional justification to more closely examine the history of the black middle class and assess historical debates regarding the group's upward mobility. The stories of the Latino and Asian American middle class are no less fascinating, of course, but deserve their full telling elsewhere. While perhaps also tempting to consider in detail other social categories such as region, ethnicity, gender, and religion, the American middle class is an all-too-rare opportunity to investigate how we as a people have been united instead of divided.

This study also adds to the ongoing conversation about the role of race relative to the origins of modern conservatism, especially in reference to the "Taxpayers' Revolt." Many historians are dating these beginnings further and further back, even all the way to the New Deal in the 1930s. In fact, a number of commentators like Thomas Sugrue in his *The Origins of the Urban Crisis* and Kevin M. Kruse in his *White Flight* have stridently contested the popular notion that a "backlash" against civil rights carried too far is what drove the conservative turn in the 1970s and 1980s.[7] To that extent, I am writing against the grain, although I am not focused on political change per se. Much of the recent and relevant literature has served to make visible the "hidden" privileges of the white middle class that were legislated into the New Deal welfare state, such as FHA-VA mortgage guarantees, the GI Bill, and mortgage interest deduction for tax purposes, which were not explicitly race-based but were administered in such a way that whites were able to take particular advantage while African Americans often were prevented from doing so. Even Social Security was unavailable to most African Americans before the 1950s due to its initial exclusion of agricultural and domestic workers, as Ira Katznelson pointed out in his *When Affirmative Action Was White*.[8] African Americans' civil rights gains arguably can be understood as implicitly calling into question such "hidden" white privileges, which surely contributed to a growing sense of white middle-class malaise.

To make it as simple as possible, I define those Americans within the middle third of net worth to be "middle class." Annual income has typically been the economic measure by which to define class in America, but I feel that net worth (the financial value of one's total assets less liabilities) is a truer criterion. It is tempting to use or include social status or the realization of certain achievements as the principal measure to define class but history has shown over and over that doing so means embarking on a slippery slope. Indeed, many definitions have been assigned to the American middle class over the years, illustrating the concept's "slipperiness" and the permeability of its boundaries. "It suggests earning enough to get by without struggling; being able to afford health care, college costs and the occasional trip to Disney World," suggested Brita Belli in 2007, taking a classic economics-based approach based on cultural markers.[9] Other, perfectly legitimate criteria have frequently been used to identify the American middle class, however. The middle class was "a body of wage earners who are able to find meaningful work and receive meaningful compensation to care for their families' physical and medical needs," suggested Frederick R. Strobel in his 1993 *Upward Dreams, Downward Mobility*, implying that belonging to the group involved more than just making a specified amount of money.[10] Much more subjective criteria can and have been used to define the American middle class, however. In his *Dollars and Dreams*, for example, economist Frank Levy wrote that being middle class relied upon "an emphasis on formal education, a preference for reasoning over physical violence, [and] an expectation of a stable career with a period of retirement," this more of a values-based model.[11] Marina Moskowitz has proposed that the middle class can be conceived as "a national community with a shared standard of living," an interesting, consumer-oriented approach to solving the problem.[12]

The difficulty in defining the middle class reflects Americans' discomfort with the idea of class in general. Even the U.S. Department of Commerce—an organization intimately familiar with facts and statistics—concluded that being middle class "is as much a state of mind and aspirations as it is a set of income levels" after conducting a study in 2008. The Department found that owning a car, having a retirement nest egg, and being able to take a family vacation were other common criteria among Americans.[13] Although it is in the business of classification, the federal government is hesitant to define the term "at least in part because class status is not a function merely of money or of other easily counted characteristics," Teresa Sullivan, Elizabeth Warren, and Jay Lawrence explained in their *The Fragile Middle Class*.[14] The Annual Demographic Survey produced by the Bureau of the Census states that the "statistical middle income" range is the middle 20 percent of all households, reluctant to mention the "C word" (class) at all.[15]

Despite our culturally determined hesitation to assign social and economic position, strong feelings have always been attached to the American middle class, explaining why there is so much concern for its fate. Because the United States was founded on the principles of democracy and equality, it makes perfect sense that "average" Americans are viewed as most symbolic of what makes this country great and different from others. The middle class reflects our national mythology of the "Everyman," an idea that is central to our national identity. While other countries, past and present, are or were structured around the existence of an upper (or ruling) and a lower (or working) class, the United States has been viewed as a place dedicated to the interests of a large middle class. People in other countries have looked down on those falling somewhere between the ruling elite and working class, seeing them as "bourgeois," while here being a member of the middle class has generally been a source of pride. (One could even make the case that being middle class is a form of patriotism.) Versus other forms of government, i.e., aristocracies, autocracies, monarchies, or socialist or communist states, a democracy or meritocracy like ours relies on the presence of a sizable, voting middle class. In order for the United States to remain powerful and stable, it is thus vital that the middle class thrives (or merely survives), standard thinking goes, hence the special status this group of Americans has always been awarded.

Indeed, those citizens who have not been middle class have consistently been viewed with some suspicion, considered somehow less "American." Both the poor and the rich contradict the constitutional precept that "all men are created equal"; that there are major class distinctions at all is seen as a violation of our national creed. The reality is that there have always been vast equalities in wealth and social status in this country, of course, but the endurance of the mythology illustrates its profound power. Any and all threats to the middle class, real or perceived, have therefore been seen as attacks on America itself, potentially dangerous acts that should not be tolerated. A look back over the past century reveals that the American middle class was almost continually "squeezed," "declining," or "disappearing," usually portrayed as victims of governmental policies favoring the rich and/or the poor. The middle class has consistently been seen as bearing the brunt of the nation's tax burden, with corporations and the rich able to avoid paying taxes through shelters and the poor lacking the financial resources to pay much or any of them.

Likewise, especially in times of economic decline, the middle class has routinely been cast as being literally "stuck in the middle," unable to afford the best things in life like the rich while too well-off to qualify for government hand-outs like the poor. Recessions and unemployment have been viewed as hitting the middle class hardest, these folks seen as being the most vulnerable to economic downturns. (The rich can afford hard times or can ride them out while the poor are already poor, the corollary to this argument goes.) Aligning oneself with the interests of the middle class has been a go-to strategy for politicians looking for votes or ways to boost their popularity, so much so that it would be hard to imagine anyone in public office or wanting to be elected having a bad thing to say about this group of Americans. Despite its profound diversity, the middle class is seen as being as American as mom, apple pie, and Chevrolet—hard working, "real" people who keep the country's wheels spinning. The irony is that much of the middle class would, if they had the chance, abandon their "average-ness" as quickly as possible to realize the nearly universal pursuit of wealth and privilege.

The cultural dynamics of the American middle class are naturally grounded in the country's unique conception of class in general. Class does not really exist in the United States, many of us believe, at least not in the way it exists in other, more hierarchical societies. And if class does exist here, almost all of us are middle class, making the notion of economic and social division unimportant or unnecessary. Polls and surveys have continually borne this out, with an inordinate percentage of us convinced we are middle class or are in the general neighborhood. This holds true for many of those who clearly belong to the upper class or under class, a good example of the populist appeal of the middle class. "Americans might more readily classify themselves as bipeds or carnivores, or proclaim their sexual orientations, than define themselves as patricians, plutocrats or gentry," Michael T. Kaufman wrote in the *New York Times* in 1989, explaining why so many of us consider ourselves middle class. In a poll conducted that year in the Northeast by the newspaper and CBS, for example, 85 percent of people said they were "middle class," 13 percent "poor," 1 percent "rich," and the remaining 1 percent "confused." Another survey completed by the National Opinion Research Center around that time revealed that 40 percent of people with household incomes of $15,000 or less labeled themselves middle class while they were by all measures poor.[16]

To further complicate things, being middle class has always been a moving target, the signifiers constantly changing. Growing up in the 1940s, for example, Kaufman viewed those who owned refrigerators as middle class as his family had only an icebox. In the 1950s, his definition shifted to owning a television set; this was followed by a series of other things or experiences—summer camp, orthodontia, even English muffins—that other families could afford but his could not. For Kaufman and no doubt many others, this materialist approach to defining class carried over to the next generation. Wearing certain kinds of sneakers, having a credit card, and traveling by plane had become the benchmarks for the middle class, according to Kaufman's adolescent children, illustrating the continually morphing nature of economic and social status in America.[17]

Although almost all Americans have wanted to be or thought of themselves as middle class, the term itself has often carried negative connotations. "For most of the century the terrible words that made people sound despicable were 'middle class,'" Russell Baker noted in 1985, the label suggesting that such individuals lacked discrimination and sophistication. "From the age of Harding to the dawn of Reaganism, it was a dreadful judgment to hear one say, 'so middle class—you're so hopelessly middle class,'" Baker added, a reflection of the nation's elitist attitudes.[18] Because the simple acknowledgment that class exists in this country poses a threat to our national identity, membership in the middle class can be seen as our natural "default setting."

While there has been increasing attention to a growing divide between "haves" and "have nots," the idea that class mobility and fluidity is an integral feature of the American Way of Life has persisted (despite clear evidence to the contrary). Belief in the American Dream—"a vision of a better, deeper, richer life for every individual, regardless of the position in society which he or she may occupy by the accident of birth," as the coiner of the term, James Truslow Adams, defined it in the early 1930s—has been a prime way we have been able to deny or cloak the unpleasant concept of class.[19] Our faith in the American Dream these last eighty years has obscured the cruel fact that we are not as different from other countries as we like to think when it comes to class mobility. "The unswerving expectation was that the onward meant upward, better meant more, and the pot at the end of the middle-class rainbow contained job security, financial well-being, and all the other fruits of society," sociologist Robert K. Merton wrote in his classic book *Social Theory and Social Structure*. "In the American Dream, there is no final stopping point," he added, finding that individuals always wanted about 25 percent more income than they had, regardless of the amount.[20] Half a century of history suggests "a better, deeper, richer life" will not be realized by many, perhaps most of us, however, the mythology of the American Dream proving to be just that.[21]

The ubiquity and endurance of the mythology of the American Dream, which I defined in my cultural history of the mythology as the devout belief that tomorrow can and will be better than today, has directly contributed to our ignorance regarding class. Americans were and are aware that some people earned and spent more money than others, of course, but this is a rather flimsy foundation for an understanding of class. Despite the occasional dustup regarding "class warfare," class-consciousness has hardly existed in this country, an ironic situation given how much weight we place on work and consumption. "Whenever we Americans discuss the issue of 'class,' we promptly throw ourselves into confusion," Irving Kristol wrote in the *Wall Street Journal* in 1979, the average man or woman on the street woefully unable to judge social and economic status. "Fortunately, most Americans never give a thought to it, are utterly incurious about it, and certainly do not discuss it at the dinner table," Kristol added, the issue simply not very important or interesting. Did income convey one's class? Occupation? Education? Family background? One's friends or neighbors? A certain way of dressing or talking? Most Americans cannot say or, more interestingly, think or care to say. Many believe that regardless of the obvious huge disparities in wealth and other indicators, we are basically a "classless" society, the first in the history of the world. One has to then wonder why so many Americans were and are obsessed with "moving up" or "getting ahead," something that suggests that some notion of class is indeed lurking in our DNA.[22]

Our democratic consumer culture has no doubt contributed to concealing the presence of class in America. Not just the middle class but many in the upper class and under class shop at the same places and enjoy the many "affordable luxuries" readily available. Retailers like Target and, to some extent, Starbucks, Best Buy, and the Gap, are national institutions, not limited to a particular income group. The "flattening" of the marketplace—enabled largely by mounting levels of consumer debt—has played a significant, underappreciated role in promoting American classlessness, I believe. Easily had mortgages (too easy, we learned) have also blurred the lines of class, and relatively affordable car leases also make it difficult to know the income or net worth of a particular driver. One does not have to be rich to drive a new BMW, for example, and one is not necessarily poor if one stops in at McDonald's or Taco Bell once in a while. The casualization of America has also made it impossible to tell who has money and friends in high places and who does not. Khakis and a denim shirt have become a standard uniform for men, even at work, a much different thing than when "clothes made the man." Sports, movies, and television are also great equalizers, with popular culture acting as a common language we all can speak. Virtually all of the traditional markers of wealth have disappeared, making each of us "middle class" even if we have $100 million in the bank or are in debt up to our ears.

The social and economic ascendance of the American middle class after World War II was actually a few centuries in the making. Recognition of a middle class in the United States hearkened back to 17th century Europe, when a social group called the "Middling" (or "Middle Rank" or "Middle Order") began to be referenced. Of a higher rank than those dependent upon the State but lower rank than those of upper standing, the "middling sorts" dedicated themselves to acquiring some level of wealth and property much like how Americans would a couple of centuries later.[23] Even though the concept of class did not eclipse that of "rank" until around the 1830s with the maturation of the United States economy, it was the equivalent of the middle class who led the nation's pursuit of independence, some have argued. "The American Revolution was a middle-class struggle involving taxes and property rights," posited Lance Morrow in *Time* in 1992, explaining why, "the middle class is essentially America itself, its soul, its promise, its culture and myth."[24]

It was the rise of the white-collar worker between 1830 and 1870 that created what sociologist C. Wright Mills called "the new middle class" in his classic work *White Collar: The American Middle Classes.*[25] Mills and later scholars agree that the American middle class took shape in the mid-1800s, as did the term itself. "Americans (or at least urban Americans) of middling economic and social position were formed and formed themselves into a relatively coherent and ascending middle class during the middle decades of the nineteenth century," stated Stuart M. Blumin in his *The Emergence of the Middle Class*.[26] Having some education and working for a salary, this (almost always male and white) individual was the prototype for today's middle-class American.[27] In her *Cradle of the Middle Class*, Mary P. Ryan showed how middle-class families became "privatized" between the Revolutionary and Civil Wars, with male and female roles now sharply delineated.[28]

In the latter part of the 1800s, "middle class" became not just a noun but an adjective, increasing its usage. "Becoming middle class was increasingly a way of doing things, a display of selective *characteristics*, a delimiting agent, a matter of discerning emphasis and attention rather than the demonstration of an undivided whole character," Bledstein noted, with any number of ways now to gain entry into the group.[29] One way was through "optimism," a core middle-class value in the 19th century, according to Jennifer L. Goloboy. The belief that tomorrow would be better than today—again, an essential component if not the primary meaning of the American Dream—was something that would help members of the early American middle class "transcend their lowly origins and find success," Goloboy writes.[30] The middle class of the 19th century was not the same as the nation's "bourgeoisie," however. In their *The American Bourgeoisie*, Sven Beckert and Julia B. Rosenbaum made an important distinction between the bourgeoisie—merchants, manufacturers, and bankers, mostly—and the middle class, as the former did not include small shopkeepers, artisans, schoolteachers, or clerks. It would not be until the mid-20th century when the bourgeoisie and middle class would merge, a phenomenon that was instrumental in forging the "American Way of Life" and supposed "classless" society of the postwar years.[31]

Although there had been a burgeoning middle class in the United States for almost a full century, its numbers swelled in the 1920s as a prosperous economy benefitted most Americans, especially urban professionals and white-collar workers. The rich got richer in the Roaring Twenties but the less well off made significant economic strides as well, forming what was the first real mass middle class in history. Millions who had never invested before were now playing the stock market, something only recently limited to the wealthy elite. Goods also once exclusive to the upper class now could be had by the middle class (again largely through consumer debt), with all sorts of entertainment and amusements to be enjoyed as well. America had a "new sub-plutocracy," *Harper's* magazine reported in 1929, something the world had never seen.[32]

While many Americans would regret being such avid investors in the stock market after the crash, most of the middle class would remain so through the Great Depression. Never before had there been such a celebration of the "common man," in fact, as ordinary Americans became symbols of the nation's enduring character. From Frank Capra films to the regionalist art movement, it was the average Joe who best represented what the country was about, what had made it great, and why it would one day be great again. (It is important to make a distinction between that "common man" and the one celebrated by Farm

Security Administration photographers and writers like John Steinbeck and James Agee; that "common man" was more often than not a sharecropper or a migrant farm worker, and thus definitely not middle class.) FDR was a supporter of the American middle class, penalizing the rich through tax policies to level the economic playing field. Providing a modicum of security to all would build the middle class, he believed, this the enduring legacy of his New Deal. The war officially ended the Depression, with plenty of high-paying factory jobs on the homefront for those not serving overseas. Besides the economic upswing, propaganda for the war encouraged all Americans to be united, something that blurred class lines. The vast majority of Americans were, or at least acted as if they were, middle class, a remarkable transformation in national identity. With the possible exception of the New Deal (specifically loans made by the new Federal Housing Administration) and WPA of the 1930s, the GI Bill was the best thing the government ever did for the middle class, allowing millions of veterans to get a college degree and move up the socio-economic ladder.

The federal government's support of the middle class carried over into the 1950s. With the Cold War raging, a stable society predicated on the "American Way of Life" was viewed as our best defense against the threat of communism. The government thus essentially subsidized the middle class by encouraging home ownership in the thousands of new suburbs springing up across the country. With as little as a $100 down payment, one could settle into one of these ticky-tacky houses and fill it up with the good things of life. "Can there have been in all recorded history as many people as materially well-off as the American middle class in the twentieth century?" asked Gorman Beauchamp in *American Scholar* in 1995, explaining that, "Modern technology democratized privilege, and we have been the primary beneficiaries."[33] Professions like social work, accountancy, and engineering rapidly expanded around mid-century, boosting the numbers of Americans with middle-class incomes.[34] Blacks too made significant strides into the middle class during the postwar years, laying the foundation for a major leap in social and economic progress over the next quarter-century.

A consumer-based economy fueled by easy credit alongside the layers of middle management in corporate jobs and a bureaucracy-heavy "military-industrial complex" virtually guaranteed that the middle class would thrive in the 1950s. In short, more Americans could legitimately claim middle-class status and adopt middle-class practices. It was ironic that it was during the heyday of the middle class that the group would begin to become the target of virulent criticism by leading sociologists, a way of thinking that continued well into the 1970s. "The images embodied in books of that period—white collar, lonely crowd, organization man, therapeutic society, one-dimension man, homeless mind, culture of narcissism—projected an enfeebled conforming without a politics, an organizational mass without a soul," wrote Bledstein, drawing on ideas put forth by Mills and by Daniel Bell in his *The Cultural Contradictions of Capitalism*.[35] Barbara Ehrenreich has carried on the tradition, if you will, of this brand of criticism directed at the middle class, or at least one segment of it. The "professional class" (more or less the upper middle class) now possessed "a meaner, more selfish outlook," she argued in her 1989 *Fear of Falling*; this group of businesspeople, lawyers, and other high achievers were "hostile to the aspirations of those less fortunate."[36]

The amazing, century-long run of the American middle class would come to an end in the mid-1960s, as what has been called the "postwar consensus" began to fragment into a myriad of coalitions or sub-cultures based on age, gender, race, and ethnicity. Major changes in the workplace—automation, new technologies, and managerial "efficiencies"—soon followed, seriously impacting both white-collar and blue-collar segments of the middle class.[37] Recession and inflation in the 1970s compounded problems for the American middle class, and the "Reaganomics" of the 1980s, i.e., corporate tax cuts, individual tax decreases, and other financial measures favoring the wealthy, were arguably equally detrimental. By the early 1990s, the middle class was "confused and dispirited," wrote Strobel, the group perhaps feeling more financial and emotional pressure than ever. The concentration of wealth at the upper end was effectively taking money out of the hands of the middle class, Strobel argued; this privatization of economic power (along with the parallel sharp decline of the labor movement) was responsible for the group's long decline.[38]

Anyone at all tuned into the media is aware that social critics on both sides of the political fence are deeply concerned about the state of the American middle class. "Arguably, the most important economic trend in the United States over the past couple of generations has been the ever more distinct sorting of Americans into winners and losers," *Atlantic* essayist Don Peck wrote in his 2011 book *Pinched*, this Darwinian process leading to "the slow hollowing-out of the middle class."[39] "America was once the great middle-class society, but now we are divided between rich and poor," observed Jeffrey D. Sachs, author of *The Price of Civilization* and director of Columbia University's Earth Institute in a recent essay for *Time*. Sachs argued that dramatic inequality in income was not just ethically questionable but bad for the economy as a whole because it left us more vulnerable to global competition.[40] Charles Murray of the American Enterprise Institute made the case in his controversial 2012 book *Coming Apart* that the erosion of the American middle class over the last half-century has left the nation without a common civic culture, the cleaving of our class system in two creating a "great divide."[41]

Conservative television and radio host Lou Dobbs has been perhaps the most vocal critic of what he has termed "the war on the middle class," seeing the group as nothing less than victims of an oppressive government and corporate culture. "America has become a society owned by corporations and a political system dominated by corporate and special interests, and directed by elites who are hostile—or at best indifferent—to the interests of working men and women of the middle class and their families," he wrote in the first paragraph of his 2006 bestseller *War on the Middle Class*. Since 2000, the middle class has been "devastated" by the political system and Big Business, Dobbs maintains, thinking the group would not survive another five years if these forces continued. Although his prediction was wrong (the middle class has not yet expired, I am happy to report), Dobbs has accurately described the uneven field on which the group has been playing in recent decades. Having "suffered in silence for too long," it was time for the middle class to fight back, he insisted, urging members of the group to "take back America."[42] And in their *It's the Middle Class, Stupid!*, liberals James Carville and Stan Greenberg made much the same case, demonstrating that concern for the American middle class is a uniting rather than divisive issue.[43]

Finally, there are clear signs that the polarization of class in America and the shrinkage of the middle class is not just a rhetorical exercise but playing out in everyday life. Both the Tea Party and Occupy Movement are much about the struggle of the nation's middle class, clear proof that the issue transcends political ideology. Even Corporate America has acknowledged the evaporation of those of average incomes. Procter & Gamble, the maker of ubiquitous brands like Crest and Tide, for example, recently adjusted its marketing plans to reflect the increased number of both higher-end and lower-end consumers and decreased number of those in the middle.[44] Will more big companies adopt a "bi-polar" marketing strategy, one has to wonder, further pushing members of the middle class into one half of "two Americas"? If so, our consumer-based society will lose much of its important egalitarian ethos, and the un-American Dream will become an even greater possibility for significant numbers of the middle class.

The American Middle Class tells its story chronologically, beginning at the end of World War II and going right up to today, when the subject of the American middle class is more newsworthy than ever. Regarding sources, the spine of the book relies on contemporary, popular magazines and newspapers, as I believe that "period" sources provide a fairer and more accurate presentation of history as it occurred than sources published decades later. As well, relying heavily upon period sources best captures the attitudes relating to the idea of the middle class at a particular time, skirting the kind of rear-view-mirror revisionism that many intellectual, social, and political histories employ. Hundreds of different sources, many of them forgotten, are used, drawing from journalists' writing of "the first draft of history." By drawing upon so many different sources, we get a truer picture of the cultural arc of the American middle class through the last half-century rather than one focused on a particular arena (such as politics, business, or the family). Journalistic sources were prioritized not only because this is a work of cultural history but, because they were typically filtered, vetted, and fact-checked, offer from a collective sense a relatively objective and balanced perspective. Scholarly and popular books and journal articles are used to frame the story and provide valuable context. Finally, also like most cultural histories, this one does not have a political agenda or even an especially fervent (and thus likely narrow) claim to make. Rather, I tell the story from what I believe to be a balanced perspective, allowing the material to drive the narrative as a good cultural history should.

The first chapter, "The Greatest Show On Earth," examines the American middle class of the postwar years, when blue-collar and white-collar Americans coalesced to form a group whose size and power was unprecedented in history. Although critically attacked as bourgeois and overly concerned with status, the middle class of the 1950s was more often viewed as a shining example of democracy at its best. Chapter 2, "The Happening," discusses how the postwar consensus based in middle-class values and centered around the "American Way of Life" broke up in the mid-1960s as the nation became more pluralistic and fragmented. Divisions along class, race, gender, and age lines tore apart the middle class, its ideological foundation crumbled by the forces of the counterculture. The third chapter, "Apocalypse Now," shows how things became significantly worse for the American middle class in the 1970s due to "stagflation," an energy crisis, and continued political unrest. Key indicators of the relative health of the middle class—the ability to buy a house and send one's kids to college—had fallen dramatically, making many pronounce that the American Dream was over.

Chapter 4 of *The American Middle Class*, "Trading Places," investigates the American middle class in the 1980s, when things went from bad to worse for the group as President Reagan's laissez-faire approach to running the country and tax policies favoring the wealthy encouraged the formation of a "haves" and "have nots" society. The fifth chapter, "Falling Down," explores the American middle class in the 1990s, a group Barbara Ehrenreich, riffing on Richard Nixon's use of the term, now considered "the silent majority." Despite having two careers, many middle-class families were now living paycheck to paycheck, struggling to make ends meet. The final chapter, "The Perfect Storm," considers the American middle class since 2000. The middle class is now at war not with other classes but with itself, evidence suggests, the upper segment trying to stay ahead of the lower that is doing everything it can to catch up. The middle of the middle class is getting smaller every day, I conclude, something that does not bode well for the heart and soul of the nation.

Notes

1 Burton J. Bledstein, "Introduction: Storytellers to the Middle Class," in Burton J. Bledstein and Robert D. Johnston, eds., *The Middling Sorts: Explorations in the History of the American Middle Class* (New York: Routledge, 2001) 1.

2 Peter N. Stearns, "The Middle Class: Toward a Precise Definition," *Comparative Studies in Society and History*, July 1979, 377.

3 Bill Wolpin, "In the Middle of the American Dream," *American City and County*, March 2010, 6.

4 Loren Baritz, *The Good Life: The Meaning of Success for the American Middle Class* (New York: Alfred A. Knopf, 1989) xi.

5 *The Good Life*, xi.

6 Nathan Keyfitz, "Consumerism and the New Poor," *Society*, January/February 1992, 42.

7 Thomas Sugrue, *The Origins of the Urban Crisis: Race and Inequality in Postwar Detroit* (Princeton, NJ: Princeton University Press, 1996); Kevin M. Kruse, *White Flight: Atlanta and the Making of Modern Conservatism* (Princeton, NJ: Princeton University Press, 2005).

8 Ira Katznelson, *When Affirmative Action Was White: An Untold History of Racial Inequality in Twentieth-Century America* (New York: W.W. Norton, 2005).

9 Brita Belli, "Welcome to Green-Collar America," *E Magazine*, November/December 2007, 27–31.

10 Frederick R. Strobel, *Upward Dreams, Downward Mobility: The Economic Decline of the American Middle Class* (Savage, MD: Rowman & Littlefield, 1993) xi.

11 Frank Levy, *Dollars and Dreams: Changing American Income Distribution* (New York: W.W. Norton, 1988).

12 Marina Moskowitz, *Standard of Living: The Measure of the Middle Class in Modern America* (Baltimore, MD: The Johns Hopkins University Press, 2004) 12.

13 "In the Middle of the American Dream," 6.

14 Teresa Sullivan, Elizabeth Warren, and Jay Lawrence, *The Fragile Middle Class: Americans in Debt* (New Haven, CT: Yale University Press, 2000).

15 Mark Mitchell, "Is the Middle-Class Squeeze for Real," *Independent School*, Winter 2006, 76–82.

16 Michael T. Kaufman, "What's Happened to Middle Class," *New York Times Magazine*, April 23, 1989.

17 "What's Happened to Middle Class."

18 Russell Baker, "Middle-Class Elitist," *New York Times*, September 15, 1985, A24.

19 James Truslow Adams, *The Epic of America* (New York: Little, Brown, and Company, 1931).

20 "The Squeeze on the Middle Class," *Business Week*, March 10, 1975, 52–60; Robert K. Merton, *Social Theory and Social Structure* (New York: Free Press, 1949).

21 Lawrence R. Samuel, *The American Dream: A Cultural History* (New York: Syracuse University Press, 2012) 13.

22 Irving Kristol, "The 'New Class' Revisited," *Wall Street Journal*, May 31, 1979, 24.

23 "Introduction: Storytellers to the Middle Class," 5.

24 Lance Morrow, "Voters are Mad as Hell," *Time*, March 2, 1992, 16.

25 C. Wright Mills, *White Collar: The American Middle Classes* (New York: Oxford University Press, 1951).

26 Stuart M. Blumin, *The Emergence of the Middle Class: Social Experience in the American City, 1760–1900* (New York: Cambridge University Press, 1989) 1, 12.

27 Daniel J. Walkowitz, *Social Workers and the Politics of Middle-Class Identity* (Chapel Hill: University of North Carolina Press, 1999) 2.

28 Mary P. Ryan, *Cradle of the Middle Class: The Family in Oneida County, New York, 1790–1865* (New York: Cambridge University Press, 1983).

29 "Introduction: Storytellers to the Middle Class," 8–9.

30 Jennifer L. Goloboy, "The Early American Middle Class," *Journal of the Early Republic*, Winter 2005, 541.

31 Sven Beckert and Julia B. Rosenbaum, *The American Bourgeoisie: Distinction and Identity in the Nineteenth Century* (New York: Palgrave Macmillan, 2010).

32 D. Aikman, "Our New Sub-Plutocracy," *Harper's*, April 1929, 570–79.

33 Gorman Beauchamp, "Dissing the Middle Class," *American Scholar*, Summer 1995, 335.

34 Frank Musgrove, "The Teen-Age Aristocracy," *The Nation*, April 26, 1965, 439–42.

35 "Introduction: Storytellers to the Middle Class," 20.

36 Barbara Ehrenreich, *Fear of Falling: The Inner Life of the Middle Class* (New York: Pantheon Books, 1989) 3.

37 *Social Workers and the Politics of Middle-Class Identity*, 3.

38 *Upward Dreams, Downward Mobility*, xi–xiii.

39 Don Peck, *Pinched: How the Great Recession Has Narrowed Our Futures & What We Can Do About It* (New York: Crown, 2011) 29.

40 Jeffrey D. Sachs, "Why America Must Revive its Middle Class," *Time*, October 10, 2011, 30.

41 Charles Murray, *Coming Apart: The State of White America, 1960–2010* (New York: Crown Forum, 2012).

42 Lou Dobbs, *War on the Middle Class: How the Government, Big Business, and Special Interest Groups Are Waging War on the American Dream and How to Fight Back* (New York: Viking, 2006) 1–12.

43 James Carville and Stan Greenberg, *It's the Middle Class, Stupid!* (New York: Blue Rider Press, 2012).

44 Ellen Byron, "As Middle Class Shrinks, P&G Aims High and Low," wsj.com, September 12, 2011.

1

THE GREATEST SHOW ON EARTH

The underlying goal of Americans is better living in all of its aspects.
President Dwight E. Eisenhower, in his January 1956 Economic
Report to Congress

In June 1953, Eric Johnston, president of the Motion Picture Association of America, delivered a speech to the Washington (State) Bankers Association. In his talk titled "The Age of the Medium Class," Johnston (who had recently left his job as head of President Truman's Economic Stabilization Agency, and had also been president of the U.S. Chamber of Commerce) praised the role of bankers throughout American history. Johnston, a clear conservative, also acknowledged bankers' important place in the fight against communism. The best way to defeat this scourge, he told the bankers, was to champion the cause of what he called the "medium class" around the world. The "medium class" was a euphemism for the American middle class, that vast group of the population who best represented the nation's values rooted in democracy and consumer capitalism. "We ought to offer an opportunity to the toilers and the tillers of the earth to take out full and active membership in the 20th century, complete with its material comforts and its spiritual values," Johnston urged the bankers, suggesting that the United States did not hold a monopoly on the idea of the middle class.[1] "The medium class is not an exclusive product of ours," he continued, explaining that:

> It belongs to an age—to the 20th century. It is the foundation of our strength, the bulwark of our society, the source of inspiration of all peoples desiring a fuller and more fruitful life. A member of the medium class may more properly be called Twentieth Century Man.[2]

The belief that a member of the middle class was the finest and noblest representative of the 20th century reflected the level of status the group was awarded in postwar America. After a decade and a half of depression and war, Americans were more than ready to enjoy the fruits of their victory over economic hardship at home and enemies abroad. The "American Century" was waiting in the wings, with the nation's middle class expected to play a literally central role in it. The early postwar years would prove to be rocky ones for the American middle class, however, as inflation made it difficult to keep up, much less get ahead, especially for those on salaries. If that were not enough, social critics set their sights on the middle class, attacking the group for its middlebrow tastes and bourgeois ways. Soon, however, the middle class hit its stride, fully realizing the prosperity and abundance it had expected and felt entitled to. As the epitome of consumer capitalism, the country's middle class was used as a weapon in the Cold War, vivid proof that the American Way of Life was superior to that of Soviet communism. Among whites, a growing African American middle class was taken as additional evidence that the nation was living up to its lofty ideals, although some blacks believed the group was an obstacle to the budding movement for equal rights. By the end of the 1950s, however, most agreed that the nation's middle class, because of its size, power, and democratic values, was a historic achievement, something no other civilization, past or present, had ever seen. The American middle class was "the greatest show on earth," one could say, a shining example for the rest of the world to follow.

A Dangerous Business

As soon as the war was over, in fact, Americans began to look to the middle class to lead the nation toward its rightful role as "the city on the hill." Businesspeople were naturally excited at the prospect of a new, very large American middle class as the postwar era beckoned. Bankers were especially delighted by the growth opportunities to be seized, envisioning millions of new customers opening up checking and savings accounts as wages soared after the war. Demand for consumer goods was high, ensuring that employment levels would remain high for some time. Unionization was spreading across the country, making many members of the working class effectively middle class, a phenomenon that would define the era.[3] More and more members of the fast growing middle class were investing some of their extra money into what was called at the time "open-end companies," or mutual funds. "The thrift savings of the nation's middle classes are getting to be a substantial factor in the great postwar growth of the professionally managed companies," the *New York Times* made note, the average yield of 4 percent considerably better than what one could get at a bank. Many or most of these Americans had little or no experience with securities, marking the beginning of Wall Street's courting of the smaller investor.[4]

Postwar inflation remained a major concern for Americans, however, especially for the salaried middle class. It took two 1948 dollars to buy what one 1939 dollar could, a situation of considerable concern for both businesspeople and civic leaders. For members of "the great middle class," a July 1948 newsletter published by the National City Bank read, inflation was "a dangerous business, ... grind [ing] them down, tak[ing] away their incentives, [and] frustrat[ing] their efforts toward security."[5] Some were seriously concerned that out-of-control inflation could lead to major political upheaval, even a dictatorship not unlike the one that emerged in Germany in the 1930s.[6] Worries about inflation would prove to be a running theme in the history of the American middle class for the rest of the century and beyond, second perhaps only to taxes as a threat to or even cause of destruction for the group. Inflation could "wipe out America's middle class," warned Eric Johnston, then the head of President Truman's Economic Stabilization agency, in 1951, a good example of how seriously declining real wages and buyer power were often taken. Johnston saw inflation as analogous to communism, in fact, the former the principal "enemy within" the nation, the latter the primary "enemy outside." Just as much effort should be taken to defeat inflation as communism, he thought, illustrating how much of a menace a weaker dollar and higher prices were considered for the middle class.[7]

With consumer spending being counted on to drive the postwar economy and serve as a key symbol of the American Way of Life, it can be understood why inflation was being taken so seriously. Even solid members of the upper middle class—$100-a-week office workers, $8,000-a-year lawyers, and $11,000 small business owners—were unable to engage in the kind of frenzy of consumption that was considered vital to national interests. "Your best customer is broke," lamented Ernest Havemann of *Nation's Business* in 1951, explaining how Americans who seemed to be doing quite well had no money in their pockets to spend on new appliances, new clothes, or even a sufficient life insurance policy. A down payment on a house or on a much-needed new car could wipe out all of one's savings, making it impossible to buy new furniture for that two-bedroom Cape Cod or ranch. A big doctor's bill or major house repairs could set oneself back for years, and already middle-class parents were losing sleep thinking about the cost of sending their children to college. Tax rates favoring those who made less money compounded the effect of inflation, making many average earners realize they had made no progress at all over the past decade despite the wartime and postwar economic surge. (Farmers and the working class had benefitted most from the prosperity.) Purchasing power ("the only thing that really counts," according to Havemann) was lower for the middle class than it was before the war, and debt from a monthly mortgage and installment payments on big-ticket items were making it impossible to climb out of the rut. "If the middle class is really our backbone, as most of us have always assumed, then we may soon reach the point where we will have a hard time standing up straight," Havemann griped, worried that the backbone may break in two.[8]

The "middle-class squeeze," as it would often be called in the decades ahead, was a puzzling and disheartening situation for postwar Americans believing their ship should and would have already come in. Lacking no necessities, members of the middle class wanted and expected no pity, but remained troubled that things had not worked out as they had anticipated. Government statistics indicating a continually rising standard of living for the nation did little to dissuade average earners from routinely worrying about money, pinching pennies, and stretching budgets as far as they could go. One was tempted to look back on the worst part of the Depression as "the good old days," when the best seats at Broadway plays cost less than $4 and breakfast at a restaurant cost around half a buck. An Irish linen suit could be had for $15 in the early 1930s, and a very decent bottle of Scotch for $3. Prices on many food items had doubled in twenty years, while one's wallet had not become appreciably thicker. Even worse, perhaps, there seemed little point in working harder to make enough money to be able to afford such niceties now. A bigger check meant even more taxes, social security, and pension payments would be deducted from one's check, not a very good incentive to spend more hours on the job. "Mr. Upper Middle Class, for so the economists seem to classify him, has understandable regrets over the predicament in which he finds himself," observed Henry F. Pringle, also writing in *Nation's Business* in 1951, a member of that group likely to be spending a lot of time thinking about "the dreams of affluence which have failed to materialize."[9]

Despite the financial woes of the middle class after the war, Americans had no qualms locating themselves squarely within the group. In survey after survey, a majority of Americans had identified themselves as middle class and a small minority as either upper or lower class. (This is another running theme in the cultural history of the American middle class.) The findings of a 1950 poll done by Richard Centers of UCLA were thus nothing new, with 88 percent of those asked saying they were middle class and 6 percent saying they belonged to one of the two other groups.[10] Such poll results were leading many to believe that the United States was a "middle-class nation," the first of its kind in history. Given the group's size and collective power, politicians were understandably eager to appeal to what they believed were middle-class values. "Like a superpower magnet, the American middle-class tradition pulls everything toward the center," wrote Holmes Alexander of the *Los Angeles Times* in 1949, surprised at what was taking place in Congress. As an example of the extraordinary magnetism of the middle class within politics, Alexander pointed to Senator Robert Taft (R-Ohio) who had been, in the reporter's words, "'centering' over a period of years." A far right conservative earlier in his career, Taft was now supporting measures for public housing, education, health insurance, and civil rights, a political position that Holmes believed made him "a seemingly indestructible figure."[11]

The same centripetal force appeared to be occurring on the other side of the aisle, Alexander believed. Senator Paul Douglas (D-Illinois), once very liberal (a Socialist, in fact), had recently voted for reductions in government spending and cost-saving modifications to the (Truman) administration's labor policy. Taft and Douglas were now not very apart in their politics, a remarkable progression given where each man had come from. The two parties as a whole had similarly moved toward the middle, resulting in what many believed to be a gridlocked, not very effective Congress. The moderating effect taking place in politics was representative of the nation's shift toward the center, Alexander concluded. "This same magnetic pull toward middle-class thinking and behavior operates upon the country at large," he observed, viewing the phenomenon as a distinctly American trait.[12]

Mid-century politicians clearly understood the wisdom of appealing to the interests of a large, ever-growing middle class. In many parts of the country, getting elected or reelected depended heavily upon maintaining a moderate position on key issues, a strategy that would become one of the golden rules of American politics for decades to come. More conservative free market capitalists did not believe that Washington represented the best interests of the American people, however, especially those of middle incomes. "For a generation the fiscal policies of the Federal government have been undermining the middle class of America and the destruction is moral as well as economic," Milton Fairman, director of public relations of the Borden Company, told the New York Advertising Club in 1952. Going back to FDR's New Deal, political leaders had overtaxed the middle class to support big spending programs, Fairman told his fellow businesspeople, with inflation further reducing the buying power of the average consumer. (The ironically named Fairman conveniently ignored how government policy put in place a variety of privileges and social supports limited to people much like him.) It was specially the IRS's progressive income tax that was lowering Americans' incentive to achieve all they could, a classic Republican view that remains very much in currency today. "Karl Marx listed a tax of this kind as the second step in his program of destroying a middle class," Fairman informed his colleagues, his reading of history questionable but a persuasive argument nonetheless.[13]

American Community

In part because of the Marxian overtones of class, in fact, educators after the war were unsure if they should teach the subject to adolescents. Would students benefit from the knowledge that social class existed in the United States? Would young people be better off knowing more about what was often called the "status system"? Was it helpful for them to be aware that there were barriers to social mobility? Social studies teachers were unsure of the answers to such questions, but knew full well that scholars and writers in a variety of fields including sociology, anthropology, and psychology were now very interested in examining the complex relationships between individuals and the groups to which they belonged. Class was a sensitive issue, however, and educators often felt they themselves did not know enough about the subject to teach it properly. Making a less advantaged student think he or she had little chance of "moving up" in life could be disastrous, they believed, as would encouraging a young person of privilege to conclude he or she already had it made.[14]

Savvier educators decided that teaching the subject of class to high school students was well worth the effort and potential risks. After reading the recent literature produced by W. Lloyd Warner and other notable researchers of the day, some teachers dove in head first, confident that greater familiarity with the subject would help students better understand the workings of society and, especially, that of their local community. A number of key points had to be covered in the curriculum, the first being that there were indeed different social classes in this country. ("Social" class was emphasized over "economic" class.) That one was born into a particular class was another fundamental concept, as was the fact that there were barriers that could make it difficult to move between classes. This was a bold idea, particularly for the times, given the power and pervasiveness of two of the nation's core myths: that we were a class-free society and, paradoxically, that individuals could rise in class through "upward mobility."[15]

As typical of postwar education in general, there was often an overt ideological agenda attached to teaching the subject of class to young people. The country's foundation in democracy afforded the opportunity (and perhaps the responsibility) for Americans of all classes to share common experiences found in public or civic life, e.g., education and the arts. Students were assigned the charge of decreasing social and economic "differences" in their respective communities—a clear attempt to broaden the middle class and, correlatively, shrink the percentage of Americans who could be categorized as either poor or rich. Each individual striving to make his or her maximum contribution to society would benefit the entire community, students were taught, the ultimate goal to lessen stratification on both a local and national basis. Teaching the subject of class to students allowed the opportunity to instill the idea that Americans' greatest strength resided in commonality rather than diversity, an important lesson in these economically jittery times.[16]

Expectedly, compared to most other subjects, class presented teachers and researchers quite a challenge. Commonly defined by sociologists as the "horizontal stratification of a population," class could mean any number of things to those in that field and related ones. Much of the perceived problem of class resided in the term's grounding in social and/or economic differences, e.g., income, net worth, occupation, group identification, consumption habits, family background, or some other measure. Further complicating matters were differences based on race, ethnicity, and religion—social divisions that were separate from but overlapped with those of class. Even those most acquainted with the subject struggled with the meaning of the term, and disagreed with how it should be used in both theory and research. Some brought an economic, and specifically Marxian, perspective to the field, while others felt the notions of class consciousness and status were more relevant. The popular belief that class did not really exist in America had not completely dissipated by mid-century, nor had the equally popular view that social mobility in this country was virtually unlimited. Finally, the term's "foreignness" and, again, Marxist connotations had historically served as a stumbling block for American sociologists, another reason why the subject of class remained problematic for anyone working in the area.[17]

Sociologists were beginning to receive a new kind of respect and even popularity after the war, however, admired for their dedication to, as *Life* magazine expressed it in 1949, "filling in a detailed picture of the American society." Sociology had begun its ascent during the Progressive era but the field's focus on the middle class in the postwar years lifted it to a new level of status. John P. Marquand's recent bestselling novel *Point of No Return* was based in part on an actual sociological study of a New England community called "Yankee City" (actually Newburyport, Massachusetts) that was spearheaded by Warner and his team at the University of Chicago. (Marquand parodied Warner's work, illustrating the degree to which Americans were now interested in matters of class.) In *Social Class in America*, Warner and his associates reported intriguing findings related to another "typical" American community, this one in the Midwest called "Jonesville" (recalling the Lynd's "Middletown" studies of the 1920s and 1930s). Soon after Warner's book was published, editors of *Life* magazine decided to take a close look at "Jonesville," in this case, Rockford, Illinois. ("Jonesville" was actually a composite of several different communities, one of them being Rockford.) Featuring photographs by Margaret Bourke-White, the article (titled "American Community") explored the idea of class in America as the media had rarely, if ever, done. It could perhaps even be said that "American Community" served as the unofficial debut of the subject of class in American popular culture from a documentary approach; a photographic essay in *Life* was the perfect vehicle to publicly address the sensitive issue of social and economic difference.[18]

"American Community" was also a great plug for Warner's book and the field of sociology in general. Readers learned there were six classes in the country ("lower-lower," "upper-lower," "lower-middle," "upper-middle," "lower-upper," and "upper-upper"), many of them no doubt wondering where they fell within the hierarchy. (Warner had used the same system in "Yankee City.") Four key criteria were used to determine an individual's class (or, as it was more often expressed, one's "social position," "social standing," or "social prestige"): the size and condition of that person's house; the neighborhood in which the house was located; his or her occupation; and the source of income (i.e., earned, inherited, or government-provided). Interestingly, amount of annual income, usually the primary determinant of class, was not one of Warner's criteria. Warner assigned numbers to each of these areas, with one's total score indicative of relative status in the community. While his methodology can now be seen as seriously flawed, such a mathematical formula served as an easy to understand, non-judgmental measure of social and economic status and, more importantly, stood as scientific "proof" that class was a simple fact of life in America.[19]

Another critical piece of Warner's study of "Jonesville" was the fact that one could move up the class ladder (with little or no acknowledgment that one could potentially move down). Class distinctions existed but economic barriers were permeable, this perhaps the real story of *Social Class in America*. "This phenomenon of social 'mobility'—the opportunity to move rapidly upward through the levels of society—is the distinguishing characteristic of U.S. democracy," *Life* gushed, "the thing for which it is famous and envied throughout the world." Warner himself appeared to have an agenda attached to his study, a function of the political framework in which he was operating. "The saving grace of the American social system is that our social positions are not fixed artificially, as they are in the so-called 'classless' society of Russia," Warner told *Life*, class here a natural, fluid byproduct of free enterprise rather than the evil, repressive thing it was within communism.[20]

While laypeople found "Jonesville" to be a fascinating examination of "the American society," those in the field found Warner's findings to be highly debatable. In fact, the sociological community was strongly divided over whether ordinary Americans even recognized social classes as real, discrete groups. Were sociologists and other academics making more out of the issue of class than existed in "the real world," in other words? Some felt definitely so, arguing that class in America was more of a pedagogical, personally defined concept than anything else. For this contingent, class was a continuum rather than a stratified social system neatly divided into clearly identifiable segments or stackable tiers. Most people viewed their local communities as rather seamless gradations of social status, they argued, taking issue with Warner and other researchers who sliced communities into distinct groups. Class divisions were not as precise and definite as their (more famous) colleagues liked to believe, they insisted, the former's brand of research interesting reading but not reflective of how Americans actually saw themselves and their neighbors.[21] Those in other fields such as anthropology and psychology also challenged the class-oriented camp of sociology. Psychologist Richard Centers, for example, saw social class purely as an individually defined concept grounded in one's attitudes rather than any kind of "system." "Social classes in their essential nature can be categorized as psychologically or subjectively based groupings defined by the allegiance of their members," he wrote in his *The Psychology of Social Classes*, seeing political and economic "tendencies" as the primary basis for community-forming.[22]

Warner and those on his side of the fence, however, completely disagreed. Social class in America was very real, they held, with not just experts like themselves but average citizens able to recognize well-defined groups. Americans identified with those of similar income levels and distinguished themselves from those of upper and lower levels, these sociologists argued, even giving the groups names. Prestige was an important part of class structure, with the various groups awarded different levels of status based on how much money they earned and how they spent it. Class was not an imaginary construct but a very real dimension of everyday

American life, they told their lesser-known colleagues, offering solid evidence from the field that appeared to back up their bold claims.[23]

The Backbone of a Country

Lending support to those academics seeing class in America as a largely constructed concept was the fact that no one could say for sure who belonged to which group. The term "middle class" in particular was proving to be challenging if not impossible to pin down, a source of frustration that would hold true for decades to come. "Like so many terms which so assuredly describe something which is real, 'middle class' is nevertheless annoyingly vague and incredibly difficult to define in exact and yet manageable detail," noted C. Hartley Grattan in *Harper's Magazine* in 1951, adding that even Marx could not achieve the task. (He, like many others, could say which people did not belong to the middle class but was not able to definitively say which people did.) Tangential or peripheral definitions abounded (e.g., those Americans who were "neither rich nor poor," "lived comfortably," or "had all the necessities and some of the luxuries"), but these were imprecise at best. Many Americans who were not even close to the median income level or of average net worth were certain they were middle class, clear proof of the haziness of the term. Researchers had variously estimated the size of the group to be anywhere from 50 percent to 90 percent of the total population, adding to the confusion. Americans famously disliked the notion of there being an "upper" or "lower" class of any magnitude, explaining the broad appeal of being somewhere in the middle.[24]

Russell Lynes, an editor of *Harper's* and the author of *The Taste-Makers*, believed that class-consciousness still existed in America at mid-century but the measures or determinants of it had recently changed considerably. Rather than wealth or family background, he proposed, it was "high thinking" that now afforded the most prestige. It was, in other words, intellectualism that carried the most social currency, Lynes argued, making people like scientists, historians, writers, and pundits the new upper class. Eggheads like Einstein and those involved with atomic energy were thus at the top of the heap, the Carnegies and Morgans of their day. As evidence, Lynes cited a current magazine ad for Calvert whiskey that featured intellectuals and artists (another elite group) as "Men of Distinction," thinking it would have been unlikely to see such a campaign before the war. "What we are headed for is a sort of social structure in which the highbrows are the elite, the middlebrows are the bourgeoisie, and the lowbrows are the *hoi polloi*," he predicted, an idea that arguably did indeed hold true for the next decade and a half.[25]

Lynes continued his discussion of the "brows," dividing middlebrow into upper and lower segments. For Lynes, writing in the magazine he edited, the American middlebrow was the American middle class, bisected according to tastes and lifestyles. Upper middlebrows took culture seriously, carefully choosing what to read (Sartre, Toynbee, the *New Yorker*, the *Atlantic*, perhaps the *Parisian Review*), where and how to spend free time (museum openings, the theater, foreign films), and what to buy (art, antiques, first editions). The friends of upper middlebrows were, naturally, other upper middlebrows, although one ideally had a few writers and artists as companions to raise the intellectual or aesthetic bar.[26]

If Lynes, a highbrow, of course, admired upper middlebrows for trying to keep up with the intellectual Joneses, he despised lower middlebrows for everything they stood for. This group was, for Lynes, "a dreadful mass of insensible back-slappers, given to sentimentality as a prime virtue, the willing victims of slogans and the whims of the bosses, both political and economic." Just as many others would soon say about the middle class, the lower middlebrow represented mass culture, as despicable a concept as one could imagine for unapologetic elites like Lynes. Advertisers exploited this group of Americans, he was convinced, knowing they were unsure of what they should like and were thus amenable to pitches for all kinds of things. (Reproductions of hunting prints were a particular favorite.) "It is a world that smells of soap," Lynes summarized the day-to-day existence of lower middlebrows, their bourgeois ways precisely what foreigners believed was wrong with America.[27]

Lynes's critique was light-hearted fare compared to the appraisal of the middle class in *White Collar*. In the 1951 book that over time came to be considered a socio-logical classic, C. Wright Mills exposed the economic and political power of the American middle class as an absolute mythology. White-collar Americans—that section of the middle class on salaries, i.e., managers, salespeople, and salaried professionals like doctors, lawyers, teachers, and professors—did not rule the nation because of their vast numbers and collective wealth as commonly believed, Mills controversially proposed. As the image on the book's dust jacket (a smallish man toting his lunch bag past an imposing office building) suggested, the typical member of the middle class was an insecure individual struggling to be recognized and desperate to climb the pyramid of what constituted "success."[28] It was the impotence of the middle class that readers found most disturbing about *White Collar*. Belonging to the group meant that one was "acted upon," Mills, a professor of sociology at Columbia University, declared, a person who was "forever somebody else's man." With the rise of this version of the middle class, the United States had become a nation of employees, he argued, the country as a whole significantly worse off. White-collar men were individuals "who had been stood up by life," Mills wrote, "small creature[s]" who were living lives of quiet desperation.[29]

The American business community not surprisingly reacted with shock and dismay upon the publication of *White Collar*. Businesspeople were typically lauded as the individuals who were leading the nation toward unprecedented prosperity and unlimited abundance, so they and journalists in the field were understandably taken aback by Mills's venom. The book was a "portrait of Mr. Nobody," *Business Week* reported in its review, a study of "hollow men" who were a far cry from the small capitalists and captains of industry of the past. That the Ivy League professor (who had argued in his previous book, *The New Men of Power*, that American labor unions had effectively joined forces with capital) was a leading social scientist made his claims all the more unsettling and difficult to dismiss. "What Mills has to say is important to any businessman who is seriously concerned with where our society is drifting," the magazine wrote, finding "a great deal of truth in the book." If the salaried middle class which included not just businesspeople but academics, staff physicians, and junior partners at large law firms was not much more than an immense body of paper pushers, as Mills saw it, the nation was hardly the dynamic force of capitalism its people liked to believe it was. The widely touted "managerial revolution" advanced by James Burnham and others was, in effect, nonsense if Mills's thesis was accurate, the American middle class simply a huge throng of powerless bureaucrats rather than the "Twentieth Century Man."[30]

Instead of being the supreme symbol of our time and place, the typical member of the middle class was thus not unlike Willy Loman, according to Mills, the sad, defeated figure of Arthur Miller's 1949 play *Death of a Salesman*. Rather incredibly, Mills recommended that white-collar Americans adopt a kind of Lomanesque hopelessness and despair, as such a perspective at least acknowledged the unfortunate realities of being middle class in postwar America. Seeing the rat race for what it was for most—an ultimately losing contest—was for Mills better than deluding oneself in the faith of upward mobility. And rather than being a big plus, which most believed it to be, the immense size of the American middle class was a distinct disadvantage, he argued. In the early and mid-19th century, the prototype of the middle class consisting of small manufacturers, merchants, professionals, clerks and bookkeepers, and well-to-do farmers possessed a strong sense of independence and the opportunity to make real economic and social progress. Urbanization and corporatization in the late-19th and early-20th century had for the most part crushed this breed of capitalists and their dreams, however, a huge shift that many failed to see. The ability for the masses to attend college had also diluted the prestige of being a member of the middle class, as had the bell-curved organizational structure of larger employers. The best days of the American middle class were over for good, Mills made clear, challenging those who believed the group was at the peak of its power and influence.[31]

Rubbing salt in the wound of white-collar Americans was their shaky financial position due to the spiraling inflation of the early 1950s. Most of the American middle class was now white-collar, government data showed, a much different story than in the late 19th century when there were many more self-employed. That the salaries of white-collar Americans were not keeping up with inflation was causing much concern among the group itself, making some think that getting a college education had been a big waste of time, money, and effort. Pay for those in the trades or working class was rising faster than that for white-collars, making the latter feel somewhat envious of those wearing denim to work. After the Depression and war, white-collar Americans were beginning to seriously wonder if their ship would ever come in, with some encouraging their children to not repeat their mistake by becoming a laborer. Would blue-collar Americans, as their economic clout continued to grow, overtake white-collar Americans in social status, flipping the composition of the middle class upside down?[32]

Fearing the answer to that question would be yes, a surprising number of white-collar Americans were changing their careers at mid-century, learning a trade to better keep up with racing inflation. College graduates in fields such as engineering and publishing were quitting their jobs and training to become "workingmen," seeing a more promising future for themselves and their families on the blue side of the middle class. Salary caps, working overtime for no additional pay, and the looming threat of losing one's job were all good reasons why white-collar workers were bailing out of their chosen professions. "I am resigning, once and for all, from the most kicked-around class in America—the salaried middle class," said one member of the group in 1950, the man's wife supporting his decision. Financial security was more important than the greater social status they (currently, at least) enjoyed, this couple and others in their position were concluding, actually feeling inferior to those carrying a lunch pail to the job. Excessive drinking and divorces were being blamed on the hard times of white-collar Americans, some of those who had been laid off eager to do any odd job that came along just to pay the bills. Some professionals were going to school on the working class by forming or joining unions, a strange development given the traditionally hostile relationship between labor and management. "This middle class, by nature, training, and profession composed of the strongest individualists and supporters of democracy should never have to doubt the promises of democracy and should be among the first to benefit from its performance," wrote Dorothy Thompson (like Johnston, an obvious conservative) in *Ladies' Home Journal* in 1950, she and many others worried that social and political unrest could result from this "un-American" state of affairs.[33]

A Bloodless Revolution

Ringing the death knell for white-collar Americans or any other segment of the middle class would prove to be premature, however, one of many similar instances to come (particularly during recessionary and/or inflationary years like 1951). Just a year later, in fact, economists were celebrating what appeared to be excellent news for the middle class as a whole. The rise in per capita real income was surpassing that of prices, giving average earners more of Havemann's "only thing that counts." Even better news was that the overall income curve was flattening, meaning the poor were getting richer and the rich were getting poorer. Government and business leaders viewed an expanding middle class, drawing Americans from both the lower and higher ranks, as the best-case scenario for economic and political reasons. "Stability," in all its incarnations, was universally placed at the top of the list of these reasons, the worst-case scenario being class upheaval or possibly even warfare.[34]

Some were even proclaiming that a "bloodless revolution" had taken place in the United States over the last two decades, when the Depression and war (not to mention five Democratic administrations) radically shifted the distribution of wealth in the country. "The trend, wherever you sample it, is toward the middle—a middle that is itself rising," noted *Business Week* in 1952, concluding that the American economy was "making everyone middle class." High employment (especially among women, relatively speaking), high commodity prices for farmers, strong unions, and robust social programs were the main factors cited for the profound leveling taking place. Economists were predicting that the "revolution" (some critics simply called it "socialism") could not be sustained at the same degree, but even that was considered good news. Too much equality would not only reduce the desire and opportunity for upward mobility, but come too close to the kind of collectivist society that was operating on the other side of the planet.[35]

Voices of capitalism were positively elated by reports that the country's classes were congregating. "The U.S. is becoming a one-class market of prosperous middle-income people," *Fortune* declared the following year, the business magazine not surprisingly delighted by the economic phenomenon that was taking place in the country. Americans were consuming three-fourths of the world's automobiles and appliances and half of its steel and oil, a clear indication of a continually rising standard of living. It was the middle class that was driving the growth, the statistics showed, the group getting ever-larger and enjoying ever-more real disposable income. Two key social trends were playing an important role in what the magazine called "the rise of a great new moneyed middle class": the baby boom and suburbanization. American families were having twice as many second babies as they did in 1940, and were heading out of the city in droves to raise those children in spacious suburban neighborhoods and houses. From a marketing standpoint at the very least, it was already readily apparent that something historic and, perhaps, revolutionary was taking place. Between the world wars, the American business community viewed consumers as belonging to either the "class" or "mass" market, the former consisting of the wealthy and the latter composed of households with little discretionary money to spend. Now, however, a new, enormous class had emerged that was not wealthy yet had a significant amount of buying power. The American middle class was the literal centerpiece of what *Fortune* believed was "probably the most sensational economic story of modern times," that story wonderful news to marketers of all kinds of products and services.[36]

Beyond its size and prosperity, the middle class of the early 1950s was appealing to businesspeople for another important reason: its perceived uniformity. Diversity along social and economic lines made manufacturing and marketing a major challenge, while commonality made each task much easier (and more profitable).

"Although the income range may seem fairly wide, the needs and buying power of the members of this group are remarkably homogenous," *Fortune* continued, going as far as to call the middle class "the new All-American market." "Sameness" was one of the businessperson's best friends, offering efficiencies in everything from design to production to selling. "Some spend more money on this thing, and some on the other," according to the magazine, "but essentially they buy the same things—the same staples, the same appliances, the same cars, the same furniture, and much the same recreation." Importantly, the rise in real disposable income among Americans was not just an economic phenomenon but a social or cultural one. "This kind of progress is erasing old class lines, and altering desires, ambitions, tastes, and even ideals," the magazine observed, the nation's population believed to be becoming more homogenous as it purchased the same consumer goods and enjoyed the same leisure activities.[37]

A year later, *Fortune* was no less ecstatic about what it now fully believed was a revolution in America's class system. Turning Mill's thesis on its head, the magazine rejoiced in the "downgrading" of white-collar professionals over the past few decades, seeing it as a key factor in the creation of what it called "the rich middle-income class." Because many more businesspeople, doctors, and lawyers were now salaried, significant numbers of Americans had moved from the lower ranks of the upper class into the upper strata of the middle class. Tremendous numbers of accountants, engineers, and teachers had also flooded into the middle class since the 1920s, making the group that much bigger. Most amazingly, however, it was the arrival of skilled, semi-skilled, and service workers into the middle-income range that was redrawing the boundaries of class in the country. (Even many laborers were earning enough to be considered middle income.) In short, the economic descriptor "middle income" was collapsing into the socially defined concept of "middle class," and this was the revolution that *Fortune* and many other observers of the scene were astonished by. "The fact is that America's booming new middle-income class consists, to a startling extent, of groups hitherto identified as proletarians," *Fortune* declared, no one (especially Marx and his colleague in communism, Friedrich Engels) predicting such a sanguine development.[38]

Company Manners

Regardless of ideological position, it could not be disputed that the American middle class had emerged as a great, if not the greatest show on Earth. Both numerically and on a percentage basis, the middle class was bigger than ever before in the early 1950s, a function of a general rise of real incomes and a more even distribution of wealth.[39] Class distinctions had been dramatically weakened through the war and postwar years, in other words, as those on both ends of the economic spectrum moved toward the middle. Many members of the lower class had become middle class (or at least middle income) during and after the war, the direct beneficiaries of a boom in manufacturing jobs. Many wealthy Americans (or "bloated plutocrats," as they had sometimes been called during the Depression) headed the reverse direction over this same period, the victims of soak-the-rich tax policies and the general decline of "Old Money."[40]

Because of these economic and social trends, many Americans in the mid-1950s assumed that the nation's population was essentially one very big middle class, an idea that simply was not true. Despite the efficiencies to be gained from a mass market, marketers in particular were quick to dispute the notion of one great uniform, faceless group of American consumers. Social and economic mobility—both up and down—still very much existed in this country, and considerable disparities existed within the middle class itself, they were eager to point out. "People are different," Nicholas Samstag, director of promotion for *Time* magazine, told the *New York Times* in 1954, he like other marketing experts not about to assume they could sell the same products and services the same way to all Americans. A recent survey had in fact shown that just 11 percent of Americans possessed almost two-thirds of the nation's discretionary income, hardly the monolithic mass market popularly believed to exist.[41]

Different or otherwise, members of the middle class now had cash in their pockets. "If the statesmen and economists are right about a solid and prosperous middle class being the backbone of a country," wrote a reporter for the *Chicago Daily Tribune* in 1956, "then the United States has never been stronger." A variety of government sources showed that 30 percent of American families (sixteen million) now had household incomes of $5,000 or more, double the number of 1948. Those in the building trades were doing especially well as the housing industry boomed. Bricklayers, carpenters, and cement masons were making as much as $8,000 a year, clearly a middle-class salary. More working wives were contributing to household incomes than before the war, giving families more money to spend. We often think of the 1970s and 1980s as the years in which women entered the workforce en masse but their mothers typically could have a part- or full-time job in the 1950s if they wanted one. (And unlike their daughters, could choose their starting and quitting times!) Having a disposable income was a completely new concept for millions of Americans who had come of age during the Depression or war, shifting their orientation from saving to spending. Buying a home was often the first order of business, a dream come true for those who always thought they would be renters. A new car was typically next on the list, this too a delightful surprise for those accustomed to driving used models. Middle-class consumers were also upgrading from discount and standard versions of products to "deluxe" and customized versions in a variety of categories, especially automobiles.[42]

The prosperity the middle class was enjoying was a surprise to those who had, a couple of decades earlier, predicted that the group would fall apart. Technological change, big business, and discord between Americans of different social and economic groups would destroy the middle class, some experts had said in the 1930s, bisecting the country into an upper and lower class. Class lines in the country in the 1950s had not become more defined but had blurred, however, moving more

Americans into the middle. (One could argue that the prediction did indeed come true later in the century when the "haves" pulled away from the "have nots.") Advances in technology and greater corporate power had in fact driven the expansion of the middle class, and those of different income levels were finding themselves in agreement on a wide range of political issues. With prosperity had come moderation, an unexpected but happy development to those who had during the dark days of the Depression seen more doom and gloom on the nation's horizon.[43]

Like Lynes and Mills before him, however, Louis Kronenberger took a close look at the American middle class and did not like what he saw. In his 1954 *Company Manners: A Cultural Inquiry Into American Life*, Kronenberger described the group as anxious, uncreative, and vulgar. The "common man" of mid-century America was literally so, he argued, lacking any semblance of aristocratic virtues such as elegance, grace, distinction, wit, and style. Popular culture consumed by a mass audience, whether Broadway theater or television, reflected this sad state of affairs. Hollywood movies were especially unsophisticated. (Kronenberger considered Sam Goldwyn, the Hollywood producer famous for his malapropisms—he once reportedly said, "I don't think anybody should write his autobiography until after he's dead"—the king of American crudeness.) The pressure to assimilate and conform had driven all individuality and eccentricity out of the American character, he believed, our lack of reflection and distaste of melancholy also making us dull people. Such charges were hardly new, of course (Tocqueville had made similar observations 120 years earlier), but Kronenberger's take on the American middle class was fast becoming a central trope in the national conversation.[44]

Academics were especially hard on the middle class. Martin B. Loeb, an anthropologist at UCLA, for example, told 500 colleagues at the 1957 meeting of the American Anthropological Association that the group had a "puritanical and bland" culture with a "packaged" way of life. "Niceness" best described them, Loeb suggested, meaning the middle class wanted to be nice, have nice lives, and be considered nice people. Some of the middle class's favorite, not at all interesting foods—the hamburger, peanut butter, and tomato soup—were apt symbols of the group, he argued, with "conformity-anxiety" a dominant trait. John P. Gillin of the University of North Carolina agreed, but thought the best descriptor of the middle class was "mechanistic" given its members' fondness for values like progress, ingenuity, efficiency, precision, and cleanliness. Conrad M. Arensberg of Columbia concurred, adding "regularity" and "respectability" to the list of values the middle class held in high regard. Because such values were taught in both school and church, it was not surprising that the group displayed such uniform (and boring) behavior, Arensberg added. In fact, the heart of American culture was so conservative and machine-like that the Soviets were using us as a model, Solon T. Kimball of Columbia University claimed, with leaders there trying to instill the same kind of sexual prudery and fixation with technology among their own citizens as a form of social control.[45]

Kimball went even further with his comparison between the middle class of the United States and those of its rival superpower. The middle class of each country shared "strikingly similar" moralities and ethics, the professor posited at the conference, an idea that no doubt raised some eyebrows at the peak of the Cold War. The United States and USSR were each grounded in the pursuit of scientific and technological development, he pointed out, a function of the core values of the lower middle class of each nation. An empirical view of the world and desire for organization among those within what was believed to be the most influential segment of the population made America and our archenemy much more alike than we cared to believe or admit. Another anthropology professor at the meeting, Leslie A. White of the University of Michigan, pushed this thesis even further, linking the rise of science and technology to the decline of religion in each country. A "cultural system which can launch earth satellites can dispense with gods entirely," he stated, the space race a fair substitute for the belief in a higher power.[46]

We Have That, Too

Such comparisons between the United States and the Soviet Union—and specifically between the middle classes of each country—were common in postwar America, especially among devout Republicans. If the United States was becoming a "classless" society, i.e., one in which almost everybody fell somewhere within a vast middle class, how were we substantially different than the quintessential classless society? Drawing a distinction between a capitalist form of classlessness and a communist (and socialist) version was a vital component of the formation of national identity during the Cold War by those with a conservative political agenda. More specifically, classlessness in the United States had to be cast as a desirable, noble pursuit, while that in Russia had to be seen as an undesirable, evil social system. The Russians, of course, saw things quite differently. Labeling Western civilization, and specifically the United States, as "middle class" was one of the worst insults Russians could conjure up, completely consistent with how the term was still defined in *Webster's Dictionary*. To the average Russian (or at least average Soviet government official), some American visitors to that country reported, being middle class signified "lacking distinction or refinement," a definition that hearkened back to a European, aristocracy-based social system. The Russian perspective was believed to be rooted in their never really having had much of a middle class, making them see such a group as having neither the sophistication of an upper class nor the discipline of a working class or proletariat.[47]

The best defense of American classlessness during the Cold War was portraying the communist system as something completely different from a classless utopia. Despite the Bolshevik Revolution of 1917, the Soviet Union was highly stratified along class lines, experts pointed out, much more so in fact than the United States. "In the Soviet Union today, class distinctions are more exact and income disparities more glaring than any in the West," *Fortune* told readers in 1953, stating that, "Class-consciousness controls the 'classless society.'"[48] There were, authorities in such matters explained, five distinct classes in the Soviet Union: a very small ruling elite, a larger group of high-ranking government officials and professionals, a still larger group of low-ranking officials and workers, the mass of laborers and peasants, and millions of what were essentially slaves. These layers formed a bottom-heavy pyramid, with the relatively few on top enjoying the best of everything and the many in the lower tiers deprived of even the most basic joys of life. Soviet society was, in short, a caste system, not at all the classless state in which citizens lived in perfect harmony.[49] "The revolution of 1917 overthrew not only what was left of the old feudal aristocracy, but also the new rising industrial and commercial bourgeoisie," E.H. Carr wrote in *The Nation* in 1955, the country having little or no authentic, recognizable middle class.[50]

Even if there was a middle class in the Soviet Union, experts also made clear, it certainly did not resemble that of the United States. The Russian middle class consisted entirely of bureaucrats, Oscar Handlin, a Harvard professor and authority on Soviet life, pointed out in *The Atlantic* in 1957, its members' jobs controlled by the state. Loyalty to the party was a must in order to get and keep these jobs, Handlin added, creating what he as an observer felt was a palpable sense of uneasiness and insecurity in both the workplace and at home. Also unlike the middle class in the United States (and some European countries), that of the Soviet Union rarely interacted with people of a higher or lower social and economic rank. Americans of all income groups and family backgrounds worked and played alongside one another, critics explained, further blurring class lines and creating a happier and more stable society.[51]

Contrasting the American Way of Life geared around the interests of the middle class from that of the Soviet Union was more often than not a contentious exercise. The most visible display was undoubtedly the "Kitchen Debate" at the Moscow Fair in July 1959, when Vice President Nixon and Soviet Premier Khrushchev sparred while standing in a model of a "typical" suburban house designed to exhibit the benefits of American-style capitalism. (Khrushchev expressed skepticism that the house would still be standing in just twenty years, while *Pravda* claimed it was hardly "typical.") Two months earlier, however, architects and builders in each country had arranged a cultural exchange in which a group of Russians could take a close look at some actual middle-class American housing. The tour took place in October that year, with sixteen Russian architects and builders inspecting homes in Bayside, Queens, and Centereach, Long Island in New York. The Russians closely inspected the blinds, wallpaper, and television sets of a cooperative apartment in Bayside, while in Centereach they toured a seven-room ranch home as well as a two-story house complete with two bathrooms and garage. "We have that, too," the Russians frequently commented, although one of the visitors admitted that he believed the houses would last a full thirty years.[52]

The Cold War helped to keep the issue of class very much alive in the late 1950s, and revived the debate over whether academics were making it out to be more important than it really was in everyday life. "Twentieth-century America is perhaps the most egalitarian society the civilized world has ever seen, yet nowhere has there been so much solemn brooding over 'class' as in this place at this time," wrote Irving Kristol in *Commentary* in 1957. Kristol (like Tocqueville) believed that greater equality was ironically making relatively slight inequalities stand out, effectively exaggerating class distinctions. Sociologists seemed overtly concerned, if not obsessed, with matters of class, he added, not exactly sure why this was so. In any case, Kristol had no doubt sociologists thought significantly more about class than did non-sociologists, the issue too complicated and convoluted for average Americans to spend much time trying to decipher.[53] Others noted the recent higher profile of American sociologists and their fascination with class. "American sociology has become the most omnivorous of all the social sciences," observed Seymour Martin Lipset in the same publication the following year, admitting he as a sociologist was similarly committed to investigating contemporary society not unlike the ways in which biologists studied living organisms. Lipset was reviewing E. Digby Baltzell's new book *Philadelphia Gentlemen*, in which the author (he too a sociologist) argued that a new kind of upper class, not unlike the aristocracies of the Old World, was emerging in the United States.[54]

While sociologists of the late 1950s seized the idea of class as the subject gained cultural currency, scholars in that field had for some time devoted themselves to studying social and economic disparity in this country. In his review of Leonard Reissman's *Class in American Society* in *Commentary* two years later, R.A. Nisbet went so far as to say that one sociologist in particular had "introduced" the idea of class in America to ordinary citizens about twenty years earlier. Tocqueville, English statesman and amateur sociologist James Bryce, and many others (also often foreigners) had made interesting observations about social class in this country, but it was Warner in his 1941 *The Social Life of a Modern Community* who established a legitimate academic field of inquiry, Nisbet believed. Warner's identification of six American social classes in "Yankee City" had created something of a dustup at a time when the United States was supposed to be, more than anything else, united. Reissman argued that this country had become significantly more hierarchical in the two decades since the publication of Warner's book, challenging the findings of more popular writers like David Riesman and William H. Whyte.[55]

More people had been talking about class, but some believed socio-economically defined groups such as the middle class had less and less influence where it mattered most. The middle class was giving up its traditional political power as Corporate America became ever bigger and stronger in the late fifties, Andrew Hacker proposed in his *Politics and the Corporation*, seeing a new kind of "corporate citizenship" emerging. Hacker, a professor of government at Cornell University, argued that the middle class was increasingly disengaged from the political process and civic life in general, not a positive development in a society predicated on democracy. Greater mobility was one reason middle-class Americans felt a stronger connection to their company than to their local community, he explained, with loyalty to one's job now more important than that to a political party or cause.[56]

Hacker clearly recognized the revolutionary effect of the corporation on American life at mid-century. "It is the large national corporation, more than any other single social institution, that has brought about this middle-class explosion," he observed, the phenomenon not limited to the coasts but taking place across the country. What was perhaps most remarkable about this revolution in the workplace was what people actually did from nine to five: produce and manage ideas and concepts rather than machines and materials, putting education at the forefront of desirable job qualifications. The profound interest in class in America, and specifically its middle class, at the end of the decade was not surprising given the fundamental shift that had occurred in the workplace. Some were comparing the expansion of the professional or managerial class to the Industrial Revolution, which had transformed the country from an agriculture-based economy to one dominated by manufacturing. In "The Rise of the Salaried Middle Class," an article published in a journal called *The Listener*, Peter Drucker traced the "managerial revolution" to World War II, when advances in technology led to the rapid growth of bureaucracy-heavy corporations. By the late fifties, the salaried middle class had become the nation's largest working group, eclipsing the number of manual laborers just as industrialism had made farmers a smaller percentage of the workforce.[57]

From such a historical perspective, it was easy to see why, as Hacker suggested, middle-class Americans were putting employment ahead of politics. With corporations often paying for workers' health care, putting money into their pensions, and even providing a social network, it was not surprising that Americans were shifting their orientation from public to private interests. Aligning oneself too closely with a particular political ideology could be a dangerous thing, some were concluding, especially if those beliefs conflicted with those of one's bosses or bosses' bosses. (Hacker cited the refusal of middle-class whites in Little Rock to make known their supportive views of integration as a recent example.)[58] With this ascendance of corporate citizenship, regionalism (or provincialism, if you prefer) was eroding in the United States, Hacker added, the middle class across the country more likely to share common values and experiences. (Hacker claimed that 60 to 70 percent of Americans were lower-middle, middle-middle, or upper-middle class.) The much bigger downside to middle-class Americans abdicating their (generally centrist) stake in the political process was the greater possibility of extremists gaining traction, Hacker concluded, the vacuum offering right- or left-wingers a prime opportunity to gain power.[59]

The Responsibilities of the Black Bourgeoisie

While critics pointed out the shortcomings of the white bourgeoisie, E. Franklin Frazier zeroed in on those of the black bourgeoisie. Initially published in France,

Black Bourgeoisie: The Rise of a New Middle Class in the United States went off like a bomb when it hit bookshelves in late 1957. (St. Clair Drake and Horace R. Cayton's *Black Metropolis*, published a dozen years earlier, had also touched a collective nerve with its examination of black–white relations on Chicago's South Side, considered the "classic" urban ghetto at the time.)[60] Most critics, black and white, generally liked the book, but were startled by the degree to which Frazier, a sociologist at Howard University, rebuked the African American middle class. "If you don't mind being cussed out, belittled, ridiculed and lambasted all at the same time, go ahead and read the book," wrote Robert M. Ratcliffe of the *Pittsburgh Courier*, thinking Frazier was courageous to approach such a sensitive subject with refreshing candor. Like many readers, Ratcliffe was initially angry at Frazier's exposé of the black middle class, feeling it was a betrayal of sorts. Upon a second reading, however, Ratcliffe came around to Frazier's argument that too many blacks were trying to adapt to and fit into white society, that (futile) effort the real betrayal to one's race. A fair share of African American readers no doubt felt that Frazier made a good point but was talking about people other than themselves, unwilling to admit they were bona fide members of the "black bourgeoisie." *Black Bourgeoisie* was actually as much a history of African Americans as a sociological critique, but it was the latter discussion that got people's attention.[61]

Frazier's attack on the black middle class came from many angles. The African American business community, in which many felt genuine pride, was in reality a social mythology, and had no impact of any significance within the national economy. Black teachers were interested more in their careers and in social climbing than anything else, seeing no reason to instill a sense of racial identity among their pupils. Leaders of the black community preyed upon the "masses" just as much as did whites, again looking out for their own personal interests first. Concern over one's social status took priority over making real contributions in fields such as science or art, hindering the struggle for equality. It was Frazier's claim that blacks were living in a make-believe world as a refuge from racism that really touched a nerve, this artificial reality a product of their own creation. "The black bourgeoisie suffers from 'nothingness' because when Negroes attain middle-class status, their lives generally lose both content and significance," Frazier wrote near the end of the book, not easy words for many readers to take.[62]

Some black critics were reluctant to agree with Frazier's view that the "new" African American middle class was simply an inconsequential shadow of mainstream society and that the group was primarily (and vainly) dedicated to gaining white people's approval. Frazier's argument that the black middle class was basically poor and powerless seemed to contradict the statistics that were widely reported in both the African American and mainstream media. It could not be disputed that blacks had made considerable economic progress since the buildup to the war in the late 1930s. African Americans' after-tax income had jumped more than 350 percent over the past two decades, this $15 billion almost equal to the value of goods the country now exported. African Americans had not been averse to spending this money. The African American market was almost as big as that of Canada, making them an increasingly attractive group of consumers for marketers to target. In certain places of the country, such as the south side of Chicago, blacks were doing especially well, slowly catching up to whites in terms of income and home ownership. How could Frazier dismiss such real progress?, some critics asked, thinking the man was doing more damage than good to African Americans' struggle for equal rights.[63]

Some in the black press were admittedly puzzled and disturbed by *Black Bourgeoisie*, completely taken aback by Frazier's thesis. The book "would be an amusing work if handled as a satire," thought Lester Granger of the *New York Amsterdam News*, "but is a poor job if considered as a serious study of the mores of the Negro middle class." Granger, like a good number of African American journalists, felt the book shined a light on the worst elements of black life, and was not at all representative of the larger population. The book could backfire by reinforcing negative stereotypes of blacks among whites, Granger worried, and possibly make African Americans' sense of self-worth lower than it already was. Ignorant whites calling blacks uncouth, irresponsible, and culturally deficient was one thing, he pointed out, but these same charges coming from an esteemed African American professor was something quite different. The late 1950s were obviously a key moment in time for African Americans (the Montgomery Bus Boycott had occurred shortly before the book's publication, and the crisis at Little Rock Central High School shortly after), making Granger think that with his book Frazier was "hand[ing] ammunition to enemies and saboteurs." Even Frazier's concept of a "middle class" was unscientific, Granger (correctly) believed, the term nebulous and constantly shifting, especially where blacks were concerned. "The Cadillac–mink coat–cocktail party behavior which so evidently distresses Professor Frazier is a passing phase of the social evolution that is going forward," Granger explained, not at all worried about the state of the black middle class.[64]

The harshest critics of Frazier viewed *Black Bourgeoisie* as downright dangerous, a severe blow to the African American community that would indeed advance the cause of the country's most vocal racists. "I have serious doubts if some of our middle class will ever recover," fretted Jesse H. Walker, the book reviewer of the *New York Amsterdam News*. Frazier had taken special aim at the "Negro press" (designating them key agents of blacks' "deep-seated inferiority complex"), a move that served only to infuriate some African American journalists.[65] "It is a shameless, pamphleteering imposture, venting Leftist spleen under the thin guise of objectivity," spat out George S. Schuyler of the *Pittsburgh Courier*, seeing no redeeming value whatsoever of this "screed." Claims that the black middle class was filled with self-hate, had no real culture, and lived irreligious, decadent lives had no basis in fact, Schuyler insisted, the professor's sociological "research" pure and utter pseudo-science. "The book should be hailed by Southern politicians, the KKK and the White Citizens Councils," he concluded, thinking "our homegrown Reds will [also] find it good."[66]

Despite (or because of) the controversy he stirred up within the African American community with his book, Frazier made the lecture rounds over the next couple of years to further put forth his view. Black fraternities and sororities were one important group Frazier made sure to reach, knowing young, educated African Americans could heed his call for what he labeled "serious leadership." "The Negro middle class does not have the same economic base and the tradition of the middle classes in other countries," he explained in his talk titled "The Responsibilities of the Black Bourgeoisie," a distinct disadvantage that required members of that group to take charge of their own destiny. Depending on white philanthropy or trying to think the way whites thought was the wrong approach, Frazier said over and over again to black student organizations and many other groups, a losing cause that would not lead to real change. Frazier thought that the black bourgeoisie could learn much from the small upper class of African Americans who had over the years pursued both knowledge and perfection within the severe constraints it faced. Although politically and socially oppressed, the black upper class was still able to create "institutions of an authoritarian character," the professor explained, something the middle class needed to do. Segregation and discrimination had effectively stunted the maturity level of African Americans, he added, emphasizing that it was due time that blacks develop their full intellectual and artistic potential.[67]

The Status Seekers

Black Bourgeoisie certainly got people's attention with its controversial ideas about the African American middle class, but it would be another book that would redefine how class as a whole in postwar America was perceived. Vance Packard's *The Status Seekers: An Exploration of Class Behavior That Affect You, Your Community, Your Future* explored the sensitive issue of class in the United States in a way like no book published before it and, perhaps, after. We were not a classless or one-class people as so many believed at the end of the 1950s, Packard compellingly argued, but rather a nation deeply divided by social and economic inequalities. Almost equal to the idea of class universality in America was the belief in fluid class mobility, i.e., that we could easily move up (and theoretically down) the ladder of social and economic status. Packard debunked both of these myths central to our national identity, an effect that many readers found disturbing. The book hit the bestseller list just eleven days after it published, proof that people other than sociologists were quite interested in the subject of class in America.[68] (John Kenneth Galbraith's *The Affluent Society*, published a year earlier, had also got Americans talking about income disparities in their "middle-class nation.")

Packard's zigging while most observers of the American scene zagged had much to do with his decision to dice up the population into multiple demographic parts. There was not one, vast middle class in America, he argued, but five classes in which it was difficult to even identify a true middle class. After sorting Americans into the Real Upper Class, the Semi-Upper Class, the Limited-Success Class, the Working Class, and the Real Lower Class (socio-economic groups that eerily resembled the alleged class structure in the Soviet Union), Packard further shredded the population by race, ethnicity, and religion, portraying the country as a patchwork quilt of colors, customs, and beliefs. Much of the remainder of the book had to do with, as the title made clear, status seeking, i.e., how Americans differentiated themselves in order to express their economic and social rank. Jobs or careers were obviously one important way we differentiated ourselves from one another and assigned degrees of prestige. Socializing, religion, politics, and education were other opportunities to establish levels of status, Packard made clear, leaving the reader with a dizzying view of America in place of the rather simplistic one he or she perhaps had. "Obstacle courses," "pecking orders," and "totem poles" were apparently everywhere one looked, according to the author, everyday life in America not a consumer paradise for the middle class but a competitive, not very enjoyable challenge. After reading *The Status Seekers*, one could not help but see America and Americans differently, the idea of a classless or one-class society much too naïve assumptions.[69]

Packard's book was the latest and perhaps most provocative critique of the nation's class system. In Europe, elites and radicals had long engaged in an intellectual discussion of the privileges and power directly linked to heredity, but such a debate seemed generally irrelevant in a society founded on, if not living up to, egalitarianism. Nineteenth and early 20th century American sociology reflected this view, focusing on social problems (poverty, unemployment, crime, child labor) rather than class. Headway began to be made in the 1920s, however, with the publication of Pitirim Sorokin's *Social Mobility* and the Lynd's *Middletown*, as well as with the development of the Chapin Scale (which measured one dimension of social status, home environment). John Dollard's *Caste and Class in a Southern Town* was an important analysis of Depression-era social class, and a number of wartime works (notably Allison Davis, Burleigh Gardner, and Mary Gardner's *Deep South*, Gunnar Myrdal's *American Dilemma*, and Carl Withers' (a.k.a. James West) *Plainville, USA*) all dealt with issues of stratification and status.[70]

It was, however, Americans' preoccupation with equality (and inequality) in the 1950s that laid the foundation for the appearance of *The Status Seekers*. Some sociologists in the early part of the decade were studying the role of class among children, and Reinhard Bendix and Seymour Martin Lipset's *Class, Status, and Power* of 1953 was an insightful (and, at 725 pages, hefty) examination of social stratification in America. Whyte's *The Organization Man* and Riesman's *The Lonely Crowd* made the issue of class water-cooler talk, and marked the beginning of a new genre of literature dedicated to national self-examination. (Psychoanalysis, the psychological theory and therapy dedicated to a deep examination of oneself, was all the rage in the 1950s, perhaps not coincidentally.) Packard not only continued this trend but added an extra dollop of social psychology to the mix, raising the emotional level of his presentation. *The Status Seekers* had an effect not unlike that of the Kinsey Report a decade earlier, when many Americans claimed to be outraged by the author's claims but literally lined up to purchase the book. If Mills' *White Collar* told readers that being middle class was something more to be pitied than envied at the beginning of the 1950s, Packard's *The Status Seekers* made a good number of readers at the end of the decade wonder if it was worth trying to move up the country's claimed ladder of success.[71]

While the thesis of Packard's book made wonderful cocktail party chatter, the business community shook it off just as it had Mills' *White Collar*. *Fortune*, which had been throughout the 1950s one of the loudest cheerleaders for an expanded middle class because of the opportunities it afforded its readers, weighed in again on the subject at the end of the decade. A mass market consisting of Americans of a wide variety of occupations and income levels was a very good thing for businesses of all kinds and sizes, especially because of its members' relatively common consumption habits. An executive making $18,000, a skilled production worker making half that, or a truck driver making a third were often living lives not all that different from each other. All (assuming they were white, of course) could very well be happily ensconced in a six-room house in the suburbs filled to the gills with the latest appliances and television set. Every summer, each might load up their big American car with their wife and two children to go camping. The wives shopped at the same kind of stores and bought similar items, while the kids attended public schools that were much more alike than different. Such a scenario would have been impossible as recently as a decade earlier, the changes occurring so fast and seamlessly that most Americans had hardly noticed, much less recognized the historical significance.[72]

Most significant, perhaps, the ballooning of the American middle class in the 1950s had fundamentally altered the geometry of social and economic status. Rather than the traditional shape signifying class structure in the United States (and many other countries)—the pyramid—it was now a diamond that best represented the country's socio-economic structure. And unlike the pyramid neatly trisected into upper, middle, and lower classes, the diamond could not be cleanly divided into segments of any kind. "The increased bunching of Americans around the middle-income levels, the increased blurring of occupational distinctions, and the increased adoption of middle class living styles by families of diverse occupational background have all tended to make the U.S. a much more homogenous society," *Fortune* observed, with ethnic, religious, and political differences less pronounced than they had been in the past. While the magazine and other sponsors of consumer capitalism were likely exaggerating the degree to which Americans' class differential had lessened in order to serve their cause, there was plenty of quantitative and qualitative evidence to support their claim. Beyond the mounds of government statistics, clothing, for example, was no longer a reliable indicator of class. Americans' favorite question to a stranger—"What do you do for a living?"—did not automatically reveal the quality of one's neighborhood or house as it perhaps used to.[73]

Still, status had hardly gone away in this middle-class dominated society, nor had attempts of differentiation from friends, neighbors, and complete strangers. In fact, just as Kristol had noted, distinguishing oneself from others was arguably more important than ever in America, a direct result of all the "sameness" within mass culture. Nuances in just about all areas of everyday life took on great significance, the means by which to assign value to how people chose to spend their time and money. Hence the keeping-up-with-or-preferably-slightly-ahead-of-the-Joneses trope commonly assigned to the decade, in which slight variations in possessions or experiences often accounted for a considerable degree of social currency. The kind of mower a homeowner used to keep his or her lawn tidy might carry a certain amount of weight, for example, as could where one chose to go on vacation. The concept of rank was heavily steeped in American culture, after all, a function of many individuals having served in the military and now working in hierarchical organizations. Despite all the rhetoric centered around equality, status seeking was an integral part of life for the middle class, as Packard had convincingly argued, an essential feature of the consumption-based American Way of Life.[74] The trajectory of the American middle class would take a dramatic turn over the course of the next decade, however, as the "greatest show on earth" faced its greatest challenges to date.

Notes

1 Eric Johnston, "The Age of the Medium Class," *Vital Speeches of the Day*, July 15, 1953, 601.
2 "The Age of the Medium Class."
3 Frank Macmillen, "Era of Big Growth Seen for Banking," *New York Times*, May 28, 1946, 36.
4 Paul Heffernan, "Thrift Accounts Aid Mutual Funds," *New York Times*, May 14, 1950, 151.
5 "Middle Class Held Inflation Victim," *New York Times*, July 2, 1948, 32.
6 "Middle Class Waning Under Inflation, Says Industrialist," *Boston Globe*, September 24, 1948, 2.
7 "Inflation Could Wipe Out U.S. Middle Class, Threatens American System, Johnston Says," *Washington Post*, September 21, 1951, 10.
8 Ernest Havemann, "Your Best Customer is Broke," *Nation's Business*, February 1951, 34–36.
9 Henry F. Pringle, "Middle-Class Squeeze," *Nation's Business*, November 1951, 42, 60–61.
10 "Work or Labor Class?", *The Science News-Letter*, May 6, 1950, 284.
11 Holmes Alexander, "The Pull Toward the Center is Exerted on Both Sides," *Los Angeles Times*, July 11, 1949, A5.
12 "The Pull Toward the Center is Exerted on Both Sides."
13 "Undermining of Middle Class Seen," *Los Angeles Times*, April 30, 1952, 14.
14 Alexander Frazier, "Shall We Teach the Status System?" *The School Review*, February 1947, 93–98.
15 "Shall We Teach the Status System?"
16 "Shall We Teach the Status System?"
17 Milton M. Gordon "Social Class in American Sociology," *American Journal of Sociology*, November 1949, 262–68.

18 "American Community," *Life*, September 12, 1949, 108–19.
19 "American Community."
20 "American Community."
21 Gerhard E. Lenski, "American Social Classes: Statistical Strata or Social Groups?," *American Journal of Sociology*, September 1952, 139–44.
22 Richard Centers, *The Psychology of Social Classes* (Princeton, NJ: Princeton University Press, 1949) 210–11.
23 "American Social Classes: Statistical Strata or Social Groups?"
24 C. Hartley Grattan, "The Middle Class, Alas," *Harper's Magazine*, February 1951, 39.
25 Russell Lynes, "Highbrow, Lowbrow, Middlebrow," *Harper's Magazine*, February 1949, 19.
26 "Highbrow, Lowbrow, Middlebrow."
27 "Highbrow, Lowbrow, Middlebrow."
28 Ben B. Seligman, "The Briefcase Man," *New Republic*, September 17, 1951, 20.
29 "Portrait of Mr. Nobody," *Business Week*, October 6, 1951, 102.
30 "Portrait of Mr. Nobody."
31 D.W. Brogan, "Rise and Decline of a Class," *Saturday Review of Literature*, September 15, 1951, 19–20.
32 Roul Tuley, "Is Your White Collar Strangling You?" *The American Magazine*, May 1951, 24–25.
33 Dorothy Thompson, "Our Fear-Ridden Middle Classes," *Ladies' Home Journal*, January 1950, 11–12.
34 "Making Everyone Middle Class," *Business Week*, October 18, 1952, 27–29.
35 "Making Everyone Middle Class."
36 Gilbert Burck and Sanford Parker, "The Changing American Market," *Fortune*, August 1953, 98.
37 "The Changing American Market."
38 "The Rich Middle-Income Class," *Fortune*, May 1954, 98.
39 "Advertising and Marketing," *New York Times*, November 21, 1952, 36.
40 "Advertising and Marketing News," *New York Times*, February 27, 1954, 24.
41 "Advertising and Marketing News" (February 27, 1954).
42 "Middle Class Strengthens Economic Role," *Chicago Daily Tribune*, January 3, 1956, D2.
43 Sumner H. Slichter, "The Growth of Moderation," *The Atlantic Monthly*, October 1956, 61–64.
44 Frederic E. Faverty, "Age of Common Man—Common Manner," *Chicago Daily Tribune*, March 21, 1954, c4.
45 Austin C. Wehrwein, "The Middle Class Mocked as 'Bland,'" *New York Times*, December 28, 1957, 4.
46 "U.S., Red Middle Classes Seen Alike in Values," *Hartford Courant*, December 28, 1957, 6A.
47 "Yes, Ours is a Middle Class State," *Boston Globe*, May 1, 1949, 10A.
48 "Soviet Society: From the Dacha Set Down," *Fortune*, February 1953, 125.
49 Harry Schwartz, "Classes of 'Classless Russia,'" *New York Times*, March 2, 1952, SM13.
50 E.H. Carr, "Soviet Society: Is There a Bourgeoisie?", *The Nation*, October 1, 1955, 277–80.
51 Oscar Handlin, "Classes and Masses in the Communist State," *The Atlantic Monthly*, May 1957, 53–56.
52 Lawrence O'Kane, "16 Russians Tour Suburbia on L.I.," *New York Times*, October 6, 1959.
53 Irving Kristol, "Class and Sociology," *Commentary*, October 1957, 358.
54 Seymour Martin Lipset, "Aristocracy in America," *Commentary*, December 1958, 534.
55 R.A. Nisbet, "The Reality of Class," *Commentary*, July 1960, 80–82.

56 "Middle Class Sterility," *Washington Post and Times Herald*, September 21, 1958, E4.
57 Reece McGee, "White-Collar Explosion," *The Nation*, February 7, 1959, 112.
58 "Middle Class Sterility."
59 Malvina Lindsay, "'Middle-Middle' Class Abdicating," *Washington Post and Times Herald*, October 18, 1958, A12.
60 St. Clair Drake and Horace R. Cayton, *Black Metropolis: A Study of Negro Life in a Northern City* (New York: Harcourt, Brace and Company, 1945).
61 Robert M. Ratcliffe, "Behind the Headlines!: 'Black Bourgeoisie,'" *Pittsburgh Courier*, January 18, 1958, A3.
62 "Behind the Headlines!: 'Black Bourgeoisie.'"
63 Roi Ottley, "'Black Bourgeoisie' Role Is Told," *Chicago Daily Tribune*, December 29, 1957, N10. For much more on blacks' consumption habits, see Robert E. Weems Jr., *Desegregating the Dollar: African American Consumerism in the Twentieth Century* (New York: NYU Press, 1998).
64 Lester Granger, "Manhattan and Beyond," *New York Amsterdam News*, August 3, 1957, 6.
65 Jesse H. Walker, "Negro Middle Class Gets Roughing Over," *New York Amsterdam News*, March 30, 1957, 4.
66 George S. Schuyler, "The Weeks Books: Dr. Frazier Toes the Line," *Pittsburgh Courier*, May 18, 1957, B2.
67 "Frazier Calls for Serious Leadership," *Atlanta Daily World*, August 22, 1958, 1.
68 A.C. Spectorsky, "Prisoners of the More Abundant Life," *New York Times*, May 3, 1959, BR1.
69 "Prisoners of the More Abundant Life."
70 Donald Cook, "Up the Social Ladder," *The New Republic*, June 15, 1959, 18–19.
71 "Up the Social Ladder."
72 Daniel Seligman, "The New Masses," *Fortune*, May 1959, 106–11.
73 "The New Masses."
74 "The New Masses."

2

THE HAPPENING

One day you're up, then you turn around to find your world is tumbling down,
It happened to me and it can happen to you.

"The Happening," the theme song of the 1967 film of the same name

On Independence Day 1964, Adam Walinsky of *The New Republic* mused about the state of the American middle class. "In present day America, the middle class is defined largely by the fact that the poor exist," he wrote, this explaining the apathy and even hostility many average earners had toward the so-called "war on poverty" being waged by the Johnson administration. Walinsky had a good, if somewhat cynical point. If the poor moved up economically and socially through the kind of massive public programs outlined in LBJ's "Great Society," the middle class would join them on the bottom rung of the nation's totem pole. The term "middle class" itself would lose all meaning, in fact, as there would no longer be a recognizable group sandwiched between a lower and upper class. For a host of reasons, the middle class was beginning to feel less than secure, and was thus keen on preserving whatever social status it still retained.[1]

The cultural vertigo the American middle class was starting to experience was part of the larger shifting of the country's tectonic plates in the mid-1960s. Not only had a beloved president been recently assassinated, but other social, political, and economic events—"race riots" in a number of cities, student sit-ins protesting the war in Vietnam, and the "British Invasion," among them—were making it seem as if the world was turning upside down. The cultural revolution of the latter part of the 1960s would indeed prove to redefine the nation and, especially, the large number of Americans considered to be middle class. The remarkable rise of what was perhaps the first real mass middle class in history was showing all the signs of having peaked, the gears of the group now beginning to go in reverse. Too big and diverse to hold together, the middle class was breaking apart into different fragments or factions, many of them based on the social divisions of race, gender, and age. A class war of sorts was going on within the African American community alone as more middle-class blacks pulled further away from those unable to escape the cycle of poverty. Many women and young people began to seriously question middle-class values and actively seek alternative ways of life, despite often being middle class themselves. (Many in the counterculture were able to rebel precisely because they had grown up to expect a degree of financial security.) By the end of the decade, indications of a burgeoning middle-class "tax revolt" could be detected, a movement that would simmer for some years before becoming a major theme of American society. For the American middle class, the 1960s marked the end of one chapter and the beginning of another, its story instrumental in making the decade a key turning point in the nation's history.

The Revolution of the Joneses

Nobody, of course, could predict the events that would transpire over the course of the next ten years and what they would mean for the American middle class. While the nation eagerly looked forward to what the 1960s would bring, social scientists and economists reflected on how far the country had come since the turn of the century. The flattening of the distribution of wealth and economic progress on all fronts over the past six decades was considered nothing short of a social revolution. Rising average family income (adjusted for inflation), increased homeownership, reduced workweek, flood of women into the workplace, higher proportion of both high school and college graduates, and escalating gross national product were all taken as signs that this really was, as Henry Luce wrote twenty years earlier, the "American Century." Most important, the nation's once sharply defined class structure had become amorphous and fat in the middle. In 1900, the country's class system was pyramid-shaped, with the working class, farmers, and poor forming the largest group on the bottom. Above was a much smaller middle class and, on top of that, a still smaller upper class. These divisions were rigid, with Americans of different classes living very different lives and unlikely to socialize.[2]

This all changed, however, as America became a much more prosperous nation. "In six decades we have grown into a decidedly middle-class society," Bruce Bliven wrote in the *New York Times* a month before JFK would be elected president, calling this radical transformation "the revolution of the Joneses." Class distinctions no doubt still existed, especially when race was added to the equation, but the United States was widely considered to be a much more homogeneous place than it used to be. "As far as the externals of living are concerned, most of us really are beginning to approach the classless society we were always supposed to be," Bliven happily reported. Mass communications—most recently television—were having an equalizing effect, sociologists believed, bridging differences by crossing demographic lines. American society was anchored by those families with "middle incomes" which, in 1960, were in the range of $4,000 to $10,000. (Having this amount of money was considered the starting point to afford non-necessities.) This lower middle class was "rapidly becoming the common denominator of almost the whole nation," Bliven maintained, the United States "one nation, indivisible" just as the Pledge of Allegiance stated.[3]

Not only was the American middle class growing from within, but both the lower and upper ends of America's class system were heading toward it socially and economically. As the working class moved up financially, it was taking on many of the behavioral trappings of the middle class. The rich, meanwhile, had shed much of their pre-World War II ostentatious ways out of both choice and necessity. High income and inheritance taxes targeting the wealthy were leveling the playing field, and conspicuous consumption was no longer in favor. Parking a huge, chrome-laden automobile in one's driveway did not carry the cultural currency it used to, and young people of all economic classes had taken to wearing dungarees nearly everywhere. It was the rise in median income since the war, however, that was most responsible for bringing down class-based barriers. Median income had risen about 50 percent in the 1950s, an astounding rate of growth that lifted much of the working class into the lower middle class. (Income growth was over 100 percent among the bottom two-fifths of the population.) Fringe benefits, most of them initiated by unions, further inflated the gains. The Marxist argument that 20 percent of a capitalist society owned 80 percent of its wealth certainly did not hold true in the United States circa 1960, especially good news at the peak of the Cold War.[4]

Bliven, a lecturer at Stanford University, had a first-hand opportunity to observe the middle class in what was perhaps its most natural habitat. Living in a new, large suburban development in California for the past few years, Bliven was convinced he was dwelling squarely in "the paradise of the middle class." Since the end of the war, Americans had headed to the suburbs in droves, of course, something that Bliven believed helped former members of the working class get over their feelings of inferiority. Although a bit small, a brand new home of one's own set amid the "crabgrass frontier" and filled with the latest appliances was a world apart from the claustrophobic confines of the city. Living and working alongside "natives" of the middle class also allowed those who had "moved up" to feel more comfortable in their new surroundings. New members of the middle class were strongly committed to sending their kids to college, this almost universally considered the best way to extend the family's social and economic progress. Three million people were attending one of the country's 1,800 colleges and universities in 1960 (Great Britain had a total of fifteen), each student and parent viewing a good education along with a sheepskin as a ticket to the American Dream.[5]

Popular culture was also proving to educate the masses and, as a result, create an informed, culturally literate middle class. In addition to all the lowbrow and middlebrow media to be found (comic books were viewed as the lowest of the low), highbrow arts and literature had seeped into mainstream entertainment. Middle-class suburbanites were hanging reproductions of the world's greatest paintings on the walls of their $10,000 colonials and ranches, lending an instant sense of sophistication to the place. While teenagers were listening to rock 'n' roll on the jukebox at the corner diner, their parents were putting Beethoven and Bach LPs on their state of the art McIntosh and Harmon Kardon hi-fis. In between episodes of shoot-'em-ups like *Bonanza* and *Gunsmoke*, one might find a broadcast of *Hamlet* starring Laurence Olivier on the big box in the living room. (The 1956 American broadcast of the 1948 British film was believed to have been seen by more viewers than all of the people who had seen the play in a theatre since it was written.) Paperback novels, especially "pulp fiction," were certainly not Shakespearean in quality, but more than a million copies of the Bard's plays sold every year in the United States. Orchestras and symphonies across the country were doing good business, with many attendees not swells in tuxes and gowns but middle-class enthusiasts of classical music. (Ground had just been broken to build the Lincoln Center for the Performing Arts in Manhattan, with President Eisenhower present at the site to declare the future complex a "great cultural adventure.") Via all these entertainment options, even *arrivistes* to the middle class had the opportunity to feel as if they were bona fide members of what some were beginning to call the greatest civilization in history.[6]

Changes in the family and home also played a key role in the flourishing of the American middle class during the postwar years. We now look back on this era as having very defined gender roles, but at the time many "average" families were proud of how both men and women participated in childrearing and house-keeping. Fathers of earlier generations would have scoffed at how domesticated men of the 1950s, especially those of the upper middle class, had become. Granddad and great-granddad each really were the "head of the household," often running their respective homes like tyrants. Men were acting less like dictators at the office as well; the new kind of corporate culture that sprang up after the war allowed little room for robber baron-style aggression. Despite the sometimes ruthless antics we enjoy seeing on television shows like *Mad Men*, men in gray flannel suits were likely to be more interested in pension plans and vacation time than fighting one's way to the top. Drinking and carousing after work have also been exaggerated in television and movies. Middle-class men were actually spending more time at home than they used to, their priority now family life rather than working overtime or pursuing risky extracurricular activities. The affordability of supposedly labor-saving devices like dishwashers and washer-dryers was changing the role of women in the home as well, as was the introduction of thousands of packaged, prepared foods. In sum, the American middle class was at the center of a host of powerful social, economic, political trends that coincided around mid-century, elevating both its numbers and status to an unprecedented level.[7]

Although large and influential, the American middle class was widely attacked on a number of fronts by many (liberal) critics. Reaching a higher income bracket and moving to the 'burbs had made the middle class soft, some complained, its generally conservative values and political views bad for the country. Conformist, obsessed with consumerism and television, overly concerned about what other people thought of them, and sheltered in the cultural wasteland that was the suburbs, the middle class was, in short, an embarrassment, according to some bestselling books. Divorce rates were rapidly rising among the middle class, as were reports of "juvenile delinquency" by adolescents growing up in middle-class families. Such social problems were not surprising, these same critics pointed out, a natural outgrowth of the group's shallowness and materialist orientation. Even if these gripes were true, others argued, the United States should be proud about the middle class and its achievements. "The American middle class is, I believe, the most resourceful, adaptable and resilient large group anywhere in the world," Bliven wrote, its members having "the highest standards in all fields that have ever characterized any major section of the population in any big country." The early 1960s would ultimately represent the zenith of the American middle class, however, as the group proved to be somewhat less resilient than Bliven believed as events of the rest of the decade and century unfolded.[8]

A Funny Thing

Throughout the 1960s, however, experts of all stripes explained how and why the American middle class had become such a force. The principal reason, many agreed, was the entry of many members of the working class into the middle class. "A funny thing happened on the way to the Great Society," wrote Ben Wattenberg in 1967, the funny thing being that "American workmen found themselves in the middle class." Over the course of the 20th century, especially in the two decades following World War II, the nation's working class had somehow become middle class, something Wattenberg (then a freelance writer) considered both "a monumental occurrence" and "a magnificent conceptual shift." Many Americans took (and continue to take) this blurring of class lines for granted but Wattenberg was not exaggerating how significant it was from a historical context. Political instability—and especially revolution—was far less likely when the numbers of rich and poor were relatively small, making a large middle class a valuable asset for any society. The postwar years had been particularly fruitful for the middle class in the United States. Between 1947 and 1964, the number of average earners increased from 19 percent to 46 percent of the population, Wattenberg estimated after reviewing census data, a percentage that was still rising. Many blue-collar workers were now earning $10,000, a figure long considered to be the dividing line between them and white-collar workers. (Fringe benefits, especially for union members, further diminished this line.) Equally important, a college degree was not necessary to reach this magic number, another sign that the economic and social barrier between the working class and middle class was quite permeable in this country.[9]

For Wattenberg, all of this evidence added up to one very important conclusion. "The blue-collar American, the fabled workingman, has arrived in Middle-Class or Middle-Income America, whichever you want to call it," he stated, this remarkable process happening without any fanfare or major political upheaval. No revolution had taken place or heads chopped off to bring this about, an amazing thing given the long, ugly history of class conflict. This new kind of middle-class American "simply arrived quietly to take due possession of a modest, mortgaged suburban home and to think about buying a second car, a pair of Bermuda shorts, a power lawn mower, and maybe even a cocktail glass with 'martooni' emblazoned on its side," Wattenberg whimsically explained. This was not at all the way great minds of the past had imagined the day when the masses would achieve a certain level of affluence and call a piece of property their own. "Workers" had not overthrown the "capitalists" in a "class struggle" as Marx envisioned; instead, as Wattenberg nicely put it, "the American working class ... *became* the middle class." Public education and the emergence of automation had surely played important roles in this transformation, but it was the labor movement that was most responsible for the scrambling of class in America, Wattenberg (an ex-union member) believed.[10]

Stewart Alsop, a writer for *Newsweek*, also noted the melding of the working class with the middle class and its historic importance. "Something has happened in this country which, as any good Marxist will tell you, can't happen," he wrote in the magazine in 1969, "the *proletariat* has become *bourgeois*." That a "proletarian" (one of the wage-earning class) was at the same time now a "bourgeois" (a person with private property interests) was not just history making but had real political implications in present day America. "Now that the working class has become middle class, the ex-working stiff tends more and more to share middle-class sentiments," Alsop observed, meaning the left had shifted significantly closer to the center. The almost four-decade run of the New Deal and its legacy appeared to be ending as a result of the American proletariat becoming the American bourgeoisie. This was very good news for the Republican Party, of course, with Richard Nixon destined to be the biggest beneficiary of this shape-shifting in class. The GOP believed it could make serious inroads in traditionally Democratic areas in Congress as well, the beginning of a new political era in the works.[11]

It was not difficult to see that the postwar morphing of class in America had all kinds of sociological implications. Some critics were going as far as to say that a new, hybrid class had been created in America, a kind of cross-pollination between blue-collar and white-collar. This new "light blue" American owned a home but, when something broke, fixed it himself rather than calling a repairman as would a white-collar person. He might own a "martooni" glass but was more likely to drink beer and serve it to friends. He liked his job and company but would strike if his union decided higher wages or additional benefits were in order. Market researchers like Burleigh Gardner of Social Research, Inc. were, not surprisingly, intrigued by this new middle-class American, intent on figuring out what products and services he or she was most likely to buy or not buy. "Blue-collar aristocrats," as Frederick C. Klein described them in *Management Review*, had become quite fond of leisure activities once associated with the upper class such as golfing, boating, and traveling by airplane. It would have been absurd for a blue-collar worker to take a two-week vacation in Mexico in the 1950s but many were doing just that in the mid-1960s, a good example of how quickly class dynamics had changed. Investing in the stock market had also become rather commonplace among this group, another case illustrating the fluidity of class in America.[12]

The American middle class was not only mercurial but, contrary to popular belief, diverse. More astute observers of the scene debunked the prevailing idea that the middle class was one big stereotypical archetype. "The new middle class is not the cohesive, conformist mass that it is cracked up to be," John Brooks wrote in *Harper* in 1966, thinking it was instead "a society of blessed and surprising contradictions." With the de-polarization of wealth over the past few decades, the middle class had become much larger and, as a result, more heterogeneous. "The new middle class is a hotbed of cultural and ideological differences and disputes," Brooks continued, its members now equally likely to be Republican as Democrat. (The middle class had been heavily Republican before the Depression and then mostly Democratic for twenty years.) As well, regional differences within the middle class were still very much in play, your typical Texan almost a different species than the average New Yorker. The middle class was so broad, in fact, that it did not feel like a class at all despite its members' devout claims of belonging to it. For Brooks, the most pronounced differences within this new middle class were that between blue-collar Americans and white-collar Americans. Brooks challenged the theory that the working class had seamlessly blended with the professional class, thinking instead that these two groups remained very identifiable. The idea that "wage earners" were indistinguishable from the "salaried" was an appealing one because it affirmed our democratic ideals but was a mythology, he maintained. "Mr. White" and "Mr. Blue," as he called them, might earn the same amount of money and share the same kind of furniture and appliances but veered in more important matters such as family dynamics, socializing, and shopping behavior.[13]

The image of the Bermuda shorts-clad, cocktail wielding middle-class suburbanite was a persistent one, however, mostly because it was so unattractive and unappealing. The suburbanite watched too much television and drank too much beer, highbrow critics complained, the group's dreams—remodeling the house, owning a boat, having a weed-free lawn—petty and vacuous.[14] As soon as the paint was dry on the new postwar homes that sprang up in the suburbs of many American cities, in fact, critics attacked their residents for their bourgeois values and lifestyle. The three Levittown communities in Long Island, Bucks County, Pennsylvania, and Burlington County, New Jersey quickly became symbols of middle-class life in America, and easy targets for urbanites predisposed to believing they were culturally sterile. After living in the New Jersey community for a couple of years, however, the notable sociologist Herbert J. Gans concluded that all the anti-Levittown rhetoric was simply intellectual snobbery. Levittowners were interested in "a kind of interpersonal vitality along with privacy and peace and quiet," he explained in his 1967 *The Levittowners*, these lower-middle-class suburbanites just not interested in the excitement and chaos of big city life.[15]

Sick and Tired

While African Americans were part of the expansion of the nation's middle class, their social and economic progress intersected directly with the critical dimensions of race and racism. At the turn of the 20th century, almost 90 percent of African Americans living in cities were doing some kind of menial labor, making those holding jobs such as a bank messenger, headwaiter at a hotel, or barber the equivalent to middle class. Work in the steel industry during World War I pushed more blacks into the middle class, but most of those jobs disappeared after the war. (The Ku Klux Klan was influential in making industries like steel all—or nearly all—white in the 1920s.) African Americans were inspired by the higher status of people of color in Europe, especially Paris, however, and viewed the "renaissance" going on in Harlem as proof that they could succeed in this country. Although the Depression would be a setback for all Americans, regardless of color, World War II served as the impetus for the creation of a sizable black middle class. With the nation now forced to acknowledge the inherent contradiction between its democratic ideals and caste-based practices, African Americans made great strides in a wide variety of fields. Social and economic progress continued throughout the postwar years, in part due to the dramatic rise of blacks attending college. The expansion of the black middle class paralleled African Americans' migration from rural communities to urban areas. One of the key indicators of middle-class status—home ownership—also grew rapidly among African Americans in the late 1940s and 1950s. About one in three African American families reportedly owned their own home in 1960, a surprising statistic given widespread discrimination and the extremely subjugated position of blacks a half-century earlier.[16]

Even before the passage of the Civil Rights Act of 1964, which outlawed racial discrimination (and segregation), a large percentage of blacks were employed in fields that put them firmly in the lower segment of the middle class. African Americans held a quarter of the jobs in government in Washington, DC when JFK became president, for example, quite impressive given that the city had been a bastion of Jim Crow. There was a long way to go, of course, as events of the 1960s would make perfectly clear, but there was little doubt that many blacks made considerable economic and social progress over the postwar years. Much of this had to do with the efforts of the National Association for the Advancement of Colored People (NAACP) and the Urban League, organizations that had since the early part of the century vigorously engaged in the war against racial injustice. With greater freedoms had come the desire and demand for full equality, however, intensifying the activities of these organizations and the civil rights movement as a whole. "There is a rapidly increasing growth of middle class Negroes all across America," observed the *Philadelphia Tribune* in 1962, these citizens "sick and tired of token desegregation."[17] The black middle class would play a key role in the movement through the decade, viewed as models for the African American community and, at the same time, vilified for not doing more to help the cause.[18]

Except for the University of Chicago team of Lloyd Warner, Allison Davis, and Burleigh Gardner, social scientists had largely ignored the interplay between class and race in America. Frazier's *Black Bourgeoisie* was considered the bible of class dynamics within the African American community, but the book was already out of date in the early 1960s because of the economic strides blacks had recently made. About 20 percent of African Americans were middle class in 1963, it was estimated, a group that tended to distance itself from the much larger lower class. "The middle class Negro often (sometimes unconsciously) disassociates himself from the lower-class Negro, not because of any personal dislike of him, but because he is symbolic of a phase in history that he wants to forget," wrote Whitney M. Young Jr. that year in *Ebony*. In addition to those who had "moved up," African Americans who had been raised by middle-class parents were clearly distancing themselves from the less well off. These younger people had typically been educated in predominantly white schools and did not have to face overt prejudice and restrictions based on race. Not belonging to the NAACP, refusing to support the Urban League, or avoiding participation in anti-discrimination activities were considered a kind of badge of honor by this generation, a good example of the social and economic split within the black community.[19]

More attention was being paid to the widening social and economic gap within the African American community as it expanded, a gap that was viewed as respectively larger than the class divisions among whites. "The bourgeoisie Negro is gradually battering his way into the clique of middle class society, but his ordinary brother is still where he was," wrote J. Pius Barbour, a Philadelphia pastor, in 1962, that place being "THE BOTTOM."[20] Tensions between the lower class and middle class were growing as members of the former accused the latter of effectively abandoning their racial identities and loyalties by focusing on their careers and enjoying their newfound wealth. Full, committed leadership from the middle class was needed if African Americans were to achieve full equality, many were saying, a house divided a much weaker one. Continued involvement in the civil rights movement was in the best interests of the black middle class as well, activists pointed out. "The educationally privileged Negro middle class will share the horrors and hardships of his more handicapped working-class brother as long as racism exists in our society and color is still the determining factor in the treatment accorded the citizens of an imperfect democracy," Young warned.[21]

The reality of racism made the determination of class within the African American community a challenging, if not impossible task. Most sociologists, in fact, believed that blacks were not really a part of the country's dominant class structure. African Americans had their own class system, they argued, one that paralleled and was somewhat analogous to the white one. A simple exercise, as one college professor was known to do, proved this. He described a typical American family in considerable detail, with students easily able to figure out they were middle class based on their income and lifestyle. But adding the fact that the family happened to be black stymied the students, illustrating that the standard guidelines regarding class simply did not apply to African Americans because of race-based preconceptions. Few would admit it, but America was still in the early 1960s a two-caste society divided less by class than race, at least in the general public's mind. Lateral movement between the black and white class structures was highly unlikely, this the thing that was proving to be so frustrating for African Americans as they moved up. Blacks and whites could make the same amount of money, belong to the same organizations, and drive the same kind of car but not be part of the same class, a legacy of hundreds of years of racism and, especially, the institution of slavery.[22] Some argued that the black middle class was fundamentally different than the white middle class because of the dimension of race and would remain so as long as the color of one's skin mattered in the United States. It was true that when white Americans moved into the middle class, they tended to lose much of their ethnic identity; this was generally not the case for blacks, who tended to retain their racial identity while they adopted middle-class values.[23]

Although sociologists generally agreed that blacks and whites had different class systems, there was no consensus regarding what percentage of African Americans were middle class. Tillman Cothran, a sociology professor at Atlanta University, believed "not more than 25 per cent of the Negro population can be called middle-class by any reasonable standards," with about 5 percent upper class. If the same criteria for the white class structure were applied, however, only about 5 percent of African Americans would qualify for middle-class status and there would be no upper class at all. C. Eric Lincoln, a professor at Clark College in Atlanta, believed that statistics were less important than values and lifestyle in determining one's class, a view that dramatically increased the percentage and number of middle-class blacks. Those with similar educations and incomes, regardless of color, shared "many of the same desires, restraints, conformities and general patterns of behavior," he wrote in the *New York Times* in 1964. A large majority of Americans, both black and white, subscribed to such values as "democracy" and "fair play" and were in pursuit of "the good life," this common outlook a fairer measure of social and economic status than racially determined data. Likewise, middle-class blacks fished, hunted, played golf, and belonged to social clubs just like whites, and children of both races took piano lessons and went to dance classes. Behavior was a better measure of class than how much money one made or had in the bank, Lincoln held, implying that many more African Americans were middle class than commonly believed.[24]

The New Middle-Class Negro

The passage of the Civil Rights Act in 1964 made it all the more important for institutions in the public eye to diversify their staffs. The Johnson administration itself took active steps to appoint blacks to high-level governmental positions, something taken as prime evidence of African Americans' class-based ascendance. (LBJ named more African Americans to prestigious posts than all previous presidents combined.) Robert C. Weaver was serving as (the first) Secretary of Housing and Urban Development or HUD (a Cabinet position), and Andrew F. Brimmer was appointed (the first black) Federal Reserve Board member. By July 1967, the President had appointed twenty African Americans to full-time executive posts, thirteen to judicial posts, and three as U.S. marshals and attorneys. (Thirty-two more were serving on presidential advisory commissions.)[25] More black congressmen were also heading to Washington. John Conyers Jr., for example, was elected to Congress in 1964, only the fourth African American to have done so. Representing Michigan's First Congressional District (Detroit), Conyers was symbolic of what *Ebony* called "the new middle class Negro," his mission to bridge the gulf between the local African American elite and those in poverty.[26]

The private sector was gradually becoming more diverse as well. The number of African Americans holding white-collar jobs doubled between the mid-1950s and mid-1960s and, given the record number of blacks in college, more were certainly to come. The dramatic rise of both white-collar and blue-collar middle-class blacks had not, however, led to equality. Redlining still existed in many neighborhoods, for example, and asking prices for houses were sometimes known to suddenly double when it was learned that the potential buyer was African American. More so than income, education, or occupation, moving into a predominantly white area was seen by many blacks as the definitive entry point into the middle class. Others were grateful for their well-paying job but had more than a sneaking suspicion they were the "token" black in the company. (A title to the effect of "Manager of Special Projects" was evidence of such "window dressing.") Negotiating the terrain between personal success and group advancement was proving to be a tricky business for many middle-class blacks, a challenge they had usually not foreseen.[27]

Like that of American Irish, Italians, and Jews in the early part of the century, the relationship between the black middle class and lower class was complex and tension-filled. Many members of the black middle class were ashamed of and embarrassed by African Americans who were poorer and less sophisticated than they, a group dynamic made even more complicated by the overarching climate of racism. While lower class blacks took pride in African Americans who achieved success, they were also apt to believe they had likely "sold out" to some extent in order to be accepted by white society.[28] Some more militant blacks believed that simply going to college would make African Americans cut their roots and encourage them to perpetuate the status quo. "Many middle class Negroes are beguiled by what they do," wrote G.C. Oden in the *Chicago Defender* in 1965, thinking such people believed they had successfully entered mainstream American life when in fact they remained the oppressed within a racist society.[29]

The recent class upheaval within the black community made these sentiments that much more intense. Class differences became magnified in the mid-1960s, as did criticism of wealthier African Americans by those in positions of some authority. For Samuel DeWitt Proctor, a regional director of the Office of Economic Opportunity (a federal government antipoverty program), the black middle class was "the people on the hill." "The angry, poor young Negroes make no distinction between the black and white rich," he told a group in New York City in 1966, the Watts riots the previous summer a good example of how race mattered less than class to the "people down in the plain."[30] Middle-class blacks generally felt the hostility directed toward them was unfair, and resented the view that they bore much of the responsibility for improving the lot of all African Americans.[31]

The two principal civil rights organizations, the Urban League and NAACP, were quick to defend the black middle class from the rising number of attacks against the group. Clarence Coleman of the Urban League considered the black middle class to be an important "buffer" between militants and the African American elite, for example, viewing the expectations of the former unrealistic and the latter as not in favor of rapid change.[32] Leaders of each organization consistently pointed out that middle-class African Americans had contributed mightily to the fight for equality since the very beginnings of the nation. "The middle-class Negro has always been the backbone of the civil rights struggle," NAACP Executive Director Roy Wilkins made clear in 1967, deeming the organization's sharp rise in life memberships a clear indication of the group's continued support. (Life memberships in the organization cost a hefty $500 at the time.)[33] Wilkins admitted middle-class blacks were probably not doing all they could, but was adamant that they did not deserve all the condemnation they were receiving. "Downgrading the Negroes in the middle class has been a sport from time immemorial," he had written in an essay for the *New York Amsterdam News* a year earlier, citing disparaging comments made by E. Franklin Frazier and the minister and politician Adam Clayton Powell as recent examples of this "sure-fire crowd pleaser."[34]

Indeed, there was considerable evidence that middle-class blacks had recently stepped up their support for equal rights. The concept and nomenclature of "blackness" (including "black power," "black pride," and "black is beautiful") had spurred a new kind of racial identity among many African Americans, and arguably helped to moderate the growing gulf between the middle class and the broader community. The rise of "Black Studies" on college campuses also served as a unifying force for all African Americans. There was no reliable data on what percentage of the black middle class was taking part in the civil rights movement, but one study found that three-fourths of the group in Chicago contributed money to the cause or participated in some other way. (One-fifth had taken part in one or more demonstrations.) Many middle-class blacks felt they were fighting for equal rights simply through their achievements, believing their success served as an example for others to follow. Others were setting up tutoring programs, serving on advisory committees to communities like Watts in Los Angeles, or going out of their way to hire people from the ghetto. These middle-class blacks were seeking "a formula whereby they can be accepted fully in a larger, pluralistic society without giving up whatever unique positive values or characteristics they possess as a group," suggested Dan Cordtz in *Fortune* in 1966, such individuals not in favor of separatism or complete assimilation.[35]

Regardless of the tensions within the African American community, it appeared that an authentic and sizable black middle class was forming a generation after the white middle class came into its own. "Another kind of 'black power' is emerging," observed *U.S. News & World Report* in 1967, that power being the "new breed of Negroes now joining America's middle class." The recent appointment of Thurgood Marshall as the first black member of the U.S. Supreme Court was symbolic of "the thousands of Negroes moving into responsible jobs," according to the magazine, citing other cases—a biochemical researcher, investment counselor, and advertising account executive—as illustrative of the trend. Black Vietnam vets were getting some of these jobs, others going to college on the GI Bill. This was a different kind of black middle class than the traditional one, the magazine pointed out. There had always been some rather well to do African American families and a large black lower middle class, but these individuals were college educated, upwardly mobile, and, most important, often working and living alongside whites. Black middle-class housewives in Washington, DC were spending much of their time playing bridge, holding tea parties, and organizing social events, much like the white middle and upper classes. Children of this new black middle class were applying to universities like Purdue and Harvard instead of Tuskegee Institute and Howard, boding well for the next generation of African Americans. Members of the group complained that many whites treated them as exceptional and tried too hard to be nice, but this was a more than acceptable trade-off for their newfound social status.[36]

Abe Foote, a Chicago insurance salesman, was a prime example of this new kind of black middle class getting lots of attention. After a twenty-year career in the Army, Foote became an agent for New York Life Insurance and, after just two years, was making more than $16,000 in 1967. (An annual income of $7,500 was then generally considered to be the entry level for the middle class.) Foote had little patience for welfare programs of any kind, and dismissed "black power" as "stupidity in its simplest form." "It really goes back to people feeling sorry for themselves instead of pulling themselves up by their bootstraps," Foote told the (pro-capitalism) *Wall Street Journal*, subscribing to the Horatio Alger school of the American Dream. Individual initiative and hard work was the way to solve the problems of the ghetto, he firmly believed, his own rise from hardscrabble beginnings proof that drive mattered more than one's color in America. Most large insurance companies had only recently hired African American agents, but were finding that many quickly became some of their top producers. Foote sold $1 million in policies the previous year, something few other first-year agents had achieved. (Much of his sales were to white families who were quite surprised when they opened their door.) Foote had just built a nine-room house in an all-white neighborhood despite being told there would be "trouble" when his family moved in. "There wasn't a bit of trouble," Foote recalled, the fact that he made sure his neighbors saw his high-powered rifle on moving day definitely a contributing factor.[37]

Still a Brother

The mainstream media's focus on the "new" black middle class obscured the less sanguine realities among the majority of African Americans. It was true that things had gotten demonstrably better in education, employment, and politics over the past decade for many blacks across the country, and progress for African Americans could be seen even in the Deep South as Jim Crow slowly eased. This was not the case in Northern ghettos, however, where things had gotten visibly worse. The gap between the growing black middle class and "slum dwellers" in a number of big cities was getting wider, cause for considerable concern within the African American community. After assessing the "race riots" that had recently occurred in Newark and Detroit, some believed a "class revolt" was brewing in which black "have-nots" would rise up against black "haves." Black rioters had torched some African American-owned businesses in Detroit, believing that proprietors had in the past treated them unfairly and were part of the "establishment." Threats were also made against well-to-do blacks and journalists covering the scene with their white colleagues. Some poor whites had joined in the looting, evidence that revolts could indeed be class-based as well as race-based in this country. With the fight for equal rights still very much in progress, moderate African Americans were understandably deeply worried about a possible class war within the black community. "Black Americans of all walks of life must pull together or face the possibility of slipping back," warned the editors of *Ebony* in 1967, urging those in the ghetto not to take their anger out on the black middle class.[38]

Many ideas for how the black middle class could and should help the lower class were proposed in the late sixties. Carl Rowan, a newspaper columnist and radio and television commentator (and ex-ambassador to Finland), saw a useful analogy in Jews around the world financially supporting Israel, something that helped the small country win the recent Six-Day War. (The United Jewish Appeal had orchestrated an urgent emergency fund campaign that netted millions of dollars from American Jews.) With a strong passion to survive, high value on education, and deep sense of community, the Jewish people offered a constructive model for African Americans to go to school on, Rowan believed. "Every factor that enabled the Jews to triumph is vital to the Negro as he wages social, psychological, and political 'warfare' in this country," Rowan wrote in *Ebony* in 1967, calling upon the African American middle class to contribute scholarship funds to needy black students. Rowan challenged doctors, dentists, contractors, entertainers, and athletes to make a $10,000, five-year pledge in order to "send an electrifying charge of hope through the tenements and hovels where hope has for too long been a stranger."[39]

Rowan's plea was gentle compared to some of the rhetoric being directed to the black middle class. "Once upon a time there was a middle-class colored American who forgot what helped him to become middle-class," began a story by Baker E. Morten in the *Afro-American* in 1965. Members of the black middle class believed they had made it on their own through hard work or getting an education, Morten explained, but it was the groundwork laid down years ago by civil rights protestors that had made it all possible.[40] "Our middle class forgets too soon," echoed David E. Sloan in the same publication two years later, of the opinion that all "black folk" had a duty to assist "our less fortunate brothers."[41] For Reverend I.D. Newman, field director of the South Carolina NAACP, the black middle class was "smug" and "aloof," warning members of the group that they had better change their ways lest they be "not accepted by whites and rejected by their own people."[42] Editors of black newspapers across the country used their platforms to make known their dissatisfaction with the middle class. "This is the class that places itself above the battle and watches the bloody confrontation not even from the sidewalks but from a television set in a sumptuously appointed parlor," a 1967 editorial in the *Chicago Defender* went, going so far as to suggest that the black middle class was as detrimental to the cause as obviously racist white Southerners.[43]

Black politicians also had the opportunity to voice their qualms about the black middle class to a sizable audience. At a meeting the following year, Brooklyn Assemblywoman Shirley Chisholm blamed middle-class Afro-Americans (as African Americans were now often referred to) for what she considered to be their "do nothing complacency." Middle-class blacks were noticeably absent at a recent trip to Albany to discuss school bussing with state officials, she informed a local group of college women. Chisholm, well known for her festive hats, was the first (and only at that point) African American female legislator in New York State, and had her eyes set on becoming the first African American female U.S. Congressperson.[44] Like the top executives of NAACP and the Urban League (who knew on which side of their bread was buttered), Bayard Rustin, executive director of the A. Philip Randolph Institute (an organization promoting unionization of African Americans), took issue with the persistent berating of the black middle class by politicians, journalists, and preachers. Some members of the black middle class who wanted to contribute to the African American community in some way were actually being rejected because of their association with the white world. "They are dismissed as either 'uncle toms,' 'bootlickers,' 'house niggers,' or 'patsies for the power structure,'" Rustin explained in a 1967 article in the *New York Amsterdam News*. Rustin seemed genuinely confused by such logic. Was a black person a "tom" simply because he or she was able to escape poverty? Did that mean that "supermilitants," as Rustin called vocal critics of the black middle class, did not want to escape poverty? Was being deprived somehow more romantic than "making it"? Blacks could not "organize" themselves out of poverty, he made clear, meaning that some engagement with the white-dominated capitalist system was necessary. "It would be disastrous and ironic if this supermilitant anti-middle class, anti-professional attitude gained wider acceptance," Rustin argued, as it played right into the hands of those who wanted to keep as many blacks as possible in poverty.[45]

The heated debate about the responsibilities of middle-class blacks to the African American community at large showed no signs of going away. "A lot of ink is being spilled on the black middle class," observed Preston Yancey in the *Afro-American* in 1967 after having seen a television commercial depicting African Americans happily working in white-collar jobs. "Get any group together and bring up the subject [and] chances are that a hell of an argument will develop in fifteen minutes," he added. Although Yancey was exaggerating somewhat ("The American colored middle class is the most complex subject in the world today," he postulated a few months after the Six-Day War and during some of the most intense fighting of the Vietnam War), he was correct about the furor the issue was creating within the African American community. More members of the black middle class were being featured in the media as success stories but no mention of activism on their part was ever included, making critics like Yancey angry. It appeared that middle-class African Americans were just not interested in establishing a base of "black power," something that just was not acceptable for people like Yancey. Unity within the African American community and aggressive action would expand blacks' political and economic power, he maintained, this the only effective way to achieve the dignity and respect they all deserved. "This is the tragedy of the black middle class," he concluded, speaking of its members' failure to recognize their important role in the continuing struggle for equal rights.[46]

Rather than simply being an ideological debate, the class conflict within the African American community played out on a local, grassroots level. In 1968, for example, middle-class blacks in Philadelphia were trying to stop the construction of a low-income development in their neighborhood, concerned that the value of their own properties would go down if it were built. "I had to work 14 hours a day and seven days a week to earn the down payment on my house," said one resident, others worried that their area would become more transient and run-down if poor blacks moved in. Local politicians were put in a tough spot in situations like this one, trying to strike a balance between the interests of those who could use some help and wealthier voters. "If middle-class [African Americans] don't let lower-class Negroes in, what kind of success do they think we will have in integrating the suburbs?" asked Philadelphia's mayor, Carl B. Stokes.[47] The animosity between lower- and middle-class blacks in Philadelphia showed no signs of relenting. A year after Stokes asked his very good question, a group called the Philadelphia Welfare Rights Organization threw the gauntlet down to members of the city's middle class by challenging them to live on a public welfare budget for a month. Interestingly, a number of individuals—a school principal, newspaper reporter, television executive, and minister, among them—accepted the dare. A single person on welfare received $147 a month (including $26 in food stamps), not a lot of money to pay the rent and all other expenses.[48] The challenge quickly spread to other cities. Fifty middle-class citizens in Richmond, Virginia agreed to "live like a dog for a week," as the *Afro-American* reported the story, literally finding out how the other half lived.[49]

The plight of the black middle class appeared to reach critical mass with the 1968 airing of a television documentary called "Still a Brother: Inside the Negro Middle Class." "The changing mood of the Negro middle class from imitation of white middle class values to greater emphasis on enduring black dignity and achievement was exhaustively detailed last night," wrote Jack Gould of the *New York Times* in his review of the ninety-minute program that aired on N.E.T. (the predecessor to PBS) just a few weeks after the assassination of Martin Luther King. Created by William Greaves and William B. Branch and narrated by Ossie Davis, "Still a Brother" began by describing how middle-class blacks were not fully accepted by their white counterparts or less privileged people of color, leaving them in an uncomfortable position. Having discovered that achieving a certain level of economic security had not brought them real equality, middle-class blacks were recommitting themselves to the civil rights movement, the documentary argued. "The program was at its best in examining the mental revolution that was enveloping the black middle class," Gould decided, "the realization that no matter what a black person's income or accumulation of academic degrees he was still not immune to humiliation solely because of color."[50] A year later, ABC aired a documentary called "To Be Black," this program also exploring the inner turmoil of the black middle class. In the documentary, two African American psychiatrists, Dr. William Grier and Dr. Price Cobbs (co-authors of the bestseller *Black Rage*), examined representative case studies from their practice. If the people featured in the show were at all typical of the black middle class, the group was generally angry, insecure, guilty, and/or frustrated, a direct result of lingering racism or uncertainty about how to act in a white-dominated society.[51]

It was ironic that blacks' sense of "twoness" was increasing at a time when many were without question making economic, social, and political gains. The expanding black middle class was triggering a schism within the African American community, making the gap between the "haves" and "have nots" that much more apparent. In the past, little criticism had been directed at the significantly smaller black middle class and its entrepreneurial ethos. Now that same ethos was often viewed as oppositional to the struggle for equal rights, casting the black middle class as "traitors to their race." By the end of the 1960s, however, many members of the black middle class had found a way to reconcile their success within the white-dominated system alongside African American activism. The "black pride" movement was continuing to serve as the bridge linking African Americans of different classes, easing a considerable amount of the tension that had existed for the last decade or so. "It's not unusual to see a black man in a three-piece suit, walking in Manhattan, acknowledge the clenched-fist salute of a black messenger hustling by with his parcels," observed Ernest Holsendolph of *Fortune* in 1969, the two parties exchanging the common greeting, "How ya doin', brother?"[52]

A greater sense of common racial identity had by no means resolved the conflict, however. Some middle-class African Americans felt uneasy or guilty about their material comforts, especially when he or she was the recipient of some kind of prejudicial remark or act by a white person. The more militant reminded members of the black middle class that they were the extension of the oppressive system every chance they could, playing upon their troubled conscience. (A sign reading "Soul Brother," as some black business owners put up on the doors of their stores in the ghetto, was no guarantee that a brick would not go through the window.) Some activist members of black professional societies would interrupt meetings to urge their colleagues to do more for the cause. Many black clergy appealed similarly to their congregations, knowing the setting could serve as a powerful incentive to contribute any way they could. "As the ranks of the black middle class increase, the question will be whether the same tensions and tearings will continue to work on its members," Holsendolph posited, accurately predicting that they would over the next couple of decades.[53]

Other African American authority figures used their professional status to shape others' views regarding the failings of the American middle class, black and white. A fair share of African American college professors were infusing their classes with a heavy dose of the "black experience," giving their mostly middle-class students a lesson in racial identity. One such African American student completely rejected his parents' middle-class values and lifestyle after a couple of years at Columbia University. The son of a college administrator, the junior was taught by his parents to work hard, ignore his skin color, and try to achieve great things. Reading the classics and listening to classical music were a couple of the family's favorite things to do. By age twenty-one, however, the psychology major refused to listen to Brahms, thinking his music was symbolic of the white patriarchy. "It's a lot of bunk," the young man said of striving for success, believing capitalism in its entirety was unfair and inhumane, especially for blacks. African Americans' concerted efforts to win acceptance by whites was "perverse," he also felt, subscribing instead to an ethos of "black self-determination." The Columbia student's friends, all black, shared his ideas, they too abandoning their middle-class roots for a different philosophy of life centered around being black in America.[54]

The Wonder of the World

For a few years now, in fact, millions of black and white middle-class adolescents and young adults in the United States (as well as in Europe and Australia) were rejecting the values and lifestyles of their parents. Through their dress, sexual behavior, work habits, and political affiliation, a good number of American college students were showing that they were not especially interested in taking part in the older generation's model of middle-class life. A "steady" job with small annual pay raises and, after forty years or so, retiring with a pension was not what these young men and women had in mind for themselves. The stereotypical middle-class approach to life outside of work was considered equally unappealing. Monogamy, marrying early, and sharply defined gender roles were contrary to the more flexible view of relationships that many young people were forming. American youth were also challenging the standard middle-class behavior of expressing one's social status through clothes and by owning certain things. Young people had always rebelled against their parents' generation in some respects, of course, but this split seemed significantly larger and deeper than those of the past. "Simply to be born into a middle-class family was sufficient assurance that one would become, in time, a middle-class adult," wrote Frank Musgrove in *The Nation* in 1965. Now, however, this was not guaranteed, a phenomenon that was proving to fracture and fragment the American middle class.[55]

As the late sixties unfolded, many middle-class parents were shocked to learn that their child had decided to follow Timothy Leary's famous petitions to "Turn on, tune in, drop out," "think for yourself," and "question authority." In New York, city officials were alarmed at the number of middle-class teenagers moving into Greenwich Village to lead "messy, miserable lives," as one policeman put it. A special unit of the city's "Youth Board" was scouring the area near Washington Square for fourteen-to-seventeen-year-olds and, if finding one, sending him or her back home after being "dried out" (of drugs). "They may dress like Village types, but you can tell they come from middle-class homes," said Deputy Inspector John O'Connor, commanding officer of the Youth Division of the city's police department.[56] Across the country, a fair number of middle-class teens were indeed dropping out of college, quitting their jobs, burning their draft cards, and heading to counterculture epicenters like Greenwich Village and Haight-Ashbury. "We no longer find the values you lived by to have any significance," one young couple told the popular writer James Michener, adding that, "we're sure you know they're phony, too." Bigger, more important things than working hard and towing the corporate line for a nice home in the suburbs, two cars in the garage, and a key to the executive washroom were out there waiting, millions of children of middle-class parents were thinking and saying.[57]

Not just middle-class parents but ministers and college professors typically had a difficult time persuading baby boomers to alter their philosophy or change their plans. Countercultural ideology advocating individuals to "do your own thing" was an attractive alternative to being pressured to go into certain fields or join "the rat race." Dustin Hoffman's character floating in his upper-middle-class family's pool in *The Graduate* seemed to say it all, the recent college grad having little interest in a career in "plastic." The movie struck a special chord among many real life Benjamin Braddocks. It "identifies the emptiness that can result from slavish adherence to middle-class values," Michener wrote of the film in the *New York Times* in 1968, these values based in the Judeo-Christian ethic and Puritanical morality, especially those related to sex. A host of other tenets of the American middle class—a belief in education, faith in upward mobility, recognition of economic and social hierarchy, desire to accumulate money and property, acceptance of responsibility, and optimistic outlook—were similarly being challenged by a fair percentage of the younger generation. Hypocrisy ("the contradiction between what the middle class says it believes and what it does," in Michener's words) was of particular concern to those seeking an alternative way of life. How could a supposedly peace-loving, democratic people justify the Vietnam War and treatment of African Americans?, activists and non-activists alike were asking.[58]

Still, members of the New Left believed that some countercultural thinking—especially that related to ending the war—could and would resonate among the American middle class. Leaders of Vietnam Summer, a national anti-war organization that operated during the summer of 1967, made a concerted effort to enlist the support of the "silent protestors" among the middle class.[59] In his 1968 *Toward a Democratic Left*, Michael Harrington went much further, petitioning the middle class to join student radicals in creating a more socialist country. A "New Majority" of liberal Democrats could transform American politics, Harrington believed, calling on those who grew up during the New Deal to join a leftist alliance. Although the middle class was not likely to leave their suburban homes to overthrow what Harrington called the "conservative coalition," the political winds were indeed blowing away from institutional authority.[60] Feeling some financial pressure, the middle class was beginning to take a few cues from radicals like Harrington. As the postwar economic machine began to run out of steam in the late 1960s, the middle class was becoming increasingly disgruntled about their taxes going toward government-funded programs for the underclass. This was most apparent in California, where a newly elected governor was fulfilling his promise to shrink bureaucracy and the welfare state. "California, under its thirty-third Governor, Ronald Reagan, is in the throes of a middle-class revolution against the poor," wrote Phil Kerby in *The Nation* in 1967, recognizing that the budgets cuts being made and new laws being passed could be the beginnings of something very big.[61]

The 1968 elections served as an ideal opportunity for what was beginning to be called "the revolt of the middle class" to coalesce. Historically viewed as representative of the establishment, the middle class was now seen as having much in common with "extremists" like black activists, striking civil servants, Vietnam War protestors, and "hippies." In a matter of just a few years, the middle-class voter had become the "forgotten man" of American politics, someone *U.S. News & World Report* considered "overtaxed, overburdened and ignored." The most remarkable thing about this emerging "revolt" was its breadth, said to encompass businesspeople, labor, farmers, retirees, and housewives. "There is in the land a certain restlessness—a questioning," LBJ had said in his 1968 state-of-the-union message, surely aware that a good part of this unease had to do with Americans' growing weariness of paying for his "Great Society." Crime, racial unrest, and the war were other major beefs among the middle class, contributing to the sense that the country as a whole was in serious decline. Youth culture's attraction to the era's notorious triumvirate of vice—sex, drugs, and rock 'n' roll—was also disturbing to many of those who had grown up before World War II. Not just politics but the nation's education system, organized religion, and the courts appeared to be imploding, a perfect storm for incumbents to lose re-election at the polls in November. "The outlook in the nation today ... borders on open insurrection or anarchy," *U.S. News* concluded, the middle class in particular looking for new leadership who could right the ship.[62]

All the major candidates running for president that year—Republican (and former Vice President) Richard Nixon, Democrat (and current Vice President) Hubert Humphrey, and Independent (and former Alabama Governor) George Wallace—accepted the thesis that unhappy middle-class voters would decide the coming election. (The recent assassinations of Martin Luther King and Robert Kennedy, along with the violence at the Democratic National Convention in Chicago, added to the sense that the nation was spinning out of control.) Nixon had begun referring to the middle class as "forgotten" Americans, good, patriotic citizens who were in no way responsible for the sorry state of the country. Humphrey and Wallace were making essentially the same argument, meaning there would be no revolution come November. While acknowledging there were definite problems (especially, for Nixon, law and order), the candidates largely ignored the deep divisions within American society along class and racial (and gender, it could be argued) lines.[63] The centrist position worked best for Nixon, who narrowly beat Humphrey. Even before Nixon moved into the White House, it seemed certain that he would continue to focus on his Middle America base. "Not since the Coolidge-Hoover era has Washington been so clearly the fulcrum of middle-class power as it will be when Nixon takes over," wrote Kenneth Crawford in *Newsweek* two weeks after the election. Crawford considered the American middle class to be "the wonder of the world," with nothing remotely like it in any other country. Like the group or not, the middle class remained the key to American politics, a fact that had undoubtedly worked in Nixon's favor.[64]

The "forgotten man" did not appear to be especially remembered during Nixon's first year in office. White, middle-class Americans were generally pessimistic about the nation's future, the results of a 1969 Gallup poll revealed, and believed that the country was in a worse place than it had been five years earlier. The middle class had a remarkable lack of faith in where the nation was headed; almost half of the respondents felt that the problems in the United States could not be solved at all. Vietnam was considered America's greatest problem, not too surprising given that the number of U.S. troops involved in the war peaked that year. (Three months before the poll was taken, *Life* magazine had published photos of the 242 Americans killed the previous week in Vietnam, something that further reduced support for the war.) White, middle-class Americans viewed racial unrest as the country's next greatest problem and, disturbingly, were resentful of the gains blacks were making. Blacks received preferential treatment in unemployment benefits, were to blame for not having jobs, and "could have done something" about the conditions in the slums, the poll reported.[65] Middle-class Americans had headed into the 1960s full of hope and optimism about what the future would bring, but now dreaded what might be coming around the corner. For the American middle class, the 1970s would indeed be a challenging decade, so challenging in fact that the group's very survival would be at stake.

Notes

1 Adam Walinsky, "Keeping the Poor in Their Place," *The New Republic*, July 4, 1964, 15–18.
2 Bruce Bliven, "The Revolution of the Joneses," *New York Times*, October 9, 1960, SM28+.
3 "The Revolution of the Joneses."
4 "The Revolution of the Joneses."
5 "The Revolution of the Joneses."
6 "The Revolution of the Joneses."
7 "The Revolution of the Joneses."
8 "The Revolution of the Joneses."
9 Ben Wattenberg, "The Century of Man," *Challenge*, March/April 1967, 26–27, 45.
10 "The Century of Man."
11 Stewart Alsop, "Nixon and the New Bourgeoisie," *Newsweek*, January 27, 1969, 96.
12 Frederick C. Klein, "Trends in Blue-Collar Spending," *Management Review*, May 1965, 45–48.
13 John Brooks, "Mr. White and Mr. Blue," *Harper*, June 1966, 88–91.
14 "The Century of Man."
15 Elmer Bendiner, "Cult of the Majority," *The Nation*, July 17, 1967, 57–58; Herbert J. Gans, *The Levittowners: How People Live and Work in Suburbia* (New York: Pantheon, 1967).
16 Carl T. Rowan, "Race in America—Past, Present, Future," *New York Times*, January 17, 1960, AD4.

17 "Vast Middle Class of Negroes Sick and Tired of Token Desegregation," *Philadelphia Tribune*, February 3, 1962, 4.
18 "Race in America—Past, Present, Future."
19 Whitney M. Young Jr., "The Role of the Middle-Class Negro," *Ebony*, September 1963, 67–71; E. Franklin Frazier, *Black Bourgeoisie* (Glencoe, IL: Free Press, 1957).
20 J. Pius Barbour, "Negro Progress an Illusion; Civil Rights Strictly Middle Class Fight," *Philadelphia Tribune*, January 30, 1962, 4.
21 "The Role of the Middle-Class Negro."
22 C. Eric Lincoln, "The Negro's Middle-Class Dream," *New York Times Magazine*, October 24, 1964, SM35+.
23 "Middle Class Status Warning by Weaver," *Chicago Defender*, May 12, 1962, 2.
24 "The Negro's Middle-Class Dream."
25 "Negroes Move Up in Government," *U.S. News & World Report*, July 3, 1967, 57.
26 Simeon Booker, "A New Face in Congress," *Ebony*, January 1965, 73–78.
27 Dan Cordtz, "The Negro Middle Class Is Right in the Middle," *Fortune*, November 1966, 174–80.
28 M.S. Handler, "Negroes Advised to Aid Their Poor," *New York Times*, February 21, 1966, 45.
29 G.C. Oden, "Dilemma of the Middle-Classes," *Chicago Defender*, September 18, 1965, 36.
30 "Negroes Advised to Aid Their Poor."
31 "The Negro Middle Class Is Right in the Middle."
32 "The Negro's Middle-Class Dream."
33 "Middle-Class Negroes Are Termed Backbone of Civil Rights Struggle," *Chicago Defender*, May 20, 1967, 4.
34 Roy Wilkins, "In Defense Of The Middle Class," *New York Amsterdam News*, June 11, 1966, 14.
35 "The Negro Middle Class Is Right in the Middle."
36 "Growing Success of Negroes in the U.S.," *U.S. News & World Report*, July 3, 1967, 54–57.
37 Stanford N. Sesser, "Nimble Negro," *Wall Street Journal*, March 13, 1967, 12.
38 "A Time for Cooperation," *Ebony*, October 1967, 150–51.
39 Carl Rowan, "An Answer to Youth's Challenge," *Ebony*, August 1967, 140–43.
40 Baker E. Morten, *Afro-American*, "The Middle Class Man Who Forgot Who He Was," July 3, 1965, 5.
41 David E. Sloan, "Our Middle Class Forgets Too Soon," *Afro-American*, November 25, 1967, 5.
42 "Middle-Class Hit By Freedom Fighter," *Afro-American*, November 4, 1967, 17.
43 "Negro Middle Class," *Chicago Daily Defender*, August 21, 1967, 13.
44 "Criticize Middle Class," *New York Amsterdam News*, June 8, 1968, 7.
45 Bayard Rustin, "The Militants and the Middle Class," *New York Amsterdam News*, October 14, 1967, 15.
46 Preston Yancey, "Tragedy of the Black Middle-Class," *Afro-American*, November 11, 1967, 17.
47 "Middle Class Negroes Battle To Keep Poor Ones Out Area," *Philadelphia Tribune*, September 24, 1968, 24.
48 Lawrence H. Geller, "Middle Class People Asked to Live Month on Public Welfare Budget," *Philadelphia Tribune*, September 30, 1969, 1.
49 "Middle-Class Persons 'Test' Welfare Budget," *Afro-American*, December 13, 1969, 17.
50 Jack Gould, "N.E.T. Program Views Negro Middle Class," *New York Times*, April 30, 1968, 95.
51 "Middle Class Blacks on ABC's 'To Be Black,'" *Chicago Daily Defender*, August 23, 1969, 35; Dr. William Grier and Dr. Price Cobbs, *Black Rage* (New York: Basic Books, 1968).

52 Ernest Holsendolph, "Middle-Class Blacks are Moving Off the Middle," *Fortune*, December 1969, 90–95.

53 "Middle-Class Blacks are Moving Off the Middle."

54 "Middle-Class Blacks are Moving Off the Middle."

55 Frank Musgrove, "The Teen-Age Aristocracy," *The Nation*, April 26, 1965, 439–42.

56 Natalie Jaffe, "City Seeks to Aid Young in 'Village,'" *New York Times*, March 29, 1966, 84.

57 James A. Michener, "The Revolution in Middle-Class Values," *New York Times*, August 18, 1968, SM20–21.

58 "The Revolution in Middle-Class Values."

59 Steven R. Weisman, "War Protest Going Middle Class," *Wall Street Journal*, September 11, 1967, 16.

60 Tom Christoffel, "For Middle-Class Candides," *The Nation*, June 3, 1968, 736–37; Michael Harrington, *Toward a Democratic Left: A Radical Program for a New Majority* (New York: Macmillan, 1968).

61 Phil Kerby, "Revolt Against the Poor," *The Nation*, September 25, 1967, 262–67.

62 "Middle-Class Revolt Brewing," *U.S. News & World Report*, June 3, 1968, 52–54.

63 "The Forgotten?" *The Nation*, September 23, 1968, 259–60.

64 Kenneth Crawford, "Middle-Class Revolt," *Newsweek*, November 18, 1968, 52.

65 "Whites Reported Pessimistic on U.S.," *New York Times*, September 29, 1969, 36.

3

APOCALYPSE NOW

We are going through the liquidation of the middle class.

Labor arbitrator William Gomberg in 1975

The numbers from the 1970 census were in, and, for "Mr. Average," as *Newsweek* put it, they were not pretty. The average American household consisted of 3.6 people, 2.3 of whom were children. The family's income was precisely $10,577, about $2,200 of which went to federal, state, local, real estate, and other taxes. Out of the remaining $8,000-plus, "Mr. Average" made payments on his house, car, appliances, often at exorbitant interest rates. With inflation, the little that was left was worth 10 percent less than it had been five years earlier, this only adding insult to injury. "Mr. Average" dreamed to send at least one of his or her 2.3 children to college, but it was unlikely they would be able to afford it. Chances were greater, in fact, that a son would be drafted by the Army, this at a time when the Vietnam War was at its peak. To use a verb President Nixon had recently made popular, "Mr. Average" was being "shafted," the system seemingly designed to work against members of the middle class in every way possible.[1]

Its foundation still shaking from the cultural revolution of the last decade, the American middle class was about to go through a gauntlet of challenges that would threaten its very existence. Spiraling inflation and a nasty recession would put an end to the country's great economic run of the postwar years, the "stagflation" of the 1970s seriously eroding the purchasing power of the middle class. If that were not enough, the middle class continued to face social and political upheaval at every turn, its confidence rattled and direction unclear. The very nature and composition of the American middle class would change considerably over the course of this decade as it adapted to an increasingly hostile environment. Said by many to be faced with possible extinction, the middle class would find shrewd ways to survive and, against all odds, maintain its status as the heart and soul of the nation.

Shabby but Respectable

For the American middle class, the 1970s began much like how the 1960s had ended. With the last notes from Woodstock still reverberating, the middle class remained very much divided along generational lines. Political orientation differed quite a bit according to age, just one factor making the middle class a much less cohesive group than it had been in the 1950s. In their 1970 bestseller *The Real Majority*, Richard M. Scammon and Ben Wattenberg reported that most middle-class voters were basically centrist, meaning politicians should avoid extreme positions on either side. And in his *The Middle Americans* published the following year, Robert Coles found that the middle class was, as the book's subtitle went, "proud and uncertain," meaning they were basically content with their lives but felt unqualified to have strong political opinions.[2]

This was entirely untrue of a significant portion of America's youth, however. University campus protesters were obviously extremely politicized, especially when it came to the Vietnam War. Rejecting their parents' values steeped in materialism and the "American Way of Life," these mostly middle-class students had the ambitious objective of forging a much different kind of society than one predicated on achieving upward social and economic mobility.[3] VISTA, the national service program dedicated to fighting poverty, served to "radicalize" a good number of volunteers and push many more to the left, the 1971 study revealed, a finding that made the Nixon administration even more critical of it. (VISTA had been formed in the mid-1960s under LBJ's administration.) Seeing poverty, racism, and war firsthand was having a profound effect on these children of relative affluence, the sociologist who authored the study found, making them angry at the Nixon administration for not doing more to help.[4]

Because the still alive cultural revolution was being led by upper-middle-class youth (and centered on some of the best university campuses), some were predicting a looming opportunity for younger members of the lower middle and working classes. Those so vehemently protesting the mechanism of consumer capitalism and the institutions that served it were, after all, not likely to join its ranks anytime soon. Filling the holes would be the children of the less well off, some were predicting, these young men and women eager and willing to move up through a good professional or managerial job. In a 1971 essay for *The New Republic*, Peter L. Berger and Brigitte Berger, each a professor of sociology, called this potential scenario "the blueing of America," something that would fundamentally alter the nation's class structure. Influenced by the counterculture but not absorbed by it like their more affluent classmates, lower-middle and working-class students would fill these positions en masse, shifting the strata of class in America. Ethnic Americans attending colleges like Fresno State and Fordham, rather than Jews and WASPs occupying buildings at Berkeley and Columbia, could very well be running corporations, landing on the moon, or even living in the White House in the not so distant future, the Bergers proposed. Much like Marx envisioned, the blue-collar masses would prove victorious, but not at all in the way he imagined.[5]

In terms of numbers, at least, the working class was already keeping the nation running. The widespread belief that the United States was a "middle class nation" or "middle class society" made it easy to forget that most Americans were, on an occupational basis, working class. It was true that white-collar workers officially outnumbered blue-collar workers (47 percent to 36 percent in 1971), but this was only because of the way the Census Bureau sorted types of jobs. Garbage collectors, waiters, and many other jobs were considered "service workers" although they were clearly more blue-collar in nature than white-collar. Farmers too were put in a separate category, this also deflating the potential percentage of blue-collar workers. Mail carriers, cashiers, telephone operators, and supermarket employees were, meanwhile, deemed white-collar by the government, inflating that percentage. (Part-time clerical and sales jobs were also considered white-collar, this too somewhat debatable, especially since many holders of these positions were women married to blue-collar workers.) After adjusting the Census Bureau's data to better reflect reality, researcher Andrew Levison reported that about 43 percent of Americans were middle class and 57 percent working class, this a clearer picture of the country's social structure based on occupation. "In a statistical sense at least, the middle-class majority is a myth," Levison flatly stated, Americans overestimating their individual and collective economic and social status.[6]

The mythology of the United States being a predominantly middle-class nation was, of course, hardly a new phenomenon. Even the flourishing of the middle class in the postwar years was more political and intellectual than economic, Levison argued, the country's social structure skewed toward the working class then as well. As in the 1970s, more Americans in the 1950s and 1960s were blue-collar than white-collar, this despite the popularity of books focusing on the social dynamics of the upper middle class like John Kenneth Galbraith's *The Affluent Society*, William H. Whyte's *The Organization Man*, David Riesman's *The Lonely Crowd*, and Vance Packard's *The Status Seekers*. Television shows like *Leave It To Beaver*, *Father Knows Best*, and *Ozzie and Harriet* had also made it appear that the vast majority of Americans lived in nice houses in pleasant suburbs where dads in suits came home every evening to find delicious dinners and precocious children waiting. Advertising had served as perhaps the loudest voice propagating the mythology that the majority of Americans enjoyed at least some degree of affluence. The truth, however, was that most Americans were now experiencing what unions liked to call "shabby but respectable" lives, i.e., a stable working-class standard of living. "It is the world of Sears Roebuck furniture,

$4 bourbon, and six-year-old cars traded in for two-year-old models," as Levison described the early 1970s version of this lifestyle, illustrating why the appeal of being middle class remained so strong. As well, the working class had no savings whatsoever, making a modicum of financial security a big part of their American Dream.[7]

Others came forth to make it clear that the popular image of the American middle class basking in material abundance was not reflective of reality. In his 1972 book *The Myth of the Middle Class*, Richard Parker offered similar evidence showing that average earners were not enjoying the consumer paradise that we liked to believe they were. Only 30 percent of American families owned a second car, for example, and many had none. The median value of a single-family home was $17,000 in 1970, hardly the kind of investment that would one day ensure a carefree retirement. Based on the numbers, a more solid claim to make was that America was a "working class nation," something most of us did not want to admit or even hear as it threatened our faith in egalitarianism and the ideals of democratic capitalism. Most interesting, perhaps, Parker went much further back than had Levison to show that wealth was unevenly distributed in this country. In fact, if there was any one constant through the nation's two hundred year history and its wide economic and political swings, he argued, it was financial inequality. (The poverty rate was essentially the same as in revolutionary times, for example.) A major overhaul of the country's tax laws would be required to turn America into the "middle class society" that was so beloved, and that was obviously not going to happen anytime soon.[8]

Lost in Space

Although it was certainly a step up from working class and a lot better than being poor, achieving middle-class status in the early 1970s was hardly cushy. Even forty years ago, wealth was concentrated at the top in the United States, far more than it had been soon after World War II. Tax and estate laws favored the already advantaged, making it difficult for anyone not currently wealthy to catch up. Even the term "middle class" was somewhat of a misnomer, economically speaking at least, as the average income was actually located somewhere within the upper end of working-class salaries. Upward mobility—another central tenet of the American Dream—was more illusory than reality for the majority, and for average earners, there was little money left over for non-essentials after all the bills were paid. The psychological implications of this gap between illusion and reality were, as one would imagine, considerable. In their 1972 book *Hidden Injuries of Class*, Richard Sennett and Jonathan Cobb discussed how many middle- and lower-middle-class Americans felt like failures despite being quite normal, both socially and economically. Even though these individuals felt like victims of forces beyond their control, they also blamed themselves for not having "made it." This group of Americans also believed they were making significant sacrifices for the benefit of their children. For them, deprivation made sense, as it increased the odds that their children would achieve the kind of success they had hoped for.[9]

As for Mr. Average, sending one or more children to college represented a primary desire among middle-class Americans. With ever-rising tuitions beyond the reach of many members of the middle class, however, some were predicting that college campuses would be comprised of the rich who could pay their own way and the poor who qualified for student aid. Since 1966, middle-class families had taken part in the Guaranteed Student Loan Program for financial assistance, but Congress had recently changed the rules of the program. Eligibility was now based on actual need rather than income, disqualifying most middle-class families from receiving the $1,500 loan.[10] With private universities now costing more than $20,000 for four years (almost twice the average annual household income), many middle-class families were opting for more affordable state colleges. Any large purchase—a new car or vacation, say—was often postponed during those four years, with some families becoming masters at budgeting. "We didn't watch dollars, we watched pennies," said one mother from Houston who put two children through college, her family's experience not that different from many other middle-class Americans.[11]

With no GI Bill to support college education as they had enjoyed, parents worried that upward mobility no longer existed for their children. Conceding that the days of rising expectations could very well be over had a profound effect on middle-class Americans. Despite Mies van der Rohe's popular adage, more (or bigger or faster) had always been better in the United States. But now, as the energy crisis made clear, making do with less was the order of the day. Cleveland Amory of the *New York Times* called this "the new game of one-downmanship" after observing a certain kind of status being awarded to values like conservation and restraint. Driving less and using less electricity had become popular things to do, a reversal of the more-is-better paradigm of consumption that had prevailed in America for so long. "Now the job is keeping down with the Jones," Amory wrote in 1973, the middle class now displaying a completely opposite style of competitive consumerism. Rather than counter the Joneses' purchase of a new Cadillac with a Lincoln Continental, for example, the Smiths were buying a mid-priced Oldsmobile after seeing that their neighbor had got a Chrysler. The upside-down battle did not end there, however. As times got even tougher, the Joneses bought a Ford, meaning the Smiths had to go out and get an economy model Chevrolet. But then the Joneses traded the Ford in for a Volkswagen, demanding that the Smiths swap their Chevy for an even cheaper Toyota. Finally, the Joneses hit rock bottom by getting rid of the Volkswagen and finding a used Mazda to drive. The Smiths got the last laugh, however, selling their Toyota and deciding to take the bus to get around.[12]

While there might have been some satisfaction playing the game of "one-downmanship," there was little reward to be found in the prospect of downward mobility. "An era of self-doubt and change is dawning for the great majority that calls itself middle class," *U.S. News & World Report* began its 1974 special report on the "squeezing" of the American middle class. Double-digit inflation and a two-year recession had escalated financial insecurities and the Watergate scandal was eroding Americans' faith in institutional authority of all kinds. Not only was disillusionment with the economy and politics on the rise, but the term "middle class" had recently become a rather disparaging epithet. Not that long ago equated with the All-American values of patriotism, hard work, and faith in the future, "middle class" was now viewed as anachronistic and stodgy. (The #1 television show between 1971 and 1976 was *All in the Family*, its protagonist Archie Bunker the very embodiment of this less than favorable image of middle-class Americans.) Reeling from the anti-establishment sentiment of the counterculture, the middle class was bearing the brunt of the economic and political turmoil of the times. There was little doubt that the century-and-a-half ascent of the American middle class had run its course by the mid-1970s, this reversal a major turning point in the history of the nation.[13]

Some looked beyond the obvious stresses of the time for the causes of the predicament of the middle class. "The psychic traumas that afflict the American middle class cannot be healed until a basic social-structural change is brought about," stated John C. Raines, a professor of religion at Temple University, arguing that the problem was rooted in our competitive and hierarchical educational system. The idea of "success" was instilled early in our lives, Raines explained, setting us up for disappointment when we learned that there were far fewer big "winners" in life than "losers." The grading system, in which the average grade was designed to be a "C," gave us an early lesson in this hard truth. Schools' real job was to teach children how to fail without complaining, Raines suggested, a terrible form of education that carried over into adulthood. Because of tax and estate laws (as well as the Old Boy Network), upward mobility was very difficult for the average American despite the popular belief that hard work would inevitably be rewarded.[14] Contrary to our rags-to-riches mythology, most of us—specifically the middle class—were destined to get a "C" in life, a notion that Raines elaborated on:

> To be a "middle"-class people is to be a people "in-between," or lost in space. Our self-respect is to be found not where we are but just ahead, where success beckons. The middle class is a class perpetually embarrassed about itself, never quite in possession of its pride. It runs from those behind—the failures, the nobodys, the ones who get pushed around; and it runs after those ahead—the successes, the people who feel content and self-confident. So those who are "middle" and live forever "in-between" are constantly emptied out, bereft of themselves. Theirs is a life lived under the endlessly measuring eyes outside, in a place full of hope and hurt.[15]

Raines considered Norman Vincent Peale as the master in tapping into this "psychic trauma" of the American middle class. The titles alone of Peale's best-selling books *The Art of Living*, *A Guide to Confident Living*, *The Power of Positive Thinking*—suggested that readers had to, in Raine's words, "fill and make potent one's inner space" in order to be truly successful. How those in the middle could do that was not terribly important (for Peale it was applied Christianity), Raines believed. In fact, Peale's leaving readers somewhat empty and unfilled was the better strategy, as this meant they would always need additional comfort and healing (and another book). Raines argued something much more systemic was needed to solve the "middle-ness" problem rather than treat the symptoms with feel-good balms. Reforming the American way of teaching would be a good start, he thought, specifically by educating students with the truth about how wealth and power worked in this country. The fact was that the overwhelming majority of us were and would remain wage-earners who in some way worked for the very small wealthy ownership class, this a long way from the idea that we were a large middle class that could climb the ladder of success with determination and fortitude. "Positive thinking" only perpetuated the mythology of the American Dream, Raines concluded, keeping the middle class in a kind of socio-economic purgatory.[16]

Not everybody believed in accentuating the negative and eliminating the positive, however. Demographer Ben Wattenberg, who, with Richard Scammon, had authored *The Real Majority* a few years back, was surprisingly optimistic about the state of the American middle class in his new book *The Real America*. "The dominant rhetoric of our time is a rhetoric of failure, guilt and crisis," Wattenberg wrote, while "the evidence of the data is the evidence of progress, growth and success." After "marinat[ing]" himself in Census statistics, Wattenberg made the case that no less than 74 percent of Americans were middle class, as high a percentage as anyone had proposed in recent memory. "The emergence of this Massive Majority Middle Class is a benchmark of major historical impor-tance," he stated, taking issue with all the naysayers claiming that the group's best days were long gone. From Wattenberg's "glass-is-half-full" perspective, American workers were more skilled and productive than ever and spent their money on useful, important things, a direct contradiction of what most critics were saying. President Ford praised the book's conclusions, happy to see that at least one authority agreed with him that things were not as bad as they seemed for the middle class.[17]

Wattenberg's claim that three-fourths of Americans were middle class (based on a complex array of variables) was clearly an anomaly. The middle class was now most commonly defined as households earning somewhere between $10,000 and $25,000, meaning it accounted for about 52 percent of the population based on income. (Thity-nine percent had incomes of less than $10,000 in 1974, while 9 percent had incomes of more than $25,000.) How much money one made was also less than reliable when determining class, however. Truck drivers and even street cleaners could earn twice the salary of a veteran teacher, proof that other factors—occupation, education, family background, and many more—heavily influenced our conception of class.[18]

While the middle class was roundly criticized for being an army of Archie Bunkers, the truth was that it was an extremely diverse group of individuals. If there was any one thing uniting the American middle class in the mid-1970s, it was the difficulty of buying and keeping up a home. The price of an average house was continuing to rise faster than the average income, making home ownership a fading dream for many of the middle class. The cost of a new house had increased 38 percent since 1969, with inflation also making appliances, furniture, utilities, repairs, and property insurance more difficult to afford. Mortgage rates had risen from 7 percent to 9 or 10 percent, and the recent energy crisis pushed gas, electric, and fuel-oil bills to record highs.[19]

With 10 percent mortgage rates and the overall cost of living rising 10 percent annually, the average American was fighting a losing battle when it came to saving money. Making money through investments was an even greater challenge, especially given the bearish stock market of the mid-1970s. Banks were offering about 5½ percent on savings accounts—exactly half the rate of inflation in 1974. U.S. savings bonds generated 6 percent a year, making them not much better. Rather than watch its savings winnow away, the middle class was trying new ways to make money or, at least, stay even. Money-market mutual (or cash-management) funds generating 11 percent to 12 percent were newly available to smaller investors, making them an attractive alternative. (Previously, only institutions and the wealthy with a minimum of $100,000 could invest in these funds, but now just $5,000 was required.) Another increasingly popular financial product was "float notes," which typically paid 1 percent more than 91-day Treasury bills, or about 10 percent. Average earners were exploring a host of other investments such as corporate bonds, Treasury securities, and tax-exempt municipal bonds. Middle-class Americans were becoming rather savvy investors, even if it was more out of necessity than choice.[20]

Like clever investing, joining a union was a good way for the middle class to keep up with galloping inflation. The labor movement in America had always been primarily working class but now more professionals and other white-collar workers were joining its ranks. Teachers, professors, journalists, musicians, actors, and government workers were hurriedly becoming members of labor unions and employee associations for the same reasons that blue-collar people had done for decades: higher pay and greater job security. Watching assembly-line workers get substantial raises while their own salaries barely moved an inch, the middle class was concluding that unions and their progressive politics were not so bad after all. Having some protection against the big layoffs going on in some industries (like aerospace) was another reason to band together. Leaders of the AFL-CIO and other unions were excited by the trend, seeing their movement as a stronger force with significant numbers of the middle class on its side.[21]

With the weakening of the traditional, WASP-based middle class in the mid-1970s, Americans who had long aspired to belong to the group had an ideal opportunity to do so. Economic and political strife had made national identity a more fluid concept, good news for those of Southern and Eastern European origin. White ethnic Americans long viewed as working class were now more often recognized as middle class as the country as a whole gained a greater sense of its pluralism. The historically WASP-oriented middle class could accommodate these tens of millions, mostly urban Italian, Greek, Jewish, Slavic, and Irish Americans, it was becoming clear, even though their income was generally less than existing members of the group. And with a genuine economic dimension, the ethnic awakening of the 1970s went beyond perceived class status. More white ethnics were attending college and starting businesses, and large corporations were finally opening their doors to first and second generation Americans. And unlike their parents who were likely to underplay their ethnicity in order to emphasize their "American-ness," this generation took visible pride in their families' roots.[22] The boundaries of the middle class were clearly shifting, a phenomenon magnified by changing racial dynamics.

A Chimera

Just as white ethnics moved into the middle class as its boundaries became more permeable, indications were that African Americans were similarly joining the group in significant numbers. Black radicals or "extremists" like the Black Panthers were making the headlines in the early 1970s, but the more important news was that the African American middle class was rapidly growing. As the numbers of black farm workers, domestics, and non-farm laborers fell dramatically from the late 1950s through the 1960s, many of these African Americans took lower-middle-class jobs such as receptionists, nurses, and truck drivers. (High military spending in the sixties, i.e., the Vietnam War, also contributed to a major shift in black employment patterns.) Income for blacks too grew over this period. Only 10 percent of black families earned more than $8,000 (inflation adjusted) in 1957, according to the Bureau of Labor Statistics, while 32 percent did by 1968. Blacks' median income was almost two-thirds that of whites by the beginning of the 1970s, another sign of a growing middle class. Except for skin color, the black middle class was starting to look a lot like the white middle class. "This black silent majority shares with its white counterpart many of the same jobs and the life-style accompanying those jobs," noted Edwin Harwood, a professor at Rice University, in the *Wall Street Journal* in 1971, African Americans equally concerned about staple middle-class issues like good schools and crime. Racism and seemingly irreversible poverty in ghettos were still major problems for African Americans, of course, but progress was being made.[23]

A closer look, however, revealed that the black middle class differed from its white counterpart in significant ways. In his *Black Bourgeoisie*, Frazier had criticized the black middle class for imitating the lifestyles of whites, something that led to "status without substance." Not only was the black middle class considerably larger and more diverse a decade and a half later, but it is safe to say that the civil rights movement had fundamentally altered African Americans' individual and collective orientation. Cultural heritage, racial pride, and social consciousness were all now part of most African Americans' identities regardless of income level or class distinction. It could not be said that there was an authentic, recognizable black middle-class culture, however, partly because many African Americans were just one generation removed from the lower class. A dual identity or W.E.B. Du Bois' "double consciousness" was thus very much part of the black middle-class experience in the 1970s. "One can observe a constant vacillation between the values and behavior patterns of the traditional Black Culture and the life styles, values and behavior patterns of the dominant white middle class," wrote Joyce A. Ladner, a sociology professor at Harvard, in *Ebony* in 1973. Ladner cited the hypothetical case of a black physician who had a deep appreciation of classical music but also retained the New Year's Day tradition of eating chitterlings, an example of how middle-class African Americans straddled different racial identities.[24]

Defining the black middle class was even more difficult than defining the white middle class. Not only did the same kind of objective (e.g., income, occupation, education) and subjective (e.g., lifestyle or "reference group") criteria come into play, but standards for judging class in the African American community were generally different than the ones used for whites. White bus drivers, policemen, and mail carriers would likely be considered lower middle class but black people having these same jobs were viewed as upper middle class. Owning virtually any home would automatically qualify an African American for middle-class status but this did not hold true for whites. The absence of an identifiable black upper class further complicated matters. Jobs requiring much education such as college professor or public school principal could be considered upper class in some black social circles, while this would not be the case for whites. In fact, education often trumped occupation as an indicator of class within the African American community, this not so among whites.[25]

Regional and local differences, especially those between the North and the South, also made defining the black middle class a major challenge. A teacher in Washington, DC would probably be considered lower middle class while one in a small town in Mississippi would be viewed as upper middle class. Class status also relied heavily upon the neighborhood in which one lived, more so than for whites, and on one's community presence. Regular attendance at church was a plus, while certain language patterns (e.g., double negatives), fashion choices (e.g., flashy clothes), and social behaviors (e.g., too much gossiping) were minuses in determining whether one was middle class. Like whites, new arrivals to the black middle class tended to rely too heavily on those behaviors that signified success.[26] Although it was an area of contention, it was tempting and logical for blacks climbing the economic ladder to look to the white middle class for cues. Not wanting to be associated with the negative connotations attached to lower-class blacks, many African Americans patterned their lives after the more affluent white middle class. "Identifying with that class, they take over its most conspicuous norms and mannerisms," wrote Nathan Hare, publisher of *Black Scholar* magazine, these individuals often overemphasizing those traits to make their higher status even clearer. Some blacks were known to drive Cadillacs to impress others but scrimped on food at home, something Hare considered "pathetic." A good number of blacks acting middle class were not really so, he believed, continually rising standards making it impossible for many to keep up.[27]

As among whites, major differences also existed among the black middle class according to generation. Many blacks under the age of thirty were wearing "Afros," for example, the curly hair displayed and viewed as a sign of racial pride and liberation from white dominance. Older African Americans tended to view the hairstyle as improper, however, emblematic of black militancy. Also like whites, the generation gap within the black middle class in the 1970s had roots in the tumultuous changes of the late 1960s. The black counterculture had been quite a different experience than the white counterculture, however, the former more about constructing racial identity than turning on, tuning in, and dropping out. Having watched the events of the civil rights movement, both violent and non-violent, play out on television, black adolescents had received a solid education in the dynamics of race in America. Now, in the early seventies, younger African Americans often felt their middle-class parents were trying too hard to adopt WASPy lifestyles and, correlatively, ignoring their own racial heritage. It was not unusual for black middle-class parents to urge their kids to spend more time with white middle-class friends and, strangely enough, less time with other African Americans. Black teenagers typically rejected this request, finding more in common with people of a similar color. College-age members of the black middle class disdained their parents' materialistic values but, at the same, often majored in fields that would someday pay well, such as law, medicine, or business. The older generation's values were peer-based, the younger generation explained, the key difference being that they viewed the good things in life as an opportunity to please oneself rather than others.[28]

Attempts to define the black middle class went back decades. Almost two decades before *Black Bourgeoisie* was published, Franklin wrote a book called *Negro Youth at the Crossways* that illustrated the complexity of class dynamics within the black community. (Hotel employees and the domestic servants of wealthy white families were part of the black upper class, Franklin maintained in the book.) In his 1968 *Black Families in White America*, Andrew Billingsley argued that analyzing black families based on (patriarchic) white middle-class standards was "completely inappropriate," challenging claims that the "Black Family" was falling apart. In 1973, however, Wattenberg and Scammon published an article in *Commentary* that presented the black middle class as "Middle Americans," minimizing the kind of cultural differences on which Billingsley and other Afro-centric writers focused. The intellectual debate reflected the jumbled ways in which class played out among blacks themselves. While lower class blacks were known to claim black middle-class status because of the stigma attached to being poor (just like whites), a fair number of African American professionals "downgraded" their class level to make it clear they retained their racial identity. After considering all the opinions, some scholars simply concluded the exercise was an impossible one. "I find no way to define 'black middle class,'" stated Ione D. Vargus, a social work professor at the University of Illinois, pronouncing, "culture and class are not fixed determinants." Even if one could neatly categorize black people by class, it would emphasize difference rather than commonality, Vargus felt, diverting African Americans from their more important struggle for equality.[29]

Alvin F. Poussaint, a professor of psychiatry at Harvard Medical School, helped add some clarity to the complexities surrounding the black middle class. Racism and, especially, the legacy of slavery made the black middle class fundamentally different than the white middle class, he pointed out, the fact that African Americans lacked a strong tradition of owning property and businesses changing the equation. Inheriting wealth was also far less common among African Americans, this too making it very likely those achieving middle-class status were the first in their families to do so.[30] Without a doubt, lingering racism made defining the black middle class that much more difficult. "Perhaps the most significant factor which makes the 'black middle class' concept a slippery one is the fact that the white community ... fails to recognize the existence of classes within the black community," suggested Robert S. Browne, director of the Black Economic Research Center in New York. Race was far and away more important to whites than class, Browne argued, a view that led experts and laypeople alike to lump all African Americans together into a single group. The black middle class was "a chimera," Browne believed, more a product of the imagination than something to be found in the real world.[31]

I Never Had It Made

Wattenberg's and Scammon's 1973 article in *Commentary* served as a lightning rod for the highly sensitive issue of race in America. In their "Black Progress and Liberal Rhetoric," the pair presented census data showing that a majority (52 percent) of blacks had achieved middle-class status. "Truly large and growing numbers of American blacks have been moving into the middle class," they wrote, the demographic shift "nothing short of revolutionary." White liberals and black leaders had ignored the significant progress African Americans had made over the last decade for political purposes, Wattenberg and Scammon argued, their intent to keep alive government assistance programs that the Nixon administration was considering or already cutting.[32] The *Wall Street Journal* and other magazines soon reported the findings of the study, elevating it from an interesting intellectual discussion to water cooler talk.[33]

The article in *Commentary* also raised quite a ruckus. Critics attacked Wattenberg and Scammon's findings, making it clear that the nation's "war on poverty" had hardly been won. Progress had no doubt been made, they admitted, but the authors' definition of "middle class" had been much too broad. Wattenberg and Scammon considered a wide range of variables, including income, education, occupation, and the number of people receiving welfare. The most important criterion they used was an annual income of $8,000 in the North and $6,000 in the South, however, to critics an absurdly small amount of money to be considered middle class. The facts suggested that the pair were indeed being generous with their definition of "middle class." Incomes of blacks were about 60 percent those of whites, and the former typically had to pay higher prices for consumer goods than the latter. Unemployment remained high for black men, particularly in large urban areas, and extreme poverty could be found in both ghettos and much of the South. Relying exclusively on census figures allowed for considerable underreporting of the poor, critics added, another major flaw in the study.[34] "Beware of those who would declare victory by falsely proclaiming that most blacks are in the middle class," warned Herrington J. Bryce, director of research at the Joint Center for Political Studies in Washington, DC, insisting that persistent economic inequality remained a fact of life for African Americans.[35] Indeed, a new Census Bureau report, "The Social and Economic Status of the Black Population in the United States, 1972," showed that many African Americans had over the past few years moved backward rather than forward.[36]

In fact, some African Americans believed that not much had changed since Frazier's *Black Bourgeoisie*. The black middle class was "in the dilemma of being a class without a real class foothold within the American structure of power," argued Earl Ofari, author of *Myth of Black Capitalism*, thinking Frazier's use of the term "black bourgeoisie" was oxymoronic. "American capitalism never has and never will permit the growth of a black bourgeoisie within its framework," Ofari continued, thinking African Americans would always be outside the ownership class. The black middle class might own some small businesses, but it would never penetrate the *Fortune* 500 to any significant degree, he argued. (Indeed, the combined revenue of the top ten black-owned companies in America was not enough to earn the magazine's 500th position in 1972.) Consisting mostly of teachers and social workers, the black middle class did not hold true power or wield institutional control, Ofari contended.[37] Such a view was hardly extremist. Shortly before his death, the baseball great Jackie Robinson rather famously said, "I never had it made," a line other African Americans viewed with great significance. No amount of talent, fame, awards, or material comforts would be enough for blacks to really "make it" in America, they believed, institutional racism too great to allow such a thing.[38]

While whether the majority of African Americans were middle class in the early 1970s was highly debatable, there were sure signs that the group was attracting some who only recently wanted nothing to do with it. Bobby Seale, chairman of the Black Panther Party, had recently run for mayor of Oakland (earning a respectable 47,000 votes) and, perhaps more shockingly, had taken to wearing a suit and tie. In the late 1960s, he and "minister of defense" Huey Newton preached a revolutionary philosophy centered around black militancy, their party deliberately ignoring the bourgeois African American middle class. Seale's views had recently changed, however, recognizing that the (now "oppressed") black middle class, with its financial resources and leadership skills, could be a valuable part of his movement.[39] Seale might have learned that a good number of the greatest African American leaders—Frederick Douglas, W.E.B. Du Bois, A. Philip Randolph, Martin Luther King, Thurgood Marshall, and many others—had been middle class. (The coiner of the term "Black Power," Stokely Carmichael, a.k.a. Kwame Ture, had also grown up middle class.) Blacks' gradual social and economic progress would not hurt the equal rights movement, both radical and moderate African Americans were concluding; in fact, it appeared that greater involvement among the black middle class would help it.[40]

To this end, editors of *Ebony* magazine made a direct appeal to the black middle class in 1973 by outlining what they felt were the group's responsibilities. Racial identity was the primary concern for all blacks in America, they held, meaning it was important not to get distracted by the pursuit of money and what it could buy. "The middle class black family which lets itself get trapped into a material bag is shirking its responsibilities to black folk," the magazine stated, the collective struggle for equal rights much more important than individual pleasures. The second responsibility of the black middle class was to family, especially by providing a good education to children so they could do even better than their parents. The third responsibility was to financially support institutions and organizations that were fighting for equal rights, and the fourth to help disadvantaged "brothers" any way they could. "The black middle class can walk tall and talk loud if blacks with more money than they ever had before in history begin to spend it in helping other blacks," the editors of *Ebony* told readers, clearly unhappy that many of them were choosing to spend their cash imitating the white middle class.[41]

White-dominated media, meanwhile, celebrated the apparent, long overdue arrival of the black middle class. "More and more blacks are achieving the American dream of lifting themselves into the middle class," proclaimed *Time* in a 1974 cover story, this group "as well heeled, well housed, and well educated as their white counterparts." For middle-class and upper-class whites, the reality of a sizable black middle class wearing the same clothes, living in the same kind of neighborhoods, and going to the same schools as themselves was good news on a number of levels. If true, the problem of racism had been largely solved, one could reasonably conclude, the rise of a large black middle class also taken as proof that upward mobility still existed in America. The welfare state and affirmative action programs of the last decade had paid off, both liberals and conservatives surmised, the nation now closer to living up to its democratic and egalitarian ideals. The now larger gap between the black middle class and black underclass was unfortunate but, all in all, a necessary consequence of progress. "The best guarantee of durable, amicable race relations in America is the continued growth of a strong, self-confident black middle class," *Time* announced, encouraged that many African Americans were finally "making a successful ascent."[42]

The rather sudden recognition of the black middle class did not sit well with some. "Recent reports of the existence of a vast middle class remind me of darting explorers emerging from the hidden depths of a strange, newly discovered world bearing tales of an exotic new phenomenon," wrote Vernon Jordan in *Newsweek* just a few weeks after the *Time* article, blaming the media for assuming that most African Americans had been spending much of their time "sniffing coke or mugging old ladies." As a result, a new African American stereotype was emerging, the executive director of the National Urban League believed, the archetypical member of the black middle class a "meek, sophisticated professional." White and, certainly, some black Americans found this image comforting, an indication that headway was being made against the primary social ills of poverty and racism. The problem was that this image was not real, Jordan felt, and the perception that it was would lessen the chances of equal opportunity rather than increase them. In addition to all the print coverage, CBS News had recently aired a documentary about the blossoming black middle class, this too wishful thinking and, ultimately, counterproductive. Without question, a black middle class existed, Jordan conceded, but it represented the minority of African Americans in 1974, just as it had in 1874. Were they white, most members of the black middle class would be considered working class, this the part of the story that the media was leaving out. "The vast majority of blacks are still far from middle-class status," Jordan, who would one day become an advisor to and close friend of President Clinton, made clear.[43]

Even if it were true, millions of blacks moving "from second-class citizenship to middle-class status," as *U.S. News & World Report* put it, hardly meant that they had "made it." The shaky economy was affecting the black middle class at least as much as the white middle class, as African Americans were often the last hired and the first fired. Becoming middle class did not guarantee that one would stay there, as any level of socio-economic status was one, nebulous, and two, a constantly moving target. Achieving a certain degree of economic status had not ended racism, of course, a somewhat rude awakening for those blacks who had assumed becoming middle class would bring greater acceptance by the white majority. Many African Americans were genuinely surprised to find that despite having a well-paying job with a well-known company they were still "treated as black," as a young computer analyst in Detroit expressed it. Some were also finding that after landing a good position their progress slowed, management apparently reluctant to award them with any real responsibility. The odds of African Americans becoming wealthy or even moving up to the upper middle class were long, giving them mixed feelings about their newfound success. Finally, some blacks who were now operating within the white-dominated world were having difficulty maintaining ties to the communities in which they were raised. For them, becoming middle class represented the crossing of a line of sorts, leaving them in a "no-man's-zone" of racial identity.[44]

New Patterns of Living

Like some black extremists, most of the white, young "rebels" of the counterculture had settled into regular middle-class life by the mid-1970s. The establishment was "the only game in town," as one expressed it, seeing that the original goals of the cultural revolution were no longer tenable.[45] However, many of the "alternative" values that had become popular during the counterculture had seeped into middle-class life. The rejection of technocracy and greater acceptance of and reliance on intuition, emotions, self-expression, and mysticism were just some of the ways in which many "average" Americans were looking beyond and going outside the conventions of middle-class norms. Most interesting, individuals were not just embracing these values attitudinally but putting them into practice. Like "hippies" a decade earlier, perfectly "square" professionals were seeking greater purpose and meaning in their lives. Some were giving up their highly paid, powerful positions to work at non-profits, others simply volunteering for causes in which they believed. A longing for a personalized sense of community was an especially powerful draw for middle-class families and individuals to make major changes in their lives. Feeling disconnected, some households were merging with others to live in more communal settings. Likewise, members of large religious institutions were joining the house church movement for a more intimate spiritual experience. These were all "serious attempts to correct dissatisfaction with the materialistic orientation, the marriage and family customs, the residential style, and the vocational and spiritual outlook basic to conventional middle-class society," noted Robert Ouradnik, a Methodist minister, in 1974, seeing members of his own congregation in Minnesota actively searching for "new patterns of living."[46]

Alternative thinking and behavior steeped in countercultural values were thus co-opted by the middle class (and the middle-aged) a decade after they alarmed more conservative Americans. Regaining a sense of self-identity in what many members of the group believed were dehumanizing times was a primary goal. The core of the postwar conception of the American middle class had been the self-contained and self-sustaining family unit ensconced in the suburbs, a way of life that was widely critiqued in the 1960s as bourgeois and conformist. Now, in the 1970s, a good number of suburbanites appeared to agree, and were swapping their three-bedroom colonial for ten acres in the country. The notion of compartmentalized roles—spouse, employee, student, etc.—too had been challenged by the anti-establishment, an idea considered not so outrageous in the 1970s. More adventurous members of the middle class were exploring ways in which to approach life more holistically, the seeds of the New Age movement firmly planted. Popular activities such as the "self-help" and human potential movements were other expressions of this quest for higher consciousness, these too rooted in the "revolutionary" principles of the counterculture.[47]

The middle class had inherited another aspect of the counterculture—radicalism. Anti-bussing activists, truckers protesting the scarcity of gasoline, and followers of Alabama governor and recurrent presidential candidate George Wallace had all earned the seemingly oxymoronic title of MARs, or Middle American Radicals. Like members of today's libertarian Tea Party, MARs were neither traditionally conservative nor liberal, viewing the government as typically working against his or her self-interests. "The MAR is an unpredictable force in American political life," Donald Warren wrote in *The Nation* in 1974, "an uneasy ally for either the Left or the Right." Both the rich and the poor were also to blame for many of the country's problems, MARs believed, each able to evade paying taxes at the expense of average earners like themselves. MARs positively despised George McGovern and everything he stood for (minorities, anti-war demonstrators, leftists, and the welfare state), and were delighted to see the Democratic senator from South Dakota get crushed by incumbent Richard Nixon in the 1972 presidential election. Although their politics were certainly different from those of the SDS (Students for a Democratic Society) and other activist groups of the 1960s, MARs also worked at a grassroots level to affect social change. "MARs may not be radicals in the conventional sense, but from now on they will certainly express their demands for participation and recognition through action," Warren observed, their own brand of political activism a legacy of the counterculture.[48]

Another, less radical sign of middle-class activism was the proliferation of public interest groups like Common Cause, the non-partisan citizen's lobbying organization promoting accountable government. Both professionals and regular folks were "fighting city hall" in a manner never really seen before in this country. (The temperance and feminism movements were heavily middle class, but this form of organized activity was significantly broader-based.) The average American was "mad as hell and not going to take it anymore," to paraphrase the famous line from the 1976 movie *Network*, more likely to protest whatever he or she thought was wrong or unfair. (The heroism of a new, very short-lived sitcom on ABC called *Karen* worked for a Common Cause-like organization.) Consumer interest groups complaining about rip-offs, mothers angry about children's television programming, and local residents resisting sprawl were a few kinds of people rising up against "the system." Rather than fighting for the ambitious goals of world peace or civil rights like protesters in the 1960s, these activists were pursuing more modest and achievable aims like stopping a high-rise development. Signature collecting had become a popular pastime for members of these interest groups who were predominantly white, middle class, and new at public controversy. Previously afraid of "getting involved," suburban housewives and their professional husbands were finding themselves passionately engaged in what was sometimes called "majority politics" (versus the "minority politics" of the sixties). No one could say with any accuracy how many Americans were part of the movement, but it was known there were several thousand public interest organizations in the country, each one dedicated to a particular issue or cause. Like Howard Beale in *Network*, the middle class was fed up with those institutions (business and government, primarily) it considered no longer reliable or trustworthy, and was determined to do something about it.[49]

Activism could certainly help but was not enough to dig the middle class out of the crater in which it found itself. "The middle class is on its way to becoming another 'lost generation' like the one that disappeared in the 1929 crash," stated *Business Week* in 1975, the hopes and dreams of many Americans being shattered. For businesses, the harsh economic and political realities posed serious consequences. Based on the assumption that the American middle class now comprised 53 percent of families (using an annual income level of $10,000 to $35,000), it accounted for 75 percent of total consumer purchases. Those in this income range bought about 80 percent of all cars, 70 percent of washing machines, 77 percent of furniture, and 73 percent of color television sets. As well, a good number of wealthy Americans "acted" middle class, meaning their consumer habits were similar or identical to the less well off. The result, marketers were coming to believe, was a fundamental shift in consumer attitudes and behavior based on this new, more challenging economic climate. "Middle-class shoppers are developing a different relationship with their money," observed market research Daniel Yankelovich, finding that the postwar "more is more" model of consumption was quickly disappearing. The broader view that growth was inherently a good thing was being rethought, the implication being that consumers would want to use fewer products and spend less money on them. Widespread criticism of the government by the middle class appeared to be spreading to large institutions of all kinds, more bad news for Corporate America. Large companies were finding that their employees' values were in flux, and not for the better. Ambitious, conscientious, hard-working, honest, and reliable employees were getting scarce, a study conducted by the American Management Association revealed, these attributes eclipsed by more personal, less productive values such as "egocentricism" and "existentialism." In short, the middle class was going through a major personality change as it adapted to the constraints and instability of the times.[50]

The weak economy and "consciousness raising" of the 1970s was altering the character of the American middle class in other ways, the most important being its size. Inflation and recession had slowed the postwar expansion of middle-class families, which, some economists argued, had increased from 20 percent of the population to 50 percent. As the middle class shrank, so did the 1950s version of the American Dream grounded in peer-based success, achievement, and material gain. The blurring of class lines that so defined postwar American culture both socially and economically was also coming to an end. The professional and personal co-mingling of white-collar workers and blue-collar workers that some considered America at its best and a resounding retort to the Communist threat was now coming apart, replaced by a more competitive paradigm. Purchasing power had emerged as a key marker of class identity, as it was discretionary income that separated the "winners" from the "losers" in a consumer society like ours.[51] The middle class and the nation as a whole were, by many accounts, splitting in two.

The New Class

The fragmentation and identity crisis of the American middle class also had significant political consequences. Many members of the middle class blamed the powerlessness they felt on the political system, thinking it was biased toward both the rich and the poor.[52] With middle-class populism in the air, pundits wondered whether 1976 would be the year in which an independent or third party candidate would make a serious run at the White House. Fed up with the bureaucracy and corruption of both major parties and their inability to solve the economic problems of inflation and high taxes, many middle-class Republicans and Democrats appeared to be open to a new kind of politician. Disillusioned, cynical, and angry, the American middle class was coming to the conclusion that traditional political solutions just did not work, opening some visible cracks in the two-party system.[53]

With the entry of Jimmy Carter in the race, however, a good chunk of the middle class had a candidate it felt relatively good about. The lower middle class was especially drawn to Carter not for his politics but for his background in farming and nuclear physics. Typical lower-middle-class occupations were automobile mechanics, television repairmen, and telephone linemen—people who worked with their hands and had an appreciation for how things were built. The peanut farmer and nuclear submarine expert was such a person, an attractive quality for other literally hands-on people. If Carter said one of his proposed policies would work, that was good enough for folks who respected a man who was able to fix something or solve a problem with common sense. Carter's honesty (a corollary of his deep religious faith) was another asset the lower middle class found appealing; the man was viewed as starkly different from the average tell-them-what-they-want-to-hear politician. Finally, Carter's not being part of the liberal elite was a plus rather than a minus for those more interested in practical matters than ideological debate. Knowing that the lower middle class comprised the majority of voters, Republican leaders were understandably very concerned about the upcoming election.[54]

With all the moaning that the middle class was getting squeezed, shrunk, or "liquidated" like the Wicked Witch of the West, few, however, were ready to admit that they themselves were no longer part of the group. Eighty-two percent of Americans polled by Yankelovich, Skelly & White in 1976 said they belonged to either the middle class or the "prosperous upper middle class," about the same percentage that had consistently responded similarly in the past. Other people were dropping into the lower class but not oneself, it seemed, a puzzling perspective that showed how deeply the idea of the middle class was woven into national identity. Much was made of regional differences (state and city loyalties remained strong, if attachment to one's local sports team was any indication) but, when it came to class, Americans had little to say. "A cloud of myth obscures the realities of American class structure," noted renowned economist Robert L. Heilbroner in the *Atlantic*, thinking a good part of this 82 percent were "fooling themselves." Even the official bible of demographics, the U.S. *Statistical Abstract*, made no mention of a "middle class" (or the "rich" or "working class," for that matter), this helping to perpetuate the mythology that class hardly existed in this country. Using the income data in the 1975 edition of the report, Heilbroner estimated 20 percent of Americans were poor, 40 percent working class, 35 percent middle class, and 5 percent upper class—quite a difference from what most of us believed or wanted to believe.[55]

The reality of being middle class could not compete with the reverent position it held in Americans' imagination. For one thing, many Americans were painfully learning that making it to the middle class did not guarantee that one would stay there. Inflation was still nipping at the heels of the middle class, the 47 percent rise in the consumer price index since 1970 almost wiping out the total 52 percent gain in median family income. (The respective inflation rates on food, cars, college, and houses exceeded the average rise in income.) Earning more money also put one into a higher tax bracket, meaning some families had less disposable income after taking into account inflation. The lines between the strapped-for-cash middle class and the poor were becoming increasingly blurry. Activities average earners once did mostly for fun—working on one's car, making home improvements or repairs, growing vegetables in the backyard, sewing clothes or building furniture, holding garage sales—were now being done to bring in or save money. Others were forgoing the supermarket and instead shopping at a food co-op on the other side of town. Businesses began offering new kinds of products and services to whom *Newsweek* called in 1977 "the middle class poor." Bankers Trust in New York introduced something called a "Miss-a-Month" loan that allowed borrowers to skip one monthly payment a year, and legal clinics that had offered their free services to the poor were now offering them to anyone who walked in the door. More people were also taking advantage of credit counseling services after finding themselves thousands of dollars in debt. And out in California, something called the "voluntary simplicity" movement was gaining traction among those subscribing to the idea that consumerism should be more about needs than wants.[56]

Something else rather revolutionary was brewing in California. Almost two-thirds of voters there approved of Proposition 13, the 1978 amendment to the state's constitution that cut property taxes by 57 percent and revenues from $12 billion to $5 billion a year. The proposition was widely hailed as the first salvo in a burgeoning "tax revolt" that would sweep the country and, as a result, put more money in homeowners' and business owners' pockets.[57] The truth was that middle-class Americans had been rebelling against local government spending for a couple of years before the passage of "Prop 13." Taxpayers were becoming increasingly angry about welfare and food stamp programs for the poor, believing they had been squeezed dry. "All across the country, the great middle class ... are lashing out at what they perceive as unfair and unfavorable treatment," *U.S. News & World Report* noted in 1977, with voters "on the warpath."[58] Many people had voted for Carter because they believed he would cut government spending and trim bureaucracy, but they had yet to see any real changes to the system. "There's a kind of pseudoconservative movement going," observed Morris Janowitz, a professor of sociology at the University of Chicago, thinking most of the middle class no longer related to traditional Democratic or Republican politics.[59]

With an apparent void (if not gaping hole) in the American political system, some recognized a rare opportunity to fill it. A "new class" consisting of upper-middle-class professionals represented the future of American politics, neoconservative intellectuals (led by NYU professor Irving Kristol) argued, an idea many—especially corporate executives—were taking to heart. This contingent looked to the rhetoric of Richard Nixon and Spiro Agnew for inspiration to counter what they believed was an anti-business sentiment on the part of the media and within academia. From the late 1960s through the 1970s, "Big Business" was looked down upon by this "new class," Kristol and others (legitimately) claimed, upper-middle-class Americans heavily swayed by the views of the liberal elite. The result had been increased consumer and environmental regulations, a situation the leaders of Corporate America sought to reverse. Promoting conservative values—principally the benefits of a free market economy—to the "new class" offered a way to get influential, successful Americans on the side of "Big Business" and, as important, get the government off its back.[60] Some, however, questioned whether such an anti-capitalist "new class" even existed, especially given the fact that its members were fully engaged in the capitalist system. The title of a book published in 1979, *The New Class?*, made that quite clear, its contributors not nearly as sure that upper-middle-class professionals held, in Kristol's words, "shared ideals, shared values, shared aspirations."[61]

Whether or not there was such a "new class," the upper middle class was clearly suffering from lingering "stagflation" (a term that had been coined by *British Economist* magazine in 1976). It was better-educated, higher income white-collar workers who were most affected both financially and psychologically by the combined effects of a stagnant economy and inflation, according to a new study. "Contrary to prevailing theory and findings, those who report the greatest negative psychological impact of stagflation are not members of the lower class, but the more affluent, better educated middle class," explained Avraham Shama, an associate professor at Baruch College, going as far to say that the middle class had become "a new poverty class." Recognizing they could no longer afford their present lifestyles, members of the middle class were, he said, "going through an accelerated change which affects their consumption patterns as well as the social system to which they belong." The result of all this change was a major sense of confusion, and the disturbing feeling that one was no longer in control of his or her life.[62] With the crossing over into a new decade, this sensation of cultural vertigo would only intensify among the American middle class, its future more uncertain than ever.

Notes

1 Stewart Alsop, "The Shafting of Mr. Average," *Newsweek*, April 19, 1971, 132.
2 David C. Anderson, "'Middle America': A Closer Look," *Wall Street Journal*, June 18, 1971, 6; Richard M. Scammon and Ben Wattenberg, *The Real Majority: An Extraordinary Examination of the American Electorate* (New York: Coward-McCann, 1970); Robert Coles, *The Middle Americans: Proud and Uncertain* (New York: Little, Brown, 1971).
3 "Toward Reconciliation," *Wall Street Journal*, September 29, 1970, 20.
4 Ben A. Franklin, "Life in VISTA Called Radicalizing," *New York Times*, May 24, 1971, 1.
5 Peter L. Berger and Brigitte Berger, "The Blueing of America," *The New Republic*, April 3, 1971, 20–23.
6 Andrew Levison, "The Working-Class Majority," *The Nation*, December 13, 1971, 626–28.
7 "The Working-Class Majority"; John Kenneth Galbraith's *The Affluent Society* (Boston: Houghton Mifflin, 1958); William H. Whyte, *The Organization Man* (New York: Simon & Schuster, 1956); David Riesman, *The Lonely Crowd* (New Haven, CT: Yale University Press, 1950); Vance Packard, *The Status Seekers* (New York: David McKay, 1959).
8 Michael Cunneen, "Rewarding John Wayne," *The Nation*, July 16, 1973, 58–59; Norman Lederer, "The Widening Gap," *The Christian Century*, October 17, 1973, 1035; Richard Parker, *The Myth of the Middle Class* (New York: Harper Collins, 1972).
9 John C. Raines, "Middle America: Up Against the Wall and Going Nowhere," *The Christian Century*, May 2, 1973, 504–7; Richard Sennett and Jonathan Cobb, *Hidden Injuries of Class* (New York: Knopf, 1972).
10 "College Squeeze Tightens on Middle-Class Parents," *U.S. News & World Report*, August 6, 1973, 26–27.
11 "The Struggle to Pay for College—How Four Families Manage It," *U.S. News & World Report*, October 14, 1974, 56–62.
12 Cleveland Amory, "The New Game of One-Downmanship," *New York Times*, 1973, 35.
13 "Squeeze on America's Middle Class," *U.S. News & World Report*, October 14, 1974, 42–45.
14 John C. Raines, "The Middle-Class Tax Burden: Incentive for Change," *The Christian Century*, September 4, 1974, 818–21.
15 "The Middle-Class Tax Burden: Incentive for Change."
16 "The Middle-Class Tax Burden: Incentive for Change;" Norman Vincent Peale, *The Art of Living* (New York: Abingdon Press, 1937); Norman Vincent Peale, *A Guide to Confident Living* (New York: Prentice-Hall, 1948); Norman Vincent Peale, *The Power of Positive Thinking* (New York: Fawcett Crest, 1952).
17 "These Folks Can Cope," *Time*, September 2, 1974; Ben Wattenberg, *The Real America: A Surprising Examination of the State of the Union* (New York: Doubleday, 1974).

18 "Squeeze on America's Middle Class."

19 "Your Own Home—A Fading Dream," *U.S. News & World Report*, October 14, 1974, 54–55.

20 "Small Investors Try New Ways to Keep Even," *U.S. News & World Report*, October 14, 1974, 63–64.

21 "More Middle-Class Workers Rush to Join Unions," *U.S. News & World Report*, October 14, 1974, 65–66.

22 "Among Middle-Class Ethnics—'A Great Deal of Bitterness,'" *U.S. News & World Report*, October 14, 1974, 46–48.

23 Edwin Harwood, "Black Progress Is Happening, Too," *Wall Street Journal*, February 2, 1971, 12.

24 Joyce A. Ladner, "The Black Middle Class Defined," *Ebony*, August 1973, 44.

25 Nathan Hare, "The Black Middle Class Defined," *Ebony*, August 1973, 45.

26 Jacqueline J. Jackson, "The Black Middle Class Defined," *Ebony*, August 1973, 45–46.

27 "The Black Middle Class Defined" (Hare).

28 Monroe Anderson, "Young, Middle Class and Very Black," *Ebony*, August 1973, 123–27.

29 Ione D. Vargus, "The Black Middle Class Defined," *Ebony*, August 1973, 46; E. Franklin Frazier, *Negro Youth at the Crossways: Their Personality Development in the Middle States* (Washington, DC: American Council on Education, 1940); Andrew Billingsley, *Black Families in White America* (New York: Prentice-Hall, 1968).

30 Alvin F. Poussaint, "The Black Middle Class Defined," *Ebony*, August 1973, 46–48.

31 Robert S. Browne, "The Black Middle Class Defined," *Ebony*, August 1973, 48.

32 Herrington J. Bryce, "Putting Black Economic Progress in Perspective," *Ebony*, August 1973, 58–62.

33 "Decade of Progress," *Time*, April 16, 1973.

34 "Decade of Progress."

35 "Putting Black Economic Progress in Perspective."

36 "The March to Equality Marks Time," *Time*, September 3, 1973.

37 Earl Ofari, "The Dilemma of the Black Middle Class," *Ebony*, August 1973, 138–43; Earl Ofari, *Myth of Black Capitalism* (New York: Monthly Review Press, 1970).

38 Lerone Bennett Jr., "Black Bourgeoisie Revisited," *Ebony*, August 1973, 50–55.

39 B.J. Mason, "A Shift to the Middle," *Ebony*, August 1973, 80–87.

40 Bayard Rustin, "The Middle Class in the Black Struggle," *Ebony*, August 1973, 144–49.

41 "Responsibilities of Black Middle Class," *Ebony*, August 1973, 180.

42 "America's Rising Black Middle Class," *Time*, June 17, 1974, 25.

43 Vernon E. Jordan, Jr., "The Truth About the Black Middle Class," *Newsweek*, July 8, 1974, 11.

44 "Blacks Find that 'Making It' Doesn't Solve All the Problems, *U.S. News & World Report*, October 14, 1974, 50–52.

45 James S. Kunen, "The Rebels of '70," *New York Times*, October 28, 1973, 268.

46 Robert Ouradnik, "The Middle-Class Quest for Alternatives," *The Christian Century*, April 3, 1974, 366–69.

47 "The Middle-Class Quest for Alternatives."

48 Donald I. Warren, "The Middle American Radicals," *The Nation*, August 17, 1974, 107–10.

49 Roger M. Williams, "The Rise of Middle Class Activism: Fighting 'City Hall,'" *Saturday Review*, March 8, 1975, 12–16.

50 "The Squeeze on the Middle Class," *Business Week*, March 10, 1975, 52–60.

51 "The Squeeze on the Middle Class."

52 "The Middle-Class Quest for Alternatives."

53 Daniel A. Mazmanian, "1976: A Third-Party Year?", *The Nation*, September 13, 1975, 201–4.

54 Robert W. Whitaker, "Populist View on Opposing Carter," *National Review*, October 29, 1976, 1182, 1197.
55 Robert L. Heilbroner, "Middle-Class Myths, Middle-Class Realities," *Atlantic*, October 1976, 37–42.
56 Susan Fraker, "The Middle Class Poor," *Newsweek*, September 12, 1977, 30.
57 Nancy Faber, "The Middle Class May Suffer in the Spreading Tax Revolt, An Economist Warns," *People*, June 26, 1978, 89.
58 "Squeeze on the Middle Class," *U.S. News & World Report*, May 2, 1977, 50–51.
59 "Outlook for Middle Class: 'I Am Mildly Optimistic,'" *U.S. News & World Report*, May 2, 1977, 56–57.
60 David Vogel, "Business's 'New Class' Struggle," *The Nation*, December 15, 1979, 624–25.
61 Irving Kristol, "The 'New Class' Revisited," *Wall Street Journal*, May 31, 1979, 24; B. Bruce-Briggs, ed. *The New Class?* (New Brunswick, NJ: Transaction Books, 1979).
62 "Middle Class Suffers the Most from 'Stagflation,'" *Marketing News*, October 5, 1979, 1, 6.

4

TRADING PLACES

I've been brought up in the middle class. I'll be damned if someone's going to take that away from me.

Laid-off Chicago steelworker working as a janitor in 1986

The Moores of Omaha, Nebraska were not happy about what a reporter writing a story about them called the "middle class money blues." Married for twenty-three years and with two young adult children, William and Rose Mary Moore were, with a $45,000 household income in 1980, firmly middle class. Five years earlier, the couple made just $31,000, but had more money to spend on unnecessary things. Now the family was living paycheck to paycheck, caught in a perpetual cycle of hard work in order to simply pay their bills. Shopping at discount stores, avoiding the meat aisle at the supermarket, and figuring out ways to save gasoline were all part of everyday life for the family. "So this is what being middle class is all about?" asked Mrs. Moore, an elementary school principal, disappointed that reaching her goal had not brought her the comfort and security she dreamed of while growing up poor. "I always felt that when I got to middle class I would really be living," she said, her husband, director of a church community center, feeling much the same way. Rising expenses and higher taxes had more than exceeded their rising income, making them feel as if they were moving backward rather than forward despite the success they had achieved. Cutting the lawn and changing their cars' oil themselves, keeping the thermostat down in the winter, and canning fruits and vegetables grown in their backyard were other ways the Moores were keeping their creditors at bay. "You work, but you don't get all the things you want," Mrs. Moore concluded, thinking, "the economic outlook is scary."[1]

Throughout the 1980s, millions of other middle-class Americans felt much the same way. The decade would turn out to be far more economically vigorous than the enervated 1970s, but prosperity was proving to be elusive for many members of the middle class. Working more but having less was a frustrating state of affairs for average earners and, more disturbingly, completely contradictory to the tenets of the American Dream. A new president with an ideology steeped in free market capitalism would indeed help turn the economy around but the good times seemed to be limited to those who were already well off. Concerns over a growing divide in America peaked in the 1980s as the middle class was squeezed in one economic direction or the other. The economic outlook would remain "scary" for much of the middle class over the course of these ten years, the decade ending much like how it begun.

White-Collar Status Panic

As the Moores of Omaha could well testify, inflation had much to do with the shaky status of the middle class. Inflation between the late 1960s and late 1970s had been arguably the worst enemy of the American middle class. Consumer prices almost doubled over an eleven-year period, meaning a worker's pay also had to at least double just to keep up (higher pay would mean a higher tax bracket). The blue-collar segment of the middle class—at least those lucky enough not to get laid off—was actually more buffered from the effects of spiraling infla- tion than the professional white-collar segment because the former tended to belong to powerful trade unions. Those belonging to weaker unions or none at all were losing ground or barely holding their own, however, imports too badly hurting their industries. White-collar workers were faring the worst, relatively speaking, as they had the most to lose. The real salaries of college professors, for example, dropped almost 10 percent over this period, and a whopping 17 percent after taxes. As the income gap between strongly unionized blue-collar workers and professionals narrowed, the latter group was again experiencing what in 1951 C. Wright Mills had called in his *White Collar* "white-collar status panic." Schoolteachers and government employees were scrambling to organize unions of their own, recognizing this was their best chance of countering inflation and remaining solidly middle class.[2]

Economic forces beyond anyone's control were having a major effect on the collective psyche of the American middle class. "Within the middle class in par- ticular, there lurks the suspicion that their dream—the American Dream—is endangered," William Kowinski wrote for the *New York Times* in 1980, the double-whammy of a recession and high inflation making those earning an average income feel broke. Many of the middle class were not sure if they should spend money while they had it on things that would soon be more expensive or try to scrimp and save. Psychiatrists were hearing more about financial insecurity from their patients, and marriages too were suffering from money problems. America as a whole appeared to be having something like a mid-life crisis, no longer sure who it was and what it should be doing. "The middle-class formula for success, along with so much else, is being called into question—not, as it was in the 1960's, for moral or political reasons, but because it may not work," Kowinski observed. If being middle class was, as Ben Wattenberg had posited in his *In Search of the Real America*, having some discretionary income, more Americans no longer qualified to be members of the group.[3]

Much of the angst the American middle class was feeling was a result of the desire for more of the good things in life and a greater impatience to get them. Making sacrifices to reap future rewards was customary for previous generations of Americans, but now this was not the case. Sustained economic growth since the 1950s had led to expectations for both immediate gratification and even bigger future rewards, a very high bar (too high, in fact) to reach. With such a view, it was not surprising that some of the middle class felt cheated and that the system was not working as it should. It was true that home values were rising, but this did nothing to resolve concerns about buying power, liquidity, and financial security in general. Losing ground and going backward were alien concepts to the middle class (and Americans in general), making the reality of "negative growth" very difficult to take. Ronald Reagan, the ex-governor of California, had been viewed by most of the middle class as an ultra-conservative, but his image was quickly improving as individuals of all ideological ilk looked to him as a potential savior of the nation's economy and the American Dream.[4]

Its standard of living eroded by inflation and taxes, the middle class was instrumental in electing the ex-movie star, much to the surprise of pundits who had initially thought the man had no chance of becoming president. Most of the middle class blamed the government for their deteriorating financial condition, and Americans were clearly ready for a different approach to how it spent tax-payers' money.[5] Not eligible for government handouts like the poor and without money to invest like the rich, the middle and lower ends of the middle class were, as *U.S. News & World Report* put it in 1981, "angry, frustrated and losing ground." Some were warning of a major tax revolt, or thinking those who worked with highly paid professionals but earned a fraction of what their bosses made (like nurses and legal assistants) would demand more money. Middle managers, secretaries, sales people, retail clerks, and construction and factory workers were also struggling, on the brink of falling from a "have" to what the media was calling a "new have not." The difference in lifestyles between the two groups was vast. "Haves" dined out, took exotic vacations, invested in potentially lucrative ventures, lived in luxurious houses or apartments, drank wine, and bought designer clothes. The "new have nots," on the other hand, ate fast food, took vacations close to home, had their savings in the bank, lived in small houses, drank beer, bought discount clothing, and watched a lot of television. It used to be somewhat of an embarrassment for a wife to work full time but that was no longer the case as the two-income family became seen as the most sensible way to keep from slipping from a "have" to a "new have not."[6]

The lifestyles of some "haves" were so different from those of the lower middle class that they soon earned a label all their own. "Yuppies" (young urban professionals) became the principal face of American bourgeois culture in the mid-1980s, a segment of the middle class consisting of a portion of the seventy-six million or so baby boomers. The standard criteria for qualifying as a yuppie were being born between 1946 and 1964 and making $30,000 a year ($40,000 for a couple), meaning only about four million (or about 5 percent) of boomers actually deserved the title.[7] Yuppies' cultural influence was significantly greater than their numbers, however, making them the target of much scrutiny. Marketers were especially intrigued by this more well-off segment of the middle class, and were up to the challenge of selling all kinds of products and services to them. "They want it all and they can pay for it, but these affluent young spenders are a demanding bunch," a writer for *Travel Weekly* warned, a typical example of the frenzy surrounding the yuppy phenomenon.[8] There were many more members of the lower middle class than younger, high-earning Americans, as some critics noted at the time, although that was difficult to tell given all the attention yuppies were getting. "The biggest economic and social bloc in modern America is not the Yuppies but the Cluppies (Upwardly Mobile Clods), that great, semi-washed lower middle class that pays most of our taxes, fights most of our wars, and watches most of our commercial programming," wrote Aram Bakshian Jr. in *National Review* in 1985, thinking it was the latter group who better reflected the country's popular contemporary morals and manners.[9]

That some members of this generation of social revolutionaries had embraced the joys to be found in consumer culture even more than their parents had in the 1950s was not lost on critics. Yuppies quickly became a cultural archetype, their penchant for certain foods (quiche, goat cheese), beverages (Perrier, white wine), activities (tennis), toys (the Walkman), drinking establishments (the "fern bar"), and clothes (the corporate uniform and running shoes, sometimes worn together) widely mocked (and envied). Dual-career couples living in a renovated townhouse and sharing the child raising responsibilities seemed to be constantly going to or returning from exercise classes at the gym, an image too precious not to ridicule. Leftists were unhappy that yuppies had abandoned their idealism for materialism, while those on the right complained about their attraction to self-indulgence and excess. Yuppies may have been middle class in a strict socio-economic sense, but they surely did not subscribe to traditional middle-class values, many agreed. But with the rise of yuppies, the middle class was new and improved, one could argue, their commitment to gender equality, the environment, and cultural diversity a legacy of their countercultural roots.[10]

Yuppies may have been the ideal target audience for many products and services, but one did not have to nibble on brie or sip Chardonnay to capture the attention of marketers. Historically treated like second-class citizens by Wall Street, not worth the trouble, for example, the broad middle class began to attract a lot more attention from brokerage houses in the 1980s. With the 1981 Economic Recovery

Tax Act, which allowed all taxpayers under the age of 70½ to contribute to an individual retirement account or IRA (originally introduced in 1974), brokers realized they had a new and enormously large group of potential investors. Brokers initially scoffed at the $1,500 annual limit on an IRA contribution, but stopped laughing when they realized how much money was collectively going into the accounts and how the nest eggs quickly multiplied. Takeovers of and mergers with brokerage houses by companies selling products and services to the mass market also played a big part in the rather sudden discovery of smaller investors, as did the concern that the upscale market was being saturated. Although they were not yet making a lot of money, baby boomers in particular had a lot of upside potential, brokers correctly concluded, making them an attractive target to bring in as clients.[11]

Brokers began to aggressively court those making about $35,000 a year—the average income of a member of the American middle class in the mid-eighties—with solicitations, mass mailings, and even cold calls. After Sears, Roebuck and Company acquired Dean Witter Reynolds in 1982, hundreds of Sears financial centers began popping up in the giant retailers' stores right next to house wares or sporting goods. Allstate insurance people and Coldwell Banker real estate agents also could be found in these "financial supermarkets," which many in the middle class found to be a more familiar and comfortable setting than a fancy office in a downtown skyscraper. Through its subsidiary, IDS/American Express, Shearson Lehman Brothers was also pursuing this "mother lode," as *American Banker* labeled the opportunity, as were Paine Webber and Merrill Lynch. The middle class had been up to that point more a group of savers than investors, but Wall Street was determined to convince Main Street it could do better than the 5¼ percent interest rate banks were offering on passport savings accounts, something average earners liked to hear.[12]

Corporate America's focus on upscale consumers went well beyond the world of finance. Retailers too had largely neglected the middle class despite the fact it still accounted for most of the consumer spending in the United States. (Those making between $15,000 and $49,000 a year accounted for 55 percent of the nation's households and 60 percent of consumer spending, according to Morgan Stanley.) Both department stores and retail chains had drifted toward the upper end of the market since the beginning of the decade, swept up by the industry's shift toward luxury and the trendy. (The style-conscious Reagans moving into the White House certainly had something to do with this.) The discount side of retailing remained strong, however, creating a vacuum in the middle. Mass marketers like J.C. Penney, Mervyn's, Zayre's, and Target were happily taking advantage of the void left by department stores and smaller chains, with industry analysts urging retailers to try to avoid getting swept up by luxury fever.[13] J.C. Penney was having a great year in 1987 by appealing to "Middle America," in fact, going against the grain by dropping prices on basic items, cutting advertising and promotion expenses, and featuring lower priced goods instead of new, expensive designer lines.[14] It may not have been very glamorous, but offering middle-class consumers good value and a wide selection of merchandise was proving to be a successful formula for retailers like Penny's.[15]

While the lower middle class watched their pennies, the upper middle class would on occasion spend money like drunken sailors. Millions of Americans with incomes between $25,000 and $75,000—some yuppies, some not—were buying Godiva chocolates, Armani fragrances, Burberry raincoats, Louis Vuitton bags, and Mont Blanc pens. Executives were initially puzzled by the high sales of their products, knowing there just were not enough rich Americans to account for the large volume. It took market researchers at Grey Advertising to identify a mass market of what they called "ultra consumers" who were responsible for most of the spending on luxury goods. "Ultra consumers" wanted the best when they could afford it and, no doubt, when they could not, maxing out their credit cards to get a Hermes scarf or pair of Gucci loafers. Emulating the rich had become a prime recreational activity for some members of the upper middle class, seeing "conspicuous consumption" as a way to separate themselves from the hoi polloi.[16] Because it conveyed wealth and status, the upper middle class had also become fond of another luxury, cocaine. Cocaine was now what *Time* called the "all-American drug," the indulgence of choice "for perhaps millions of solid, conventional and often upwardly mobile citizens." "A veritable blizzard of the white powder is blowing through the American middle class," the magazine reported, the drug perfectly suited for the go-go times.[17]

The Social Glue

Needless to say, a $380 Burberry jacket, $250 Louis Vuitton purse, or $200 Mont Blanc fountain pen were all well out of the reach of the lower middle class. Some believed, in fact, that the writing was already on the wall for these members of the middle class. As millions of high-paying jobs in manufacturing, mining, and construction disappeared in the early (and recessionary) 1980s, many economists were predicting that blue-collar workers would have a much tougher time earning a middle-class wage in the future. Lots of new service industry jobs were being created, but these were lower paying, barely above the minimum wage. These same economists foresaw that it would increasingly require two adults in a family to support a middle-class lifestyle (or one adult working two jobs), a prediction that would turn out to be 100 percent correct.[18] Those of the persuasion that America should be a "fair" or "harmonious" society were especially disturbed about the apparent polarization of the workplace and, consequently, the country itself. Occasional slowdowns in economic growth could be expected, as could periods of high unemployment, but this cleaving of the nation in two seemed more systemic and permanent. If nothing else, a big middle class was needed to consume all the products American businesses made, as the numbers of the wealthy were simply too small to support the economy.[19]

Even though he arguably played a major role in creating these hard times of the American middle class, President Reagan again appealed to the group as he ran for a second term. Seeing which way the winds were blowing, the Democrats too jumped on the (white) middle-class bandwagon in the run-up to the election. A new breed of "Democons" seemed to be in the works as the party gravitated toward the interests of "average Americans" rather than espouse "fairness" and "compassion" for the underclass. The traditional party platform grounded in social equity, public justice, and progressive reform was yielding to, as Democratic National Committee chair Paul G. Kirk Jr. expressed it in late 1985, "the unifying common interest themes of family, of work, of education, of fiscal pragmatism and economic opportunity, of equality and competitiveness, of patriotism and a more secure future." Public opinion research was showing this is what the majority of voters wanted to hear, making the 1986 presidential election a battle for the middle class.[20]

However, things looked bleak not just for the blue-collar segment of the American middle class but also the white-collar segment. As a widening economic divide between the rich and poor became more evident during President Reagan's second term, the implications for the entire middle class were becoming clearer and clearer. The late 1970s were the last years in which economic inequality among Americans declined, according to economists Bennett Harrison, Chris Tilly, and Barry Bluestone, reversing a thirty-year trend. The wealthiest Americans were earning an ever-growing share of national income, government statistics showed, and the poorest a continually shrinking portion. Based on the pattern of income distribution in the country, some economists were predicting that the American middle class would disappear completely, leaving an affluent minority and poverty-stricken majority.[21]

The apparent shrinking of the American middle class hit critical mass in the mid-1980s, as a flood of media attention to the issue raised public concern. New jobs were being created at the top and at the bottom, the general thesis went, America's "declining middle" the result of a fundamental change in the occupational structure of the country. A two-tiered society could very well lead to political and social unrest, some were warning, the presence of a large middle class the only thing preventing Marx's predicted revolution between the rich and poor.[22] "A healthy middle class is in fact the social glue that holds our society together," the esteemed economist Lester Thurow wrote in 1984, arguing that, "other societies may be able to survive divided into rich and poor but we Americans simply don't have the historical roots that make this possible."[23] If that were not enough, the disappearance of the middle class, with its tremendous purchasing power, might wreck the entire economy. The loss of jobs in "smokestack" industries (automobile manufacturing, blast furnace and basic steel products, and iron and steel foundries), the rise of the low-paying service economy, and the emergence of high-tech were all contributing to the bipolarization of the national workforce, supporters of this view argued. McDonald's now employed more people than General Motors, a telling sign of the times.[24]

Was this "ungluing" of America really true, or simply an imagined scenario put forth by the more liberal distressed by President Reagan's laissez-faire economic policies? The reports of the death of the American middle class were greatly exaggerated, a growing number of researchers were beginning to say after taking their own hard look at the numbers. "We see no evidence that jobs associated with the middle range of society are disappearing," said Ronald Kutcher of the Labor Department in 1984, pointing out that the service sector went well beyond flipping burgers. The argument that new high-tech jobs were wiping out large numbers of manufacturing jobs also was not true, some studies were showing.[25] (Apple's landmark "1984" commercial for its new Macintosh computer might have had something to do with the fear that technology would subjugate the masses.) One study in particular suggested that all the fretting about the middle class was much ado about nothing. According to government statistics from 1973 and 1982, there was no polarization in income, Neal H. Rosenthal pointed out in *Occupational Outlook Quarterly* in 1985. In fact, average earners' real income grew over this ten-year period, he reported, although no more recent numbers were yet available.[26]

Rosenthal's analysis was a breath of fresh air to those thinking the shrinkage of the middle class was largely a myth created by the liberal media. "Thank you, Neal Rosenthal," wrote Robert J. Samuelson in *Newsweek* soon after the article by the Bureau of Labor Statistics economist was published. "The theory's wrong and needs demolishing," Samuelson happily reported, firmly believing the popular argument that middle-income jobs were rapidly being replaced by high-paying and low-paying work was "a pure case of social theorizing by stereotype." General anxiety about the country's economic future had triggered a panic attack that the middle class was going away, he suggested, this mass hysteria unwarranted given the facts. The proportion of workers with middle-income jobs had hardly changed between 1973 and 1982, Samuelson reiterated, the much-bally-hooed "polarization" of America simply not true. Advocates of the theory were politically motivated, he contended, admitting the country had economic issues but not of the magnitude liberals were claiming.[27]

Others in the business of business challenged the claim that America's middle class was vanishing and that society was being cleaved in half. In 1986, William Baldwin wrote a scathing article in *Forbes* making the case that not only was the middle class not getting poorer but that the richer were not getting richer. Both of these assertions were conjectures based on flawed statistical analysis, Baldwin held, something other conservatives relished hearing. Even the way liberals defined the middle class was all wrong, he argued. Thurow had suggested any household earning 75 percent to 125 percent of the median income was middle class, seemingly as good a definition as any. But such a definition (resulting in about 24 percent of the population, down from 28 percent in 1967) would make a fireman in Los Angeles upper class and an English professor in Oregon lower class, Baldwin pointed out, a perfect example of how liberals like Thurow were trying to make the middle class a relatively narrow or "skinny" group. Conservatives like Baldwin liked to define the middle class in broader (or "fatter") terms because it proved that America was the "middle class nation" they envisioned and that President Reagan's economic policies were not dividing the country into "haves" and "new have nots."[28]

Nothing like the Draconian measures Thurow recommended in his new book *Zero-Sum Solution* to correct the inequitable distribution of income in America was necessary, Baldwin and the likeminded felt. "The reality is somewhat less dramatic," Baldwin explained, of the opinion that the MIT professor was using "Chicken Little's income statistics."[29] The flood of lower paid, younger, and female workers into the job market and the dramatic rise of single-parent families in the 1980s were the real reasons for the big swing in income, defenders of the Reagan administration argued, seeing the situation more in terms of demographics than politics. Assuming these revisionist critics were right, one could conclude that laissez-faire capitalism worked, a tacit endorsement for a "just-get-out-of-the-way" style of government. It was hard to ignore the inverse effects President Reagan's public policies were having on the rich and poor, however, with liberals making a reasonable case that a dwindling middle class was leading to social instability. "Unless … growth produces an equitable distribution of benefits, something is deeply wrong with democratic capitalism," wrote Robert Kuttner in *Business Week* in 1985, thinking, "a shrinking middle class is a call for action."[30]

The Hourglass Economy

Whatever one thought of democratic capitalism, it was not hard to find evidence that the United States was well on the way to becoming a two-tiered society. Again, most retailers were scrambling to one side of the market or the other, and product categories ranging from food to clothing to furnishings all seemed to be splitting into a high-end and a low-end. It was, however, the common struggle for the standard elements of the American Dream—a house, a new car, and a college education for one's kids—that illustrated that a new chapter in the nation's history was being written. Baby boomers' monthly payments on their average-priced cars were typically higher than their parents' mortgage payments, a good example of how out-of-whack things had become. "America's middle class is in a fix," *U.S. News & World Report* pithily put it in 1986, the metaphor of trying to climb a descending escalator an apt one. Despite the recent tax cuts, big-ticket items remained out of reach for many caught up in the receding economic tide. Working more for less was resulting in an all-time high of consumer debt, as many Americans refused to give up the things to which they had become accustomed. Some felt, however, that things were not as bad for the middle class as it seemed. "The upper boundaries of desires have climbed, and that's changed the criteria for what it takes to stay in the middle class," Ben Wattenberg suggested, boomers' parents never having the opportunity to buy things like VCRs, CD players, or home computers. Other things once considered luxuries—having a second car, owning a boat, or going to Europe—were now not unusual, more support that the bar to be middle class had been raised over the course of a generation.[31]

Even if being middle class now meant something much different than twenty or thirty years earlier, there were hard reasons why it was more difficult to "keep up." The simplest reason was that there were a lot more people vying for jobs and creating a generally more competitive climate. As Landon Jones discussed in his *Great Expectations: America and the Baby Boom Generation*, the seventy-six million or so twenty- and thirty-somethings were jockeying for a limited number of jobs, not to mention pay raises and promotions. Job security was fast becoming a distant memory, the prospect of having a single employer for a lifetime remote at best. And with both partners in a marriage now working, childcare was proving to be a major drain on net income. The biggest difference by far, however, was the price of a home. As late as the early 1970s, one could buy a decent home for $30,000 in many parts of the country and get a mortgage with a 6 or 7 percent interest rate. In 1986, that same home would likely cost $200,000 and require a 10 percent interest rate, effectively doubling the percentage of gross monthly income going toward it. Down payments had risen proportionately, another barrier to achieving the classic middle-class symbol of owning a home.[32]

Americans were willing to concede the fact that the nation was not really a universally "middle-class society," as we liked to believe, but the vanishing of a sizable and stable group of average income earners was too much to accept. What was America without the middle class?, many asked, our very identity hanging in the balance. The issue of class polarization was becoming a highly heated one among economists and other wonks, with those on the left ringing alarms about where the country was going and those on the right claiming the system was working the way it should. The huge wave of baby boomers entering the workforce accounted for the downward shift in income, people at organizations like the Brookings Institution and the Conference Board explained, the middle class to be restored as the largest generation in history aged and made more money. The statistics spoke for themselves, however, making their interpretation more of an ideological and political exercise than an academic one. A visual depiction of income distribution still resembled the classic bell curve but, over the last decade, the center had flattened somewhat while the left and right ends had gotten taller. (Economists referred to this as "the hourglass economy," while politicians preferred "the dumbbell economy.") Fears of both ends of the economy becoming taller than the middle accelerated through the decade as the income divide showed no signs of diminishing.[33]

Stephen J. Rose's graphic depiction of Americans according to social and economic status did little to allay these fears. In 1978, Rose, an economist, created a poster called "Social Stratification in the U.S." that illustrated Americans' income, occupation, family structure, and racial composition. Using little human figures rather than statistics, the poster caught people's attention, especially for showing the country's extreme distribution of wealth. Women and blacks collectively earned about 60 percent of what white men did, the poster also revealed, this too more alarming when presented in visual form. Rose updated the poster in 1986 and published it as a book called *The American Profile Poster*. Once again, many were shocked to see how just a few little figures accounted for much of the nation's wealth. The second edition of the poster also depicted the changes that had taken place over the past eight years. About 5 percent of the little people had gravitated toward the low-end of income and about 3 percent toward the high-end, meaning one, the middle class was shrinking, and two, wealth was becoming more concentrated among the financial elite. (The poster relied on Bureau of Labor Statistics.) By almost any measure, inequality was growing in America, exactly what critics of the Reagan administration's economic policies and social programs had been saying all along. "*The American Profile Poster* is a bleak, statistically meticulous and even-tempered presentation of trends that ought to alarm anyone except the minority of beneficiaries from the Reagan revolution in social and tax policy," wrote Robert Lekachman in the *New York Times Book Review*, concluding that, "America seems en route to becoming a dual society."[34]

Part of the strong disagreement about the status and fate of the American middle class was due to the ambiguity of the term itself. Statistically, "middle class" signified median income, although this number and range was much disputed. The Tax Reform Act of 1986 classified all Americans with incomes between $20,000 and $50,000 as middle class, but even this simple and clear definition was not universally accepted.[35] The term meant much more than earning a certain degree of money, of course, this explaining why the term remained so fuzzy. Lifestyle, purchasing habits, even one's vision for the future revolved around the words "middle class," with specific designators—owning a home, sending one's children to college, and some discretionary income for a second car or annual vacation—firmly set in the American mindset. It was these benchmarks to consider oneself a member of the middle class in good standing that had become more difficult to achieve, a direct result of falling income levels in real (inflation-adjusted) dollars. While conservatives pointed to the "baby boom factor" for why average earners were bringing home less money, liberals were confident that public policy was a leading cause. Lower taxes for the affluent and less spending on social programs tilted the national distribution of wealth, the democratically-inclined believed, a perfect recipe for pushing both the upper and lower ends of the middle class out of the group. But even lefties admitted the shift began before Ronald Reagan took the presidential oath, meaning more than politics and economics were at work. "Structural changes," principally globalization, "de-industrialization," the technological revolution, and the decline of unions, were no doubt playing an important role in the collapse of the American middle class, making one wonder if anything could be done to stop or even slow it.[36]

The question of whether or not the middle class was doomed intensified as more numbers were produced supporting each side. "When the drift was first spotted in the early 1980s, it stirred only academic interest," *Time* noted in 1986, but now the alleged slippage of the American middle class was "spark[ing] a fervent debate." According to Census Bureau data, the proportion of households earning between $15,000 and $50,000 decreased from 65 percent in 1970 to 58 percent in 1985, after adjustments for inflation, evidence that the middle class was indeed relatively smaller. Unlike the Bureau of Labor Statistics data, however, these figures showed that most of these households had drifted up rather than down. (Five percent of the spread went up while just 2 percent went down.) In the case of two average earners getting married, two middle-class households were lost and one upper-middle-class created, another fly in the statistical ointment.[37] In one of the more authoritative studies, economist Katherine L. Bradbury of the Federal Reserve Bank of Boston found not only that "the general perception of a shrinking middle class is correct," but about four times as many families fell out of the group than rose above it between 1973 and 1984. Bradbury had defined the middle class with incomes between $20,000 and $50,000 in 1984 dollars, perhaps this accounting for the different findings. It was not demographic trends but rather "the complex workings of the economy itself" that were reducing the numbers of middle-class Americans, the study published in the *New England Economic Review* posited, the rumors of the group's decline not exaggerated.[38]

If there was any definitive conclusion to make, it was that the "shrinkage theory," as it was sometimes known, was heavily reliant on how one defined the middle class. The very idea of a "middle class" was a generally arbitrary one, the "fervent debate" plainly revealed, a mash-up of economic and psychological categorizations that were as subjective as objective, if not more so. Lawrence Lindsey, an economist at Harvard, threw out the numbers in entirety. "A middle-class person is someone who expects to be self-reliant, unlike the upper class with its unearned wealth or the lower class with its dependency on society," the professor held, obviously favoring a qualitative approach over a quantitative one. From this perspective, the American middle class was "bigger than ever," Lindsey added, not at all on life support as most of his colleagues insisted. "It is only because the middle class is so sacred in the U.S. that even its potential shrinkage is so controversial," *Time* observed, few if anyone believing that the group need not exist.[39]

The passion on both sides of the debate revealed how strongly many felt about the American middle class. The mere possibility that the middle class was in retreat was, perhaps more than anything else, surprising. After all, much of the mythology of the American Dream of reaching the middle class had been real over the last century and a half. All kinds of factors—free or cheap land, greater educational opportunities, affordable housing, and a consistently growing economy (albeit with a few big hiccups)—made upward mobility not all that difficult, especially if one was white and male. The notion that class lines were becoming more rigid and that luck or fate was playing a more important role in the trajectory of one's life was a difficult thing to take. An end to the economic boom of the last few decades was a rude awakening and, on a grander scale, antithetical to the American faith in perpetual progress. It was simply unthinkable that an older generation was better off financially than a younger one and, in particular, that a good number of American families were losing their middle-class status. Lots of attention began to be paid to "the largest inheritance in history," the passing of this great wealth from the Depression/World War II generation to their baby boomer children the only way many of the latter would remain middle class.[40]

Something in the Refrigerator

For African Americans, achieving the American Dream of becoming middle class had special resonance. Much had changed in the three decades since E. Franklin Frazier wrote in *Black Bourgeoisie* that the black middle class "lacks a basis in the American economic system." Thirteen percent of African Americans were middle class in 1960 but nearly a third were in the late 1980s, a clear sign of progress. Two-thirds of black professionals, managers, and white-collar workers were first generation middle class, sociologists estimated.[41] There was still an undeniable income gap between the black middle class and the white middle class due to lingering racism but it was getting smaller every year, a direct result of the civil rights movement and affirmative action. In addition, the black middle class was increasingly operating within the broader, pluralistic society rather than just within the African American community, a sign it was indeed now part of the nation's "economic system." African Americans were even more uncomfortable talking about class than whites, however, the subject a divisive one and subservient to the much bigger issue of race.[42]

The cultural dynamics surrounding the black middle class remained complex. Different standards were often used to sort blacks into the middle class than for whites, for one thing, a reflection of race-based attitudes and discrimination. And while white white-collar workers were almost always considered middle class, this was not the case for black white-collar workers. Blue-collar and semi-skilled African Americans typically made more money than black salespeople and clerical workers, meaning moving into such a white-collar occupation for them represented downward rather than upward mobility. (Frazier had used occupation to determine class status, while W.E.B. DuBois had used family income in his important work *The Philadelphia Negro*.) Based on Census Bureau data and Congress's definition based on income, 29 percent of black households were middle class (versus 44 percent of white households) in 1987. (Eighty percent of black middle-class households were families, the remaining 20 percent consisting of single people.) Despite the fact that the number of African Americans in professional, managerial, and technical occupations doubled in the 1970s, the black middle class (like the white middle class) was shrinking rather than growing. A couple of recessions, double-digit inflation, and the shift from high-paying manufacturing jobs to lower-paying service jobs had hurt African Americans particularly hard.

Additionally, the black middle class was paid less than its white counterparts in many occupations, and a higher percentage of the former worked for the government rather than in the private sector. Most significant, perhaps, was the wealth disparity between the black and white middle classes. The median net worth of the former was less than a third of the latter, a statistic suggesting that, despite all the attention paid to income, wealth was equally important in determining class.[43]

The lifestyles of the black middle class, which often mimicked those of the white middle class, became rich fodder for popular African American comedians such as Dick Gregory and Redd Foxx. An African American setting the table with "silverware" rather than knives and forks was a clear signal that one was a member of the black middle class, Gregory joked, an act designed to show others one's sophistication. Those new to the middle class worked especially hard to prove that they had reached a higher rung on the ladder of success, something that was not lost on keen observers of the social scene like Gregory and Foxx. "Buppies'" (black urban professionals) discovery of trendy foods like quiche and crepes made good-natured teasing, these sometimes served right alongside traditional "soul food" such as greens, "chitlins," and cornbread. Bread and spaghetti had suddenly become "croissants" and "pasta" for this group, Gregory noted, with "little bitty pieces of food they call hors d'oeuvres" served before the main course. Foxx, meanwhile, quipped that any African American ahead of his or her car and house payments and "hav[ing] something in the refrigerator" was part of the black middle class. Having life insurance and a couple of thousand dollars in the stock market were for Foxx other indications that one had crossed the class line.[44]

Middle-class black families' leaving their neighborhood for a more affluent and whiter one was taken more seriously, however, a possible sign that they were effectively abandoning their race.[45] "When many blacks make it to the middle class they move to the suburbs and just maintain their black skin," said Catherine Hughes, owner of a radio station in Washington, DC, believing such a relocation leads them to "take on a white mentality."[46] Many cities across the country offered a perfect solution, however. Neighborhoods like Hamilton Heights in New York City, Baldwin Hills in Los Angeles, MacGregor Park in Houston, Cascade Heights in Atlanta, and Chatham in Chicago were havens for middle-class blacks who preferred to live among their own. Safe, quiet, and well-cared for, these areas were considered ideal by professionals who often worked with whites but wanted to spend their free time around other blacks.[47] The revival of Harlem as a middle-class neighborhood was something of a phenomenon considering its steep decline in the 1960s and 1970s. Turn-of-the-century brownstones were being restored to their original glory by black college professors, writers, lawyers, and actors who knew a good deal when they saw one. Middle-class whites too were trickling into the neighborhood in the mid-eighties, drawn to the area by what was without a doubt the best real estate opportunities in Manhattan.[48]

More generally, it was important for blacks who had "made it" not to, as the expression went, "forget where you came from." Leaving "brothers and sisters" behind was a sensitive issue in the African American community, viewed by many as working against the unity that was vital to an oppressed group. African Americans of all economic strata believed staying involved in and giving back to black causes was important if not essential, a heavy emotional burden for some who had reached the middle class. Of course, working predominantly with whites and achieving a certain income level did not mean automatically losing one's attachments and connections to the black community. Many embraced DuBois' concept of "dual consciousness," shuttling back and forth between the white and black worlds with relative ease. Other middle-class African Americans were frustrated that more blacks had not moved up the ladder as they had, and felt they had no obligation to anyone.[49]

While how blacks "acted white" made a good standup routine, many Americans were truly interested in whether the majority of African Americans were achieving middle-class status. Race remained one of the country's most divisive issues, and it was a simple fact that the color of one's skin was closely linked to how much money one earned. Overall, African Americans made considerable economic progress in the early 1980s, with the black middle class one of the fastest growing demographic segments in the country. (A prime factor was black women entering the workforce during these years.) The black middle class was growing at a much greater rate than the white middle class, in fact, in part because they had so much catching up to do because of discrimination.[50] Some whites did not understand why a good number of blacks remained poor, however, and were therefore happy to see evidence suggesting more were "finally making it." Many African Americans also took great pleasure in hearing about blacks' success stories, something the editors of *Ebony* certainly understood. Not unlike *Life*, the monthly magazine for the African American market was consistently upbeat, positive, and self-affirming, its editorial slant leaning decidedly toward values steeped in aspiration and achievement. In 1987, the magazine ran a series of articles under the banner "Faces of Middle Class America" that focused on individuals or families who were professionally accomplished and were living "the good life." As prime examples of "black bourgeoisie" culture, these articles were clearly intended to not only entertain readers but to serve as inspiration for other African Americans.

Looking back, one would not know that *Ebony*'s "Faces of Middle Class America" series appeared at a time when the middle class was being torn apart at the seams. Attractive families living in nice houses somehow had the time and money to enjoy leisure activities like tennis and golf, take skiing vacations, and pursue some form of creative expression such as music or ballet. Volunteering time to local civic organizations was also important, a sign of these families' commitment to their community. Ivy League-educated men held prestigious, high-paying corporate jobs, while women either worked outside the home or were housewives, a throwback to an earlier generation of middle-class Americans. (Unlike June Cleaver or Harriet Nelson, a stay-at-home mom had a graduate degree and had left corporate life once baby came along.) More than anything else, however, family "togetherness" and giving back to the black community was emphasized in the articles, reassuring readers that despite their success the individuals featured had not become self-absorbed and had retained their African American identity.[51] Work and school took precedent, with keeping as busy as possible the recipe for happiness.[52] When a single person was featured in *Ebony*'s "Faces of Middle Class America" series, he or she was an old-fashioned sort who enjoyed wholesome activities like reading and watching old movies when not rapidly climbing the ladder of success at work or, conversely, a social butterfly.[53] Driven, motivated, and grabbing life by the horns, the people depicted in the stories proved that not just black celebrities and athletes could realize the American Dream but ordinary, hard-working folks.

Not everybody was happy to see this rosy portrayal of black middle-class life. "The Black middle class occupies a precarious and ambiguous position in the United States today," posited Nathan Hare, chairman of the board of a company called the Black Think Tank, of the opinion that Americans of all races generally found the group pretentious and overly occupied with consumerism. Redd Foxx and Dick Gregory's observations were obviously over the top and designed to be funny but, according to Hare, not too far off the mark. It was true that the black middle class was sometimes referred to as "bourgies" (short for bourgeoisie), "Black Anglo Saxons," "oreos," and "coconuts," all derogatory terms referring to the group's alleged attempts to imitate the lifestyles of the white middle class (and specifically yuppies). Members of the black middle class typically viewed themselves as role models for the African American underclass, a view that the latter often did not share. More militant civil rights activists flatly believed that the black middle class was selling out, i.e., giving up the fight for a more equal society in exchange for a (white-provided) well-paying job and the things it could buy. Most troubling to Hare and others, the black middle class looked to white society to create their identity, and thus had no real opinions of their own. Black middle-class men getting romantically involved with white women was an especially sore spot to people like Hare. In short, the black middle class was striving for recognition and validation by whites, a pathetic and ultimately hopeless pursuit that was bad for African Americans as a whole.[54]

Members of the black middle class, naturally, disagreed with such a harsh assessment. First of all, they asked, why did they have to defend their choice of lifestyle when the white middle class did not? Even the label "black middle class" was fundamentally erroneous, they added, as it implied there was a black upper class. No such class existed in America, at least not one connected to "old money." Income level was the only true determinant of being part of a "black middle class," making the kind of sharp criticism from people like Hare absurd. Members of the black middle class were proud of their efforts to help the less fortunate, whether it be through financial assistance or by serving in civic, professional, fraternal, and religious organizations. The middle class was as assertive as any group of

African Americans when it came to fighting for equal rights, some were quick to point out, not about to allow extremists like Hare to diminish their sizable role in serving the black community.[55]

Critics such as Hare would have been pleased to learn that the steady rise of the black middle class was stalling in the late 1980s. Serious inequities persisted, making some think that blacks' social and economic ascendance over the past generation may have peaked. Middle-class African Americans' wages and salaries often continued to be lower than whites in the same occupations, and blacks were more frequently unemployed. In the corporate world, very few blacks had moved beyond middle management, and none had yet become CEO of a major company. (Herman Cain was in the running at Godfather's Pizza.) The Reagan administration had not been a fan of affirmative action, making some companies pull back on such programs. "You have black people who have reached the middle class, but a high proportion of them are struggling to meet the standards of that class," said Bart Landry, a University of Maryland sociologist and author of *The New Black Middle Class*, finding economic insecurity to be greater among African Americans than whites. Blacks' educational gains also appeared to have hit the wall, something that did not bode well for their future. Like the white middle class, the black middle class appeared to be moving backward rather than forward, the 1980s turning out to be great for a few but challenging for the many.[56]

Falling from Grace

On paper, at least, it would seem that the bulk of the American middle class should have been thriving in the late 1980s. Unemployment was at a fourteen-year low, inflation was a third of what it was in the early 1980s, and even the October 1987 stock market plunge had not done any long-term damage to the economy. Still, more Americans believed the middle class was worse off economically as a result of President Reagan's policies, according to a 1988 *Time* poll. (Reagan had famously asked, "Are you better off than you were four years ago?" in a 1980 debate against incumbent President Jimmy Carter.) "Though the wealthy are doing noticeably better, most middle-class Americans feel squeezed," the magazine reported, the benefits of the eighties boom not distributed evenly.[57] Among younger people especially, job insecurity, the inability to own a home, and the belief that it was unlikely that one would do as well as one's parents were creating the sense that the middle-class standard of living was slipping away. The media was fueling this pessimistic outlook, giving lots of coverage to factory closings, corporate layoffs, and farm bankruptcies. The fall of the Berlin Wall and collapse of the Soviet Union were just a few years away, but there remained a widespread feeling that American capitalism was in serious decline.[58]

A spate of books about the American middle class was published in the late 1980s, all of them attempts to better understand the reasons for the group's discontent. In his 1988 *Middle American Individualism*, leading sociologist Herbert

Gans argued that individualism was the core trait of "middle Americans," explaining why the loss of control over their lives due to economic factors was proving to be such a crisis. Unlike social critics like Richard Sennett and Christopher Lasch, who believed that materialism, hedonism, and selfishness were indelibly linked to middle-class individualism, Gans argued that most Americans were simply more discerning and sophisticated than previous generations.[59] Barbara Ehrenreich had a more unflattering view of middle Americans in her *Fear of Falling* published the following year. As the title of her book made clear, the professional middle class had a profound fear of falling (and failing), a fear so great it was the principal guiding force in these peoples' lives. The middle class's elitism and self-absorption was a direct result of their fear of falling downward socially and economically, she claimed, calling for them to get over this dread so they could become more caring and inclusive individuals.[60]

In her *Falling from Grace: The Experience of Downward Mobility in the American Middle Class*, Katherine S. Newman explored the emotional and psychological impact of moving backward socially and economically. Expectedly, prolonged unemployment was a major blow to those believing they would be rewarded for hard work, especially among men conditioned to think they should be the family's breadwinner. Some of those who found themselves "falling from grace" went to great lengths to hide the fact from neighbors, friends, family members, and, most tragically, themselves. The financial shenanigans of Wall Street's "paper entrepreneurs" were much to blame for the downward mobility of the American middle class during the Reagan years, Newman argued, their manipulation of companies via mergers and leveraged buy-outs having devastating effects on the lives of real people.[61]

Loren Baritz, however, believed the crisis the middle class was facing was simply business as usual. From its very beginnings the middle class had been dissatisfied and discontented, the Amherst professor suggested in his *The Good Life*, with some kind of serious threat always dashing its members' hopes and dreams. A never-ending series of events—the wave of Eastern European immigrants in the late 19th and early 20th centuries, the rise of mass consumer culture in the 1920s, the Depression, World War II, postwar conformity, the counterculture, and the economic calamities of the 1970s—made "the good life" an elusive pursuit for the majority of the middle class, he argued. Still, most Americans considered themselves middle class or aspired to be part of the group, making one wonder what the draw was if things had been continually so bad for them.[62]

Whether victims of economic forces or the cause of their own troubles, the middle class was, the majority agreed, shrinking. Some did not view this necessarily as a bad thing, however. While getting smaller, the middle class was getting richer, according to economists like Marvin Kosters of the American Enterprise Institute. Putting a positive spin on the squeezing of the group, Kosters and economists at the Brookings Institution produced numbers showing that real family income was rising rather than declining. How was this possible, when all evidence suggested that average earners' income was not keeping up with inflation? By working more, of course. "Forget reports of its demise," announced *Changing Times* in reporting these economists' analyses, "the middle class is alive and well and living on two incomes." A family having to work two or more jobs was now just a fact of life to remain middle class, in other words; the way to get there had changed but the destination had not. "The need to rely on two incomes doesn't make middle-class status any less real than it used to be, just different," the magazine explained, a curious way to look at the issue.[63]

Keeping up a middle-class lifestyle now relied heavily on meeting other criteria. In addition to having two jobs, it was important that a couple had already purchased their house. Few families earning an average income (the middle three quintiles, or 60 percent of households) could afford to buy a first home and, even if they could, their mortgage would undoubtedly make them "cash poor." Sending kids to public school or a state college was also key, as the tuition of private education would all but eat up after-tax incomes. Finally, it was imperative that no family member come down with an illness that required long-term, uninsurable medical treatment. (Even being covered for 80 percent of medical costs and having to pay the remaining 20 percent, as many HMO policies required, could break a family's bank.) The cost of these three big-ticket items—real estate, education, and health care—had considerably exceeded the inflation rate, making it increasingly difficult for such families to maintain one's economic and social status.[64]

The outpouring of concern about middle-class families over the past decade led one reporter to try to meet a particular one face to face. In an interesting exercise, Michael T. Kaufman of the *New York Times* went looking for the archetypical middle-class family in New York City in 1989. "I expected it would be a bit down market from the TV Huxtables and a little upscale from Archie Bunker, and the children would be called Tiffany and Jason and names like that," Kaufman proposed, surprised to find that the search turned out to be a lot more difficult and complicated than he thought it would be. How much money would this family make? What neighborhood would they live in? What would they do for a living? Income was just one indicator of class status, he quickly learned, with those of "middle income" making anywhere from $32,000 to $53,000 a year in the city. Middle-class neighborhoods also varied significantly, Kaufman discovered, each ZIP code in the city (he focused on Queens) often having quite different houses, shops, and cars. Occupation too provided no definitive solution to finding the quintessential middle-class New York City family, leading Kaufman to try to identify one through consumption habits. This also led to a dead end, however, making him give up his ambitious quest. "I finally concluded that the middle class, whatever it is, is not a single, precisely delineated group," he explained, no particular family truly able to represent all of its members.[65] As the nation entered the last decade of the 20th century, the American middle class would become even more amorphous, its story going in unpredictable directions and taking new twists and turns.

Notes

1 "Middle Class Money Blues," *Ebony*, August 1980, 72–76.
2 Paul Blumber, "American Incomes Today," *Current*, February 1980, 17–22.
3 William Kowinski, "The Squeeze on the Middle Class," *New York Times*, July 13, 1980, A27; Ben Wattenberg, *In Search of the Real America: A Challenge to the Chaos of Failure and Guilt.* New York: G.P. Putnam, 1978.
4 "The Squeeze on the Middle Class."
5 "Why the Middle Class Supports Reagan," *Business Week*, May 18, 1981, 132–36.
6 Lawrence Maloney, "America's Middle Class," *U.S. News & World Report*, March 30, 1981, 39–45.
7 Barbara Ehrenreich, "Is the Middle Class Doomed?" *New York Times Magazine*, September 7, 1986, 44+.
8 Steve Noveck, "What do These Yuppies Want?", *Travel Weekly*, November 30, 1986, 44+.
9 Aram Bakshian Jr., "Soap and Sympathy," *National Review*, July 26, 1985, 51–52.
10 "Arise, Ye Yuppies!," *The New Republic*, July 9, 1984, 4.
11 Jon Freidman, "A Middle Class Mother Lode," *American Banker*, April 18, 1985, 12.
12 "A Middle Class Mother Lode."
13 Sidney Rutberg, "Analyst Hits Neglect of the Middle Class in Retailing Trends," *WWD*, April 3, 1986, 8.
14 Jill Curry, "One Year Later at J.C. Penney," *Chain Store Age—General Merchandise Trends*, February 1987, 35+.
15 Les Gilbert, "Retailers Ponder the 'Middle Class'; Identity, Income Questioned," *HFD—The Weekly Home Furnishings Newspaper*, March 9, 1987, 8.
16 Jaclyn Fierman, "The High-Living Middle Class," *Fortune*, April 13, 1987, 27.
17 Michael Demarest, "Cocaine: Middle Class High," *Time*, July 6, 1981.
18 "Declining Middle Class Projected," *Dun's Business Month*, July 1984, 13.
19 Bob Kuttner, "The Declining Middle," *The Atlantic*, July 1983, 60–64.
20 "The Democons," *The Nation*, December 14, 1985, 635+.
21 "Is the Middle Class Doomed?"
22 Lester C. Thurow, "The Disappearance of the Middle Class," *New York Times*, February 5, 1984, A3.
23 Lester C. Thurow, "The Gap Gets Wider in US Standard of Living," *American Banks*, October 22, 1984, 18+.
24 Neal H. Rosenthal, "Is the Middle Class Shrinking?", *Occupational Outlook Quarterly*, Fall 1985, 15+.
25 "The Myth of the Vanishing Middle Class," *Business Week*, July 9, 1984, 85–86; Monroe W. Karmin, "Is Middle Class Really Doomed to Shrivel Away?", *U.S. News & World Report*, August 20, 1984, 65.
26 "Is the Middle Class Shrinking?"
27 Robert J. Samuelson, "The Myth of the Missing Middle," *Newsweek*, July 1, 1985, 50.
28 "Middle Classicism," *National Review*, April 25, 1986, 19.
29 William Baldwin, "Chicken Little's Income Statistics," *Forbes*, March 24, 1986, 68+; Lester C. Thurow, *Zero-Sum Solution: Building a World-Class American Economy* (New York: Simon & Schuster, 1985).
30 Robert Kuttner, "A Shrinking Middle Class Is a Call for Action," *Business Week*, September 16, 1985, 16.
31 Beth Brophy, "Middle-Class Squeeze," *U.S. News & World Report*, August 18, 1986, 36–41.
32 "Middle-Class Squeeze"; Landon Jones, *Great Expectations: America and the Baby Boom Generation* (New York: Coward McCann, 1980).
33 "Is the Middle Class Doomed?"

34 Robert Lekachman, "Squeezing the Middle Class," *New York Times Book Review*, May 4, 1986; Stephen J. Rose, *The American Profile Poster* (New York: Pantheon, 1986).

35 Dr. Robert B. Hill, "The Black Middle Class Defined," *Ebony*, August 1987, 30–32.

36 "Is the Middle Class Doomed?"

37 Stephen Koepp, "Is the Middle Class Shrinking?" *Time*, November 3, 1986, 54–56.

38 Gene Koretz, "The Middle Class Isn't What It Used To Be," *Business Week*, November 17, 1986, 26.

39 "Is the Middle Class Shrinking?" (Koepp).

40 Robert Kuttner, "The Patrimony Society," *The New Republic*, May 11, 1987, 18–21.

41 James E. Ellis, "The Black Middle Class," *Business Week*, March 14, 1988, 62–70.

42 "Moving Up at Last," *Harper's*, February 1987, 35–46.

43 "The Black Middle Class Defined"; W.E.B. Dubois, *The Philadelphia Negro: A Social Study* (New York: Schocken Books, 1899).

44 Walter Leavy, "A Comedic Look at the Black Middle Class," *Ebony*, August 1987, 68–72.

45 "A Comedic Look at the Black Middle Class."

46 Ian Austen, "In a Class of Their Own," *Maclean's*, January 20, 1986, 22.

47 "The Black Middle Class—Where It Lives," *Ebony*, August 1987, 34–40.

48 Theodora Lurie, "The Middle Class Returns to Harlem," *Maclean's*, February 25, 1985, 8.

49 Alvin F. Poussaint, M.D., "The Price of Success," *Ebony*, August 1987, 76–80.

50 Andrew F. Brimmer, "Income and Wealth," *Ebony*, August 1987, 42–48.

51 "The Vinsons of Stamford Take Time Out for a Baby," *Ebony*, August 1987, 156–58.

52 "The Collins Family Believe in Togetherness in New Orleans," *Ebony*, August 1987, 150–55.

53 "Bonnie Jenkins is Single and Living in Washington, D.C.," *Ebony*, August, 146–48; "Architect Craig Stark Puts His Hope in the Future of Miami," *Ebony*, August 1987, 144–45.

54 Nathan Hare, Ph.D., "Is the Black Middle Class Blowing It? Yes!," *Ebony*, August 1987, 85–86.

55 Regina Jollivette Frazier, "Is the Black Middle Class Blowing It?. No!," *Ebony*, August 1987, 89–90.

56 "The Black Middle Class"; Bart Landry, *The New Black Middle Class* (Berkeley: University of California Press, 1987).

57 George G. Church, "Are You Better Off?", *Time*, October 10, 1988, 28–30.

58 Jerry Flint, "Too Much Ain't Enough," *Forbes*, July 13, 1987, 92–102.

59 Michael Schudson, "Middle American Individualism: The Future of Liberal Democracy," *The Nation,* June 4, 1988, 794+; Herbert J. Gans, *Middle American Individualism: The Future of Liberal Democracy* (New York: Free Press, 1988).

60 Kenneth F. Kister, "Fear of Falling: The Inner Life of the Middle Class," *Library Journal*, August 9, 1989, 152; Barbara Ehrenreich, *Fear of Falling: The Inner Life of the Middle Class* (New York: Pantheon Books, 1989).

61 Marilyn K. Dantico, "Katherine S. Newman. 'Fear of Falling: The Inner Life of the Middle Class,'" *Social Science Quarterly*, September 1989, 799; Katherine S. Newman, *Falling from Grace: The Experience of Downward Mobility in the American Middle Class* (New York: Free Press, 1988).

62 Nicholas Lemann, "The Good Life: The Meaning of Success for the American Middle Class," *Washington Monthly*, May 1989, 58; Loren Baritz, *The Good Life: The Meaning of Success for the American Middle Class* (New York: Alfred A. Knopf, 1989).

63 "Is the Middle Class Getting Squeezed?" *Changing Times*, March 1989, 30+.

64 "The Stretching of the Middle Class," *The Economist*, September 17, 1988, 29.

65 Michael T. Kaufman, "What's Happened to Middle Class," *New York Times Magazine*, April 23, 1989.

5

FALLING DOWN

I am not economically viable.

Bill Foster (Michael Douglas) in the 1993 film *Falling Down*

If the 1993 film *Falling Down* (in which an unemployed engineer snaps in an almost *Taxi Driver*-like fashion) was a bit over the top in capturing the angst of the American middle class, perhaps a joke going around a few years later did a better job. President Clinton encounters a voter on one of his campaign trips, and asks for the man's support. "Why should I vote for you?" the obviously peeved man asks the incumbent president, to which Clinton answers, "Because I created millions of new jobs in my first term." The irate man quickly responds, "Yes, and I've got three of them."[1]

Funny or not, the joke (reportedly based on a true story) reflected the frustration many of the middle class felt even as the economy was turning around in the mid-1990s. Unlike in the early part of the decade, there were indeed many jobs to be had, but most of them involved asking customers if they had any coupons when paying for their Big Mac or oil change. High-tech jobs in Silicon Valley were also waiting to be filled, but there were only so many Americans in 1996 who knew hypertext or C++ programming languages.[2] "Flexibility," rather than loyalty, had rather suddenly become the key to successful employment in the country as more Americans found themselves competing in the global economy. Around the same time that the Berlin Wall came down, the postwar dream of a lifetime job and all the benefits it afforded also imploded, making many of the American middle class feel adrift and dislocated. Words like "deskilling," "outsourcing," and "downsizing" had entered the lexicon of workers, with a growing sense that one was, like Bill Foster in *Falling Down*, no longer "economically viable." Rather than justifiably believing they represented the heart and soul of the nation's economy, members of an ever-smaller middle class were concluding they were now useless and dispensable. The falling down of the America middle class in the 1990s went well beyond matters of self-worth. "The shrinking of the middle class is particularly worrisome for those concerned with the fate of democracy, for it is the class that has historically been the backbone of liberal democratic regimes," wrote Jean Bethke Elshtain in the *New Republic* in 1996, concerned that civic life as we knew it was disappearing in this new economic order.[3]

A Kind of Free-Floating Anxiety

The unhappy state of the American middle class in the 1990s had roots in the preceding years and decades. Just as "the eighties" effectively ended in 1987 with the "Black Monday" market crash, so did the economic momentum of the middle class begin to reverse in the fall of that year. A recession officially began in July 1990, according to government statistics, but higher taxes had started to eat into the net incomes of typical middle-class families a few years earlier. The middle class had also overextended itself in the greed-is-good decade, and was now literally paying the price through high interest payments. Cutting back was now the order of the day, the last decade of the century and millennium beginning to look like it would end with more of a whimper than a bang.[4] In the fall of 1991, Vice President Dan Quayle urged Americans to "be more upbeat, more positive," words offering little comfort to those thinking there would be precious little under their Christmas trees in a couple of months. "A kind of free-floating anxiety has gripped the great middle class, even those holding well-paying jobs with two cars in the garage," wrote Larry Reibstein in *Newsweek*, the worst-case scenario a major medical catastrophe that would put most in even deeper debt. Smelling blood, more Democrats were thinking of entering the presidential race, knowing George Bush was very vulnerable.[5] "Bush, like Reagan before him, favors the wealthy, tolerates the poor, and has forgotten the largest group in the middle," said a self-identified Republican from North Carolina, thinking he and everyone else in the middle class were being "taxed to death."[6]

The American middle class was definitely being squeezed in higher education due to rising tuitions at private colleges and universities. Although qualified for acceptance at such schools, many high school graduates could not afford to pay the $20,000 or so annual tuition nor were they eligible for financial aid. Stuck between a rock and a hard place, these students were likely to choose one of the elite, more affordable state universities such as University of Michigan or UCLA. This in turn bumped many other smart middle-class students to second- or third-tier schools, a domino effect that *U.S. News & World Report* called "the great college tumble." (Some college officials called the phenomenon "the middle-class melt.")[7] Moderate-income families were also having to take out loans to fund a child's college education, this too part of a "downward migration" in higher education in America. Federal "Pell grants" were limited to low-income families, and the Bush administration was trying to get Congress to make eligibility for them even tougher in order to cut government spending during the recession. Applications to and attendance at community colleges were, not surprisingly, way up, as more middle-class students with excellent grades settled for what they could afford.[8]

Who and what was to blame for the "downward migration" in education and, more generally, the "free-floating anxiety" of the middle class? Not everyone was so sure that the 1980s had been as devastating on the American middle class as was popularly believed. In a kind of economic autopsy, all sorts of "experts" juggled the numbers this way and that to determine if most Americans made gains during the decade or just the rich (an exercise that continues to this day). Those on the right, not surprisingly, tended to think that the much-ballyhooed decline of average families during the Reagan years was overstated if not outright false. Michael Novak of the American Enterprise Institute, writing for *Forbes* in 1992, suggested that simply examining median income would reveal whether the middle class made gains or experienced losses. Median income rose more than $2,000 in inflation-adjusted dollars between 1981 and 1989, he reported, meaning more Americans did better under Reagan (and Bush) than worse. Partisan politics (and the liberal media) were the cause of all the gnashing of teeth, he argued, the fact that bad news was more interesting than good also playing a part in the bending of truth. "Since 1970 the middle class has expanded upward in a very rapid fashion," Novak concluded, directly contradicting the majority who were convinced that the last two decades were a big slide for most Americans.[9]

Kevin Phillips, who was purportedly a devout Republican (he had helped Richard Nixon win over Southern Democrats in 1968), certainly agreed that the income divide of the 1980s had hurt the middle class. In two books, *The Politics of Rich and Poor* and *Boiling Point*, Phillips described how the rich got richer that decade and the effect that had on the country's political landscape. The under-cutting of the middle class during those years was a "quiet devastation," he suggested in the latter book, even some of those making as much as $150,000 a year not really secure because of high taxes and few benefits.[10] Regardless of what and whom was to blame, there was a consensus that the middle class was suffering in the early 1990s as another presidential election neared. "The recession has left the great American middle class feeling frayed and sobered and vulnerable," wrote Lance Morrow in *Time*, believing that, "fear and anger are eating like acids at the electorate."[11] "The middle class is now scared," agreed Mortimer B. Zuckerman in his *U.S. News & World Report*, comparing the situation to that in the 19th century when thousands of American skilled craftsmen lost their jobs to new machines that could produce goods faster and cheaper.[12]

Indeed, telling a good number of middle-class white men in the early 1990s that their lives had been rapidly "expanded upward" as Novak claimed would elicit guffaws or something much worse. Like the fictional character Bill Foster in *Falling Down*, those who had lost their good jobs often felt a sense of rage that went well beyond pure economics. "Virtually no one in the major media speaks for those disaffected middle-class whites who, though making up a majority, see themselves as increasingly marginalized in a nation where 'protected' minorities have become a privileged class and traditional values are under officially sanctioned (not to mention subsidized) siege," wrote film critic Terry Teachout in *Commentary*. Rush Limbaugh had made a very successful career by speaking for this sizable group, of course, and the mainstream media was starting to pay attention to this now ironically disenfranchised demographic. *Newsweek* had just published a cover story on "White Male Paranoia," and *Fortune* did the same on white-collar unemployment just a week before *Falling Down* opened, suggesting the plight of the "downsized" middle class worker was reaching critical mass.[13]

It was the inescapable reality of contraction that felt so alien and distressing for the American middle class. Looking back, an ever-expanding middle class was one of the pillars of postwar prosperity and optimism, something that was considered one of the nation's proudest achievements. That the American middle class was large and would continue to get larger was also ammunition against communism, clear evidence that our system was in the best interests of the majority. Our version of class based on a kind of "cultural equality" devalued foreigners' version predicated on social and economic stratification, and proved that Marx had some certainly interesting theories but it was capitalism that actually worked. Best of all, perhaps, the postwar American middle class accommodated both white-collar and blue-collar workers, another retort to Marx and his intellectual descendants subscribing to a fundamentally divisive workplace based on class. The peaceful coexistence between white-collars and blue-collars applied not just at work but in their personal lives as well. Middle managers and their public sector equivalent could happily live alongside blue-collar workers, another important symbol of economic (if not social) equality. A middle class, both real and imaginary, subsumed the working class (and its politics), with enough abundance believed to go around for nearly everybody (at least nearly all white people).[14]

Although this model began to self-destruct in a cultural sense in the early 1960s, it would be another decade before its economics fell apart. "Something happened to this expanding middle class around 1973," wrote Jack Beatty in the *Atlantic* in 1994, with median family income (adjusted for inflation) now decreasing. The energy crisis, a shift from a manufacturing-based economy to a service-oriented one, Wall Street's short-term demands for dividends, a decline in public education, and lower spending on public infrastructure all negatively impacted the nation's economy over the next two decades. Virtually unlimited abundance now just a happy memory, the middle class diverged, its blue-collar (and "new-collar") component falling further and further behind white-collar workers in wages and salaries. Beatty and many others believed the two-decades-long breakup of the American middle class transcended economics, creating what he called a "civic void." "The crisis of the middle class is of commanding gravity," he wrote, seeing it as the country's most important issue. "Anti-politics" were one direct result, a pervasive cynical attitude destabilizing the relationship between the government and the people. Unless and until the economy improved, Beatty was not optimistic that this civic void would be filled. "What we have here, in short, is a circular, self-generating crisis for which it is hard to come up with convincing efficacious solutions," he bemoaned, seeing little reason to be bullish on the future of the American middle class.[15]

Living on the Edge

While insightful, such analyses ignored the fact that there really was no longer one giant American middle class as there was (or might have been) in the postwar era. Given how broadly the middle class was now generally defined (households with incomes between $25,000 and $100,000), it could be expected that the economic situations between the lower and upper ends varied dramatically. Most families close to a six-figure income were typically holding their own despite the early 1990s recession but those bringing in half or less of that were bearing the brunt of the downturn. Millions of the American lower middle class were struggling to pay their mortgages or rent and their children's college tuition although they were not poor or unemployed. This segment of the middle was "living on the edge," Mark Levinson of *Newsweek* wrote in 1991, with "making ends meet" a constant effort. There was little or no chance of taking a vacation or saving money for retirement, making many wonder why they were working so hard. A good number of these folks were living below the standard that their parents had, giving them a bleak view of their future prospects and those for their own kids. (Polls showed that the lower middle class was as pessimistic about the future as those living in poverty.) Unlike the upper middle class, the lower middle class had not shared in the bounty of the 1980s, setting them further back from the rest of the pack. The concept of decline, both in real terms and relative to one's expectations, was simply not part of many Americans' vocabulary. Anger was the natural reaction, with politicians, those better off, and people getting government handouts all targets of their deep resentment.[16]

Statistics relying on averages also obscured the vast differences between the lower and upper middle classes. The gap in incomes expanded significantly in the 1980s, but viewing the American middle class as one enormous group masked the wide division within it. The upper segment went one way and the lower went another, in crude terms, a trend that was continuing in the early 1990s. Democrats blamed Reaganomics on this splitting of the middle class, but it was the "stagflation" of the early 1970s that triggered the distancing of the two segments. It was then that wages, adjusted for inflation, began to drop, the beginnings of what would become, two decades later, essentially two American middle classes. An income of $50,000, once thought of as a boatload of money, was now for many families just enough to scrape by. Delaying home improvements and car repairs, leaving the lights off as much as possible, renting a video instead of going to a movie, or even cutting out beef from the weekly shopping list were not unusual ways for the lower middle class to save money. Plans to have another child were often abandoned, one of the sadder aspects of this economic parting of the ways. Those without college degrees were more apt to be in tough straits, not surprisingly, with one's level of education strongly linked to income. Weaker labor unions had not helped matters; blue-collar workers simply did not have the bargaining power with management that they once had.[17]

Although there was no doubt that the lower middle class was more likely to be living on the edge, it was clear that many members of the upper middle class were hardly living extravagant lifestyles. Families bringing in $75,000 in the early 1990s could typically afford a nice home in a nice neighborhood and a couple of cars but were foregoing luxuries and saving nothing, a troubling fact of life. The upper middle class was justifiably worried that the Clinton administration and Congress would target it to lower the deficit and reform health care, its size and income level making it ripe for the picking. After taxes, insurance, mortgage payments, utilities, and gasoline, many upper-middle-class families had less than $10,000 for food, clothing, and other necessities. Such families felt that they just were not getting their money's worth when paying the government about half of their gross income. Taxes were notoriously high in most European countries but citizens there received free health care, university educations, and other subsidies, a fair return on investment. Eighty-four percent of readers of *Money* magazine felt their federal tax dollars were not being well spent, a sign that many middle-class Americans simply did not trust the government, at least regarding its economic policies.[18]

Alan Wolfe of Boston University also believed that the American middle class had cleaved in two by the early 1990s, but not based on economic status. The two American middle classes held distinct sets of moralities and outlooks on life, he argued in 1993, the disparity thus less about money than values. What Wolfe called the "old" middle class ascended in the postwar years, when a large number of Americans made significant gains against the backdrop of a relatively steady and strong economy. Rising incomes, bigger and better houses, and the familiar trappings of consumerism were all part of what many viewed as the realization of the American Dream, as was sending children to college and retiring to a warm place. "Many people in this generation became middle class just by showing up," noted Wolfe, American society geared to allow most citizens, especially white men, to enjoy economic and social mobility. Just as the good times evaporated for this sizable group of Americans in the early 1970s, however, a new and different kind of middle class emerged. Through hard work and sacrifice, many urban white ethnics with civil service or unionized blue-collar jobs, college graduates working in service industries, African Americans, and immigrants now achieved middle-class status. These contrasting and even clashing groups altered the economic, political, and social character of the nation, Wolfe held, the old and new American middle classes competing not just economically but culturally.[19]

Having struggled to earn their privileges rather than have them handed over on a silver platter, the new middle class of the 1970s and 1980s saw things quite differently than their predecessors, according to Wolfe. While the old middle class was engaged in the civic or public sphere, especially when it came to politics, the new middle class was primarily dedicated to private interests. Religion was highly secularized for the old middle class while the new was not averse to traditional, even fundamentalist faiths. The old middle class had learned how to manage their careers, focusing on process, while the new was more interested in producing things. The old middle class was open to bilingualism and multiculturalism in general while the new middle class, ironically, had more of a "love it or leave it" philosophy regarding national identity and loyalty. Given these basic distinctions, Wolfe concluded, it was important to view the American middle class not as a single, monolithic entity but as a dualistic one with dissimilar and often conflicting views and aspirations.[20]

The Wimpiest Term in the Lexicon of Social Taxonomy

Whether there were one or two middle classes, it remained those with average incomes whose votes were most sought after by politicians. Just as in the 1980 presidential election campaign, both Democrats and Republicans aggressively wooed the middle class by offering tax cuts in the 1992 campaign.[21] Incumbent president George Bush and the Democratic candidate, Arkansas governor Bill Clinton, were each also promising job security and better schools for Americans, all key hot buttons for a beaten down middle class. "Our politicians have scanned the huge expanse of national need and determined, in time for the great U.S. election campaign of 1992, that they will pledge themselves to resuscitation of the middle class," wrote Fred Bruning for *Maclean's* in February of that year.[22] Bush, an icon of the wealthy elite, was also trying to appear more middle class by doing things like sharing a pizza with factory workers and petting a cow while campaigning in New Hampshire in January of that year.[23]

Based on what Reagan had promised and then delivered, however, Bruning was not swayed by Bush's Everyman stunts or either party's rhetoric. Twelve years of Reagan and his successor had led to higher unemployment and a recession, hardly the prosperity he vouched for when campaigning against incumbent Jimmy Carter. "When the politically ambitious—Democratic or Republican—start braying about the middle class, it's a sure bet someone is about to be fleeced," Bruning warned, having heard this story before. Politicians knew the term "middle class" encompassed virtually all Americans' income levels and lifestyles, and that most of us believed we were in the mainstream or wanted to be considered part of it. Typical American activities—having a pizza delivered or going to the movies on the weekend, say—were taken as signs of one's "middle-classness," this despite having millions in net worth or being in debt. Suspicious of the wealthy and either fearful of or holding disdain for the poor, Americans' natural inclination was to lean toward the socio-economic center regardless of personal circumstance.[24]

Americans' clinging to the idea that almost all of us were middle class, something that was likely unique in the world, functioned as a powerful leveling force that reinforced the nation's egalitarian spirit. A vice president of a regional bank and a successful electrician made about the same amount of money, but it was likely two such individuals had different attitudes and opinions regarding any number of important issues. Still, they were each "middle class," making them seem more similar than they probably were. The same could be said to be true of those over forty and those under, homeowners and renters, blacks and whites, and even men and women. Much was made about the country's political stability because of the checks and balances of our two-party system, but on closer inspection it was perhaps this nearly universal membership in the middle class that kept us from splintering into hundreds of discordant subcultures. As a fundamentally multi-cultural society, perhaps the most diverse on the planet, the unifying effect of our common belonging to the middle class could not be overestimated. "It is in the middle class that the nation locates its center of gravity, its values, its work force, its soldiers, its leaders and above all its voters," Morrow of *Time* proposed, thinking that "American democracy means middle-class democracy."[25]

Politicians' appeals to the middle class certainly sounded great in speeches, but it was actually more the working class that was listening. More than 90 percent of Americans considered themselves middle class, recent polls showed, although just 60 percent actually qualified based on annual income.[26] Vincente Navarro, a professor at Johns Hopkins, argued in *The Nation* that the majority of Americans belonged not to the middle class but to the working class if one's financial identity was defined by hourly wages. Such workers represented more than half of adults, according to a study by Erik Olin Wright of the University of Wisconsin, a fact most politicians did not recognize, at least publicly. Navarro felt that the discourse focusing on the middle class was obliquely racist, a means of marginalizing minorities who accounted for significant numbers (and the fastest growing segment) of the working class. "By referring to a mythical middle-class majority as an entity separate from 'the others,'" he wrote, politicians were delivering a "divisive message." More broadly, it could be said, Americans' preference to think of themselves as more middle class than working class helped to minimize not just the nation's immense economic differences but our profound cultural diversity as well.[27]

While some believed using the term "middle class" rather than working class was linguistic trickery, others warned that politicians were speaking in a kind of code when making promises about who was going to get taxed and how much. "Candidates who talk about taxing the rich are really aiming straight at the middle class wallet," advised Novak in 1992, seeing a global trend away from the left that always seemed to serve the interests of the wealthy.[28] The fastest rising taxes were actually state and local income, sales, and property taxes, which had nothing to do with the federal government. Escalating property taxes (presumably based on the increasing value of one's home) were especially frustrating as it was difficult to tell what one was getting for the additional money. If anything, public schools were getting worse rather than better, many felt, with some feeling the need to put their kids in private school. Between higher property taxes and private school tuition, once nicely growing savings accounts and IRAs were sitting dormant, with all money that came in going out just as quickly. Middle-class families were thus often faced with a decision with existential overtones: should we scrimp to try to put a few dollars away for retirement, or seize the day by enjoying life with the little money one had (or borrowed on credit cards)?[29]

Separate from the tax issues, politicians always seemed to be "rediscovering" the middle class, Meg Greenfield of *Newsweek* observed, as if it was something new and alien. It was absurd that the vast majority of Americans could go missing, and that each new sighting of them during a campaign was treated as major news. "Where does the middle class go in between times?" she joked, adding that the term's very definition was used differently by different candidates. Some politicians (much like non-politicians, especially the media) referred to a group of Americans with a particular range of income, while others defined it by a certain set of cultural characteristics. Sometimes the term was a politically correct way of meaning "white people," Greenfield thought, like Navarro, and other times it signified anyone outside the New York–Washington–Los Angeles elite. (Lewis Lapham of *Harper's* concurred, thinking the phrase "the forgotten middle class" was "a euphemism for the modestly affluent and well-to-do, the not-poor and the non-black.")[30] Ironically, on occasion the term meant the (white) lower class rather than the middle class, a good example of how confusing or at least fluid the concept of class was in America. Attempts for politicians to appear as regular folk by doing "middle class things," e.g., eating at a local restaurant or shopping for socks at J.C. Penney (the latter something George Bush had also done), only made them seem more non-middle class, Greenfield felt. Americans easily saw through such playacting, knowing that a rich, powerful man stopping for a piece of pie in their town was Public Relations 101.[31]

In mentioning the word "class" at all, however, politicians were in some respects breaking one of our cultural taboos. America was not supposed to have rigidly defined economic and social classes like those in Europe, according to our national creed, the concept of an aristocratic elite or an oppressed proletariat in opposition to our firm faith in equality. Throughout the nation's history, class signified foreignness, and invoked the dangerous ideas of revolution and communism. But by limiting themselves to the term "middle class" (versus "upper class" or "lower class"), candidates were actually reinforcing the American mythology of classlessness rather than challenging it. Because most Americans liked to think they were middle class or in the general neighborhood, any mention of the words promoted unity rather than divisiveness. Much or all of the term's potential political power had at some point been drained away, something both George Bush and Bill Clinton knew very well. "Middle class is the wimpiest term in the lexicon of social taxonomy, meaning little more than not rich, not poor," thought Barbara Ehrenreich in 1992, seeing the term now as essentially synonymous with "normal."[32]

However, while perhaps not class-conscious, Americans were extremely status-conscious, Ehrenreich was quick to point out. Driving a Chevrolet and owning a Mercedes were two very different things, we all knew, the latter conveying a level of success (and perhaps intelligence) that the former did not. It was during the 1980s that our collective status-consciousness spiked, she argued, the distinction between the lifestyles of the rich and famous and those of the growing numbers of homeless too vast to ignore. It was that same decade when the middle class as a whole felt it was losing some of its status, as prices rose and income levels stayed constant. In terms of lifestyle, remaining "middle class" required being almost wealthy, somewhat contradictorily, a troubling trend that carried over into the early 1990s.[33]

Governor Clinton was thus in the right place at the right time when he made his bid for the presidency. "The election of 1992 marked the eruption of a powerful new force only beginning to make its mark in American politics: widespread frustration over the decline of middle-class prosperity," wrote Kevin Phillips ten days before the inauguration, the economic downturn sparking pervasive and intense dissatisfaction with the state of the union. (75 to 80 percent of Americans felt the country was on the "wrong track" polls showed). A bad job market and sinking home values were ideal conditions to sway middle-class voters, something that Clinton fully exploited in his campaign speeches. The rich "were getting the gold mine while the middle class got the shaft," he said in one of them, the tax rate on average incomes another sore spot. (Bush's raising of the taxes of middle-class families, despite his claim to read his lips that he would not, did the incumbent no favors in the campaign.) "In the name of all those who do the work, pay the taxes, raise the kids and play by the rules—in the name of the hard-working Americans who make up our forgotten middle class, I accept your nomination for President of the United States," Clinton had said to the Democratic National Convention in July 1992, that he happened to be from Hope, Arkansas only adding to his credibility.[34]

W(h)ither the Middle Class?

The populist movement centered around the interests of the middle class that cohered during the 1992 election did indeed appear to mark a watershed moment in American history. Much like how Teddy Roosevelt's third-party Progressive platform in 1912 and FDR's New Deal in 1932 successfully attacked the excesses of capitalism, Clinton's promise to rebuild the prosperity of ordinary Americans went beyond ordinary politics. The quarter-century postwar boom was officially ending, creating an opportunity for virtually anyone who boldly challenged the status quo. What made the movement so powerful was that not just inner city and working-class Americans liked Clinton's message but also suburbanites and college graduates who had been laid off. In "W(h)ither the Middle Class? A Dynamic View," a chapter in *Poverty and Prosperity in the USA in the Late Twentieth Century*, Greg Duncan, Timothy Smeeding, and Willard Rodgers argued that suburbanites were actually affected more by the recession than urbanites as the latter were more likely to hold relatively secure government or government-related (versus corporate) jobs. Believing downward mobility could simply not happen to them, suburbanites facing bankruptcy and the loss of their homes were especially open to a new regime predicated on remembering the "forgotten" middle class. And unlike the Great Depression, when almost all Americans took an economic hit, the rich appeared to be not just surviving these tough times but thriving, magnifying the discontent among the middle class. Fears that the nation was on the way toward becoming a highly stratified country like Brazil paved the way for the man from Hope to deliver just that to the American middle class.[35]

Peter G. Peterson, the billionaire businessman and ex-Secretary of Commerce, believed the middle class was getting off too easy, however. Although unpopular, if not anathema, to demand that the middle class make large financial sacrifices in order to balance the budget and reduce the deficit, Peterson boldly suggested doing just so. Coddling the middle class as newly elected President Clinton was doing might be an effective way to remain well liked but was absurd from a financial perspective. "Most Americans, emphatically including the middle class, will have to give something up, at least temporarily, to get back our American Dream," he stated in *The Atlantic Monthly* after juggling the numbers. Entitlements were the big problem, he prophetically wrote in 1993, the government's commitments to Social Security, Medicare, and tax breaks a looming disaster. It was the middle class, not the poor as popularly believed, that represented the primary beneficiaries of these entitlements, a fact that seriously endangered the nation's economic future. "The middle class is at the heart of our budget problem—and must be at the heart of the solution," Peterson insisted, estimating that this large group of Americans received 80 percent of total benefit dollars. Going after the rich and helping the poor was all fine and good, but it was those falling somewhere in between that would have to pay higher taxes and/or accept a reduction in entitlements to keep the United States solvent. Peterson's argument may have been not just fiscally prudent but made sense on a cross-cultural basis. Although beleaguered, the American middle class remained the richest in the world and paid far lower taxes than middle-class citizens of most other countries.[36]

Hard numbers backed up Peterson's conviction that the middle class should not get a free ride if America wanted to be fiscally healthy. "Politicians may talk about raising taxes only for rich people, but to raise any significant amount of revenue the pols would have to attack the middle class," agreed *Forbes* in its analysis of where most of the nation's money was. Soaking the rich made good headlines but did not generate nearly enough cash to pay the country's bills, a fact that both Republicans and Democrats usually ignored, especially if they were running for office. Placing surtaxes on millionaires or raising the tax rates on the highest earners—steps Bush and Clinton had respectively proposed—fell well short of, say, doubling the taxes of those in the middle. "Politicians tax the middle class for the same reason some people rob banks," explained Peter Brimelow, as "that's where the money is."[37] Middle-class Americans could of course decide to move to another country or not work as hard to escape the tax hike but each was unlikely, meaning they remained the best source to raise money if economics (versus politics) ruled the day.[38]

Defenders of the middle class argued that this group of Americans was already paying more than their fair share of taxes, however, the financial burdens in real people's lives missing from the IRS's tidy charts and tables. In their *America: What Went Wrong?* (based on a series of articles originally published in the *Philadelphia Inquirer*), Donald Bartlett and James Steele argued that the tax system was fundamentally rigged against ordinary Americans. The articles and book became something of a phenomenon, with a PBS documentary featuring Bill Moyers created out of the bestseller. (Then presidential candidate Bill Clinton had called the bestseller "must reading.") Many readers agreed with the Pulitzer Prize-winning reporters' thesis that the American middle class was effectively "dismantled" during the 1980s. Not just corporations but the government enacted policies that hurt average income earners, they held, a series of events that showed no signs of reversing.[39] Around the same time, Sylvia Nasar of the *New York Times* also wrote a number of articles about the economic favoring of the wealthy at the expense of the middle class, adding to the outpouring of public interest in the issue.[40]

Bartlett and Steele said much the same thing in their follow-up book, *America: Who Really Pays the Taxes?* and extended their treatise by making the case that the rich often found ways to avoid paying taxes while the middle class was left footing the bill.[41] Changing one's name, incorporating oneself in the Cayman Islands, or paying oneself large dividends in order to claim deductibles losses were all strategies the wealthy used to lower (or completely eliminate) their taxes.[42] Those on the right attacked Bartlett and Steele's methodology, however, claiming that the Carter years had been much tougher on the working class than during Reagan's two terms. "The rich *did* get richer during the Eighties, but not without making others richer also," argued Ed Rubinstein in *National Review*, claiming that "the longest peacetime economic expansion in U.S. history took place" on the Gipper's watch.[43] The middle class may indeed be hurting now, he and other hard-core Republicans insisted, but Reaganomics was one of the best things to ever happen to the American people.

The Radical Middle

Whatever one chose to believe about the past, raising taxes on the middle class to get the country out of the hole it had dug for itself in the present would be politically suicidal, and was unlikely to happen soon. "The middle class is growing increasingly cantankerous," noted Lawrence Kudlow in *National Review* in 1994, unhappy it was carrying a higher tax burden than upper-income earners.[44] The middle class complained about government (over)spending, but did not want entitlements like Social Security and Medicare touched, a Catch-22 with which Clinton (and his two successors) continually struggled. (His proposal of a "New Covenant," in which citizens would have to offer something in return for their entitlements, never really gained traction.)[45] Much like how he and incumbent president George Bush promised tax cuts for the middle class in the 1992 campaign, Bill Clinton proposed a "Middle-Class Bill of Rights" in 1994 to try to win votes and stay in the White House for another four years. With its "Contract for America" already in place, however, the Republican Party had positioned itself as the party for the middle class, making the run-up to the 1996 election an interesting one.[46] "Both Republicans and Democrats have set out to placate the increasingly anxious, economically squeezed and angry middle class," observed Kenneth T. Walsh of *U.S. News & World Report*, each party knowing these voters represented the key to winning elections and gaining support on particular issues.[47]

President Clinton, in fact, embarked on a road trip to middle-class communities around the country in early 1995 to court the affections of voters concerned about taxes and jobs. Getting reelected might prove more difficult than holding some town meetings and demonstrating he was just a country boy at heart by buying some apple butter at a roadside stand in Kutztown, Pennsylvania, however.[48] Census Bureau data showed that median household income had shrunk through the early 1990s, leading many pundits to predict that a "radical" middle class would emerge and vent their anger at Clinton at the polls.[49] The concept of a "radical" middle class first emerged in 1968 to explain support for presidential candidate George Wallace, and was used again in 1992 to describe Ross Perot's populist appeal. (The similar idea of "radical centrism" was first used by sociologist Seymour Martin Lipset in his 1960 book *Political Man*.) Now again a "radical" middle was in play, journalists like *Newsweek*'s Joe Klein believed, thinking that nationalistic Americans repulsed by both classic liberalism and far right conservatism would have a big effect on the upcoming election.[50]

Klein's 1995 cover story for *Newsweek*, "Stalking the Radical Middle," certainly gave many the impression that Clinton was in a similarly precarious position as Bush was four years earlier. Rather than favor the upper class, however, Clinton was in cahoots with special interests, lobbyists, foreign leaders, and the underclass, the radical middle supposedly believed, the latter getting a free ride through welfare and food stamps. The radical middle class was bipartisan, Klein believed, the common denominator being disgust with the American political system as a whole. Klein was not the only one to propose something big was afoot. As many as two-thirds of Americans felt alienated from Washington, Gordon S. Black and Benjamin D. Black, co-authors of *The Politics of American Discontent*, posited, a true movement in the making. Colin Powell used a softer term for this group of Americans—the "sensible center"—but his concept of an infuriated middle class wanting a third party to emerge that served its interests was basically the same. In short, the radical middle wanted the system cleaned up (and overhauled), the budget balanced, and civility restored, all reasonable demands but a lot to ask for given the inflexibility and lethargy of Washington.[51]

A third party was thus just waiting to be born, Klein and others felt, one that appealed to centrist voters sick and tired of politics as usual. Given its sensible stance predicated on social liberalism and fiscal conservatism, was such a group really "radical," Michael Lind asked in the *New York Times*, or more of a "moderate" middle? Lind believed there were actually two groups in the "middle," the moderates and radicals separated by class and degree of anger. Moderates tended to be upper middle class and generally accepted the system, while radicals were lower middle class and would be happy to see the current system tossed into the trash and something very different forged. There were then two other parties in waiting, Lind concluded, progressive moderates and populist radicals too dissimilar to coalesce into a single movement.[52]

The political rhetoric overstated both the devastation the American middle class had experienced and their rage, however. Imports, automation, and corporate cuts had certainly wiped out many jobs among the middle class by the mid-1990s, and hourly wages had not kept up with inflation for three decades. Still, spending was up among the middle class over the last decade, as was home and car ownership. A higher percentage of Americans had major appliances like air conditioners and dishwashers than ever before, and the average house was getting bigger. In short, living standards and buying power were up among those defined as middle class, these fifty-three million households (or three out of five Americans) not as impoverished as politicians liked to make out.[53] Indeed, by the time the actual election rolled around, the prospect of a bitter middle class had largely dissipated. The now favorable economy (and rising stock market) had cooled voters' anger about the state of the nation, it appeared, making the reelection of Clinton a virtual certainty. Clinton's shift toward the center halfway through his first term also increased his appeal to moderates, a lesson a future incumbent Democratic president would learn well.[54]

While Clinton's reelection campaign turned out to be anticlimactic, it did prompt Democrats to rethink what their party should be about. Long-time progressive journalist Richard Parker, for example, believed that Democrats should focus their attention not on the poor and excluded but on the middle class, quite a shift in direction. Historically, progressives were dedicated to improving the lot of the working class and economically disadvantaged, but Parker argued it was time to officially change their orientation. Recent presidential elections had proved that success in politics relied heavily on embracing a populist kind of centrism and, specifically, speaking to the interests of the middle class. Trying to complete the social legislation of the New Deal of the 1930s or Great Society of the 1960s was living in the past, he believed, explicit loyalty to the middle class the party's future.[55] Ramesh Ponnuru of the *National Review* thought the president had already largely achieved this. The most important dimension of Clintonian-style politics was "the attempted retooling of the Democratic Party as the servant of middle-class interests through the mechanism of government," he wrote within days of the president's reelection. Through broad-based social initiatives rather than safety nets, Clinton pollster Stan Greenberg had envisioned a few years earlier, Democrats could and should be the party not just for the "have-nots" but everybody.[56] For now, at least, the Democrats had claimed title to better serving the needs of the politically powerful American middle class.

The Web of Comforts

Even the U.S. Government could not magically reinvigorate a still reeling middle class, however. Guarantees and perks the middle class had relied upon for decades were simply no more. "The web of comforts that muscular U.S. companies and a benevolent Uncle Sam provided the American middle class for 60 years is dissolving before your eyes," Joseph S. Coyle of *Money* wrote in 1995, seeing job and income security as a thing of the past. Global competition had made the postwar job-for-a-lifetime extinct, and company-paid pensions were being replaced by voluntary plans funded by workers. Dreams of retiring early were rapidly fading among the middle class, and being able to pay for health care had emerged as Americans' number one concern, according to a poll by the magazine. And despite President Clinton's reassurances that Social Security would be around when they did retire, many were having their doubts, thinking their future checks would likely be, as the saying went, "in the mail."[57] Children with no health insurance were increasingly coming from middle-class families, statistics showed, another "web of comfort" that was vanishing. Companies were making it more difficult for employees to include their families in health care coverage, one of many cost-cutting measures to improve bottom-lines. The number of uninsured Americans overall continued to grow, many of them not poor but middle class who simply could not afford to pay escalating premiums. A program similar to Medicare, the national health insurance program for the elderly created in the 1960s, was clearly needed, but how to pay for it was proving to be a political football.[58]

The woes of the American middle class somehow defied conventional measures indicating that the economy was strong. Unemployment and inflation were low, yet most Americans were not optimistic about the future, according to polls. Anxiety lurked beneath the surface of prosperity, with a constant fear that one could suddenly be jobless in this era of downsizing. And if one did get laid off, it was unlikely that one would make the same amount of money, studies showed. In addition, part-time and temporary employment had exploded in America over the last couple of decades, a disturbing trend for those wanting to work full-time (and receive not just the higher pay but the benefits that afforded). Moonlighting was also up significantly; the percentage of Americans holding multiple jobs far exceeded that of any other industrial nation. If many of the middle class were struggling just to keep up in a good economy, what would happen when another recession arrived, as it inevitably would?[59]

For at least one journalist, Lynn H. Ehrle, that question was moot. The American middle class was not struggling, Ehrle argued, but that was only because it no longer existed. "The American middle class has disappeared," the freelance writer wrote in the *Humanist* in 1996, basing this bold claim on readily available Census Bureau data. Like others, Ehrle believed the demise of the middle class began in the 1970s, as purchasing power became weakened by stagflation. Safety nets and a sharp rise in two-income families disguised how sick the middle class was in the 1980s. By the early 1990s, however, the household income gap that had ballooned between an upper and lower class could not be missed. Egregious tax policies, the exporting of jobs, massive layoffs, union busting, and automation were the nails in the coffin of the middle class, the nation now composed of a small upper class and a large lower class. Whether measured by household income or net worth, the American middle class was now a "myth," Ehrle seriously claimed, a fact the media and politicians refused to recognize because it was a frightening idea. Faith in a vast "middle" was essential to maintaining our national identity, but the sad truth was that we now had only a narrow top and wide bottom. The good news was that the middle class could be brought back to life, but Ehrle was not hopeful that the government and corporations would make much of an attempt to help resuscitate it anytime soon.[60]

While most journalists did not think the middle class had gone belly up, many did believe it was on life support. "If calling America a middle-class nation means anything," Paul Krugman wrote in 1996, "it means that we are a society in which most people live more or less the same kind of life." The problem for Krugman was that we were that kind of society around 1970, describing what took place in the United States over the last quarter of a century as a "spiral of inequality." If the downward spiral of the middle class began about 1970, it accelerated in the 1980s. The "Reagan Revolution" really was one, he agreed, but not in the way conservatives liked to believed. The revolution that began with Reagan's election was dividing Americans, not uniting them in a common cause, and this rift was continuing to grow. Krugman lived in Palo Alto at the time, a place in which the enormous disparities between the wealthy and the poor could not be missed. The technology boom had made the boundary between an upper and an under class that much more extreme, so much so that many younger people assumed the town, and many others in the United States, had always been that way.[61]

This just was not true, however. In Palo Alto and hundreds of communities across the country a generation earlier, a managerial class and a working class lived, worked, and played closely together, their incomes not that far apart. (Skilled blue-collar workers actually often earned more than white-collar middle managers.) CEOs of typical Fortune 500 companies made about thirty-five times that of an average employee in 1970 while in the mid-1990s it was 150 times, this alone evidence that a select group of Americans had taken the high road while a lot more had taken a lower one. Foreign imports, information technology, the decline of unions, and high tax rates on the middle class were all partly to blame, Krugman thought, but the larger cause was a shift in the nation's values. The nation's egalitarian ethic had disappeared, he had concluded, this the primary reason for our spiral of inequality. Truly scary scenarios could be conceived should inequalities continue to spiral over the course of another generation. "Imagine a Blade Runner-style dystopia, in which a few people live in luxury while the majority grovel in Third World living standards," he envisaged, offering a variety of strategies to avoid such a nightmare. Until another FDR and unifying force equivalent to World War II came around, however, economic policies would have to serve as the best way to reverse the spiral and revive the middle class.[62]

The $20 Meal

It was difficult for those in the American middle class to resist comparing their economic situation to those of their parents when they were the same age. Only one parent, usually the dad, worked full-time a quarter-century ago but, with a desk job or high union wage, that was all that was necessary. Now both parties in a married couple each often held full-time jobs, if they were lucky. New kinds of software were replacing middle managers, this just one way corporations were "streamlining" their organizations. Thinning executive ranks had become the focus of many American companies, especially those which had recently undergone a merger or acquisition. If dad's job was eliminated for some reason, the company would typically find another one for him within the organization. This was fast becoming an obsolete practice, however, as it defeated the whole purpose of cutting costs. Even with the distressing gender biases of the times, it appeared that one's parents had it a lot better around 1970, at least when it came to buying power. Maintaining the jump in real income and living standards that mom and dad had enjoyed would prove to be an unsustainable proposition as Europe and Japanese competitors caught up to and then surpassed our manufacturing capabilities in many industries over the next couple of decades.[63]

Comparing consumer culture circa 1970 and in the mid-1990s was apples and oranges, however, making things seem gloomier for the current middle class than they really were. Things were more affordable back in the day partly because of the things we were using, the upscaling of American culture still to come. Keds had evolved into Nikes, the five-channel television set into a five hundred-channel multimedia device, and the Ford Pinto into a Honda Accord, with no comparison between the consumption habits of the typical American middle-class family in 1970 and one a quarter-century later. Being middle class now was a lot more complicated and cost a lot more than once upon a time in America simply because products and services were far superior. Dining out had become routine rather than the special occasion it used to be, and vacations in Cancun and Caribbean cruises had largely replaced the Great American Roadtrip to a national park or Aunt Sally's in Iowa. The average middle-class family's lifestyle in the 1990s would be considered extremely luxurious in 1970 if time travel (and all kinds of other events defying the physical laws of the universe) were possible, this fact essential in judging how good or bad things were for most Americans at the end of the 20th century.[64]

While consumerism, perhaps more than any other part of American culture, had progressed over the past few decades, marketers were no longer treating the middle class as one very large group. Although there were still some iconic brands that continued to serve one big American market (Pepsi and Ivory soap, say), they were more the exception than the rule. Many companies were offering different product lines for an upper middle class and a lower middle class, both shaping and reflecting the growing economic divide in the country. One Winnie-the-Pooh line of items could be found in upscale stores like Nordstrom's and Bloomingdale's while another was sold at Wal-Mart, for example, an intentional strategy by the Walt Disney Company to segment the middle-class marketplace. With the middle of the middle class losing both numbers and purchasing power, it made sense to target the upper and lower ends that were each growing in population and discretionary income. The mass market, once the bullseye of business, had eroded and polarized just as the middle class had. PaineWebber was, in fact, advising investors to put their money into companies that were following a "Tiffany/Wal-Mart" strategy and avoid those "that serve the 'middle' of the consumer market." Roper Starch, the market research firm, had just published a report called "Two Americas" showing that our society was sharply divided along economic, educational, and technological lines. Restaurants too were going one way or the other. "The $4 meal is doing all right, and the $50 meal is doing all right," said economist Lester C. Thurow, but "the $20 meal is in trouble."[65]

The segmentation of the American marketplace paralleled the historical path of the middle class to a remarkable degree. Mass marketing ruled in the postwar years, when economic disparities within a large middle class were relatively narrow. Niche marketing strategies developed in the 1970s and 1980s, decades in which the middle class began to fragment into clearly identifiable upper and lower segments. Now, in the 1990s, when a "middle" middle class was difficult to detect, marketers were rushing to the margins where the action was. Two tiers of products ranging from cars to computers and services ranging from banking to telecommunications were being sold, both their relative quality and advertising geared to class distinctions. One did not have to look further than the retail landscape to see that the days of a homogeneous assemblage of American consumers were over. Middle-of-the-road department stores were either disappearing or banding together to stay alive (the Macy's Group was quickly gobbling up local and regional players), while both discount and specialty were thriving.

Customers who once frequented chains like Sears, Montgomery Ward, and J.C. Penny were now shopping at K-Mart or Neiman-Marcus. The implications of this bifurcation of the marketplace went beyond one group of Americans owning a superior Winnie-the-Pooh plush toy, some believed. "This new dual world affects far more than just the way goods are sold," David Leonhardt wrote in *BusinessWeek*, thinking, "it has become yet another force tearing at the country's fraying sense of community." Mass marketing in the 1950s and 1960s was a unifying force, Leonhardt suggested, while current marketing strategies were contributing to the sense that there really were "two Americas."[66]

These Are the Good Old Days

While the nation may have been divided in two, the economic boom of the late 1900s sparked by the dot-com bubble appeared to be just what the American middle class needed. The state of the middle class remained either dismal or rosy, however, depending on whom one listened to. "Income distributionists," i.e., those who argued that the rich should be taxed at much higher rates to create a more even playing field, looked to recent Census data to make their point. Incomes were declining among the poorest Americans in real dollars even in the now good economy, while the incomes of the richest continued to rise. By 1998, 20 percent of Americans raked in about half of all earnings, up from 46 percent in 1990. "Income disparities between the top fifth of families with children and families at the bottom and middle of the income scale have grown substantially over the last two decades," reported the Center on Budget and Policy Priorities, a classic view among the more liberal.[67]

Conservatives could not dispute these numbers or the loss of middle-class jobs but were able to look at the situation much differently. Income mobility still very much existed, for one thing, meaning people who were poor a couple of decades ago were unlikely to still be poor. Family incomes had risen over the past quarter-century when adjusted for average household size, another fact the "class warfare lobby" tended to ignore. Another explanation for why the middle class appeared to be disappearing was that they were moving up rather than down the economic ladder, conservatives pointed out. Fewer families qualified as middle class based on their income levels than in decades past, in other words, this a good thing. Asset holdings also had grown significantly over the past couple of decades, something that did not show up in income statistics. (Many elderly, for example, were income poor but asset rich, making it difficult to say which class they belonged to.) Finally, when the value of fringe benefits like health care, pensions, and vacation time were added, wages were rising instead of falling, another reason reports of the death of the American middle class was greatly exaggerated. "For the vast majority of Americans, these are the good old days," believed Stephen Moore of the Cato Institute, countering those who claimed the heyday of the middle class was in the rear-view mirror.[68]

One reason why the middle class was likely doing better than some critics claimed was, a little oddly, that it simply did not account for a large share of the nation's financial assets. It was true that there were more investors than ever in the stock market because of the popularity of mutual funds, 401(k)s, and IRAs. (Forty percent of American households owned some stock in 1995.) But even collectively the middle class did not own enough stock to get hurt much in a bear market like the one in 1998 (or gain much in a bull market). A study by NYU economist Edward N. Wolff showed that the wealthiest 10 percent of American households earned a whopping 85 percent of the stock market gains of about $3 trillion between 1989 and 1997. (The richest 1 percent earned half of that, rather incredibly.) The middle class just did not have enough money to make much difference on Wall Street, in other words, meaning the exposure of the average investor was minimal. Homes, not stocks, was where most of the financial assets of the middle class resided, making even a severe market slump not terrible news for ordinary folks.[69]

Despite not having a significant piece of the nation's financial pie, many members of the American middle class were determined to live as if they did. For a good number of Americans, in fact, being middle class or appearing as such to others was simply not good enough. While between the 1930s and 1950s most rich Americans unconsciously or consciously minimized their wealth to look "ordinary," the opposite had been true from 1960s on. In the "downsized" 1990s, a sizable portion of the middle class was living beyond its means, afraid to be seen by friends and colleagues (or admit to themselves) that they were part of the hoi polloi. Keeping one's McMansion and the BMW in the driveway was imperative to some although they were no longer making the big bucks they had in the go-go eighties. Some were even raiding their IRAs or giving up their health insurance in order to maintain their luxurious lifestyles, the thought of being truly middle class unacceptable if not abhorrent. Dropping down in class was considered embarrassing and shameful in this country, Julia Schor explained in her *The Overspent American*; seeing us as a competitive people prone to defining our identity not in absolute terms but relative to others. The "upscaling" of the nation had made it harder to keep up, making some of the middle class take desperate measures to seem more well off than they really were.[70]

Based on Alan Wolfe's research, however, the intense peer pressure some of the middle class felt was largely unnecessary. In his 1998 *One Nation After All*, Wolfe found that most members of the middle class had adopted a philosophy of cultural relativism or secular humanism—a fancy way of saying they were non-judgmental. "Middle-class Americans have added an Eleventh Commandment: 'Thou Shalt Not Judge,' he wrote in the book, suburbanites particularly inclusive. Wolfe's survey revealed that most suburban Americans subscribed to the "I'm OK, You're OK" school, obviously influenced by a couple of decades of warm and fuzzy self-help wisdom (or just Oprah Winfrey). When it came to what one did for a living or the kind of relationship one was in, Middle America felt "to each his own," rather refreshing news after decades of suburbs bashing. Schor's finding of overspent Americans was no doubt equally valid, but such people were likely trying to "Keep Up With the Joneses" (or one step ahead of them) because of their own insecurities rather than from outside forces.[71]

The make-believe universe of American pop culture no doubt fueled the desire of some of those firmly middle class to surround themselves with the trappings of the upper class. In movies and on television, ordinary Americans were somehow able to enjoy luxurious lives, the flourishing wealth culture of the times obviously influencing Hollywood screenwriters and directors. In the 1998 film *Stepmom*, for example, Susan Sarandon and Ed Harris make their way between their fabulous SoHo loft and gorgeous 19th century colonial in the suburbs in a Land Rover and BMW, not exactly your typical upper-middle-class lifestyle. Having no money did not prevent the young couple in *The Parent Trap* from getting married on the QE II and then staying at a lavish winery in Napa Valley and posh mansion in London (with butlers at the ready in each). And in *You've Got Mail*, Meg Ryan lives in a beautiful apartment on the Upper West Side although her bookstore is going under. Audiences responded well to all these films, however, suggesting that real life members of the middle class liked to see people similar to themselves living much like the rich.[72] Two popular television shows of the late 1990s—"Friends" and "Mad About You"—also blatantly skirted the realities of New York City real estate, their middle class characters living in plush flats while holding down working-stiff jobs.[73] "With a few exceptions, TV characters are upper-middle class, or even rich," Schor noted, thinking popular culture distorted our sense of normalcy.[74]

As the American Century drew to a close, the fate of the middle class was as uncertain as ever. Would the chugging economy keep chugging, or were the current good times artificially inflated by the emergence of a revolutionary new medium and a wild stock market? Only time would tell, of course, as the excitement of entering the 21st century and Third Millennium brought forth new kinds of challenges and opportunities for the American middle class.

Notes

1 Jean Bethke Elshtain, "Lost City," *New Republic*, November 4, 1996, 25.
2 Marc Levinson, "Not Everyone is Downsizing," *Newsweek*, March 18, 1996, 42–44.
3 "Lost City."
4 Ed Rubenstein, "Middle-Class Malaise," *National Review*, December 2, 1991, 16.
5 Larry Reibstein, "That Sinking Feeling," *Newsweek*, November 4, 1991, 18–21.
6 Lance Morrow, "Voters are Mad as Hell," *Time*, March 2, 1992, 16–20.
7 Jane Bryant Quinn and Virginia Wilson, "The Middle-Class Melt," *Newsweek*, December 17, 1990, 49.
8 Thomas Toch and Ted Slafsky, "The Great College Tumble," *U.S. News & World Report*, June 3, 1991, 50.
9 Michael Novak, "Middle-Class 'Meltdown'?", *Forbes*, January 20, 1992, 94–95.

10 Mickey Kaus, "Singing the Same Old Song," *Newsweek*, February 8, 1993, 59; Kevin Phillips, *The Politics of Rich and Poor: Wealth and the American Electorate in the Reagan Aftermath* (New York: Random House, 1990); Kevin Philips, *Boiling Point: Democrats, Republicans, and the Decline of Middle-Class Prosperity* (New York: Random House, 1993).

11 "Voters are Mad as Hell."

12 Mortimer B. Zuckerman, "Who Does Feel Your Pain?" *U.S. News & World Report*, December 26, 1994, 126.

13 Terry Teachout, "Movies and Middle-Class Rage," *Commentary*, May 1993, 52–54.

14 Jack Beatty, "Who Speaks for the Middle Class?", *The Atlantic Monthly*, May 1994, 77–80.

15 "Who Speaks for the Middle Class?"

16 Mark Levinson, "Living on the Edge," *Newsweek*, November 4, 1991, 23–26.

17 "Living on the Edge."

18 Frank Lalli, "Help for the Middle Class Living Paycheck to Paycheck," *Money*, June 1993, 7.

19 Alan Wolfe, "Clash of the Middle Classes," *Harper's Magazine*, October 1993, 20+.

20 "Clash of the Middle Classes."

21 George F. Will, "Ahoy! Is That a Middle Class?", *Newsweek*, November 4, 1991, 80.

22 Fred Bruning, "Beware the Defenders of the Middle Class," *Maclean's*, February 10, 1992, 15.

23 Susan Dentzer, "George Bush's Search for the Middle Class," *U.S. News & World Report*, January 27, 1992, 12–13.

24 "Beware the Defenders of the Middle Class."

25 "Voters are Mad as Hell."

26 "George Bush's Search for the Middle Class."

27 Vincente Navarro, "The Middle Class—A Useful Myth," *The Nation*, March 23, 1992, 361, 381.

28 Michael Novak, "Getting the Message," *Forbes*, May 11, 1992, 92–93.

29 Denise M. Topolnicki, "The Pain of the Middle-Class Tax Squeeze and What You Can Do About It," *Money*, April 1992, 80–86.

30 Lewis H. Lapham, "Winter of Discontent," *Harper's Magazine*, April 1992, 7–11.

31 Meg Greenfield, "Rediscovering 'Real People,'" *Newsweek*, January 20, 1992, 62.

32 Barbara Ehrenreich, "Double-Talk About 'Class,'" *Time*, March 2, 1992, 70.

33 "Double-Talk About 'Class.'"

34 Kevin Phillips, "Down and Out—Can the Middle Class Rise Again?", *New York Times Magazine*, January 10, 1993, 16–18.

35 "Down and Out—Can the Middle Class Rise Again?"; Dimitri B. Papadimitriou and Edward N. Wolff, eds., *Poverty and Prosperity in the USA in the Late Twentieth Century* (New York: Palgrave Macmillan, 1993).

36 Peter G. Peterson, "Facing Up," *The Atlantic Monthly*, October 1993, 77–90.

37 Peter Brimelow, "The Tax Tree," *Forbes*, May 11, 1992, 106–7.

38 Laura Saunders, "Follow the Money," *Forbes*, October 26, 1992, 138–40.

39 Connie Goddard, "Looking at What Went Wrong with America," *Publishers Weekly*, February 10, 1992, 22; Donald Bartlett and James Steele, *America: What Went Wrong?* (Kansas City, MO: Andrews McMeel, 1992).

40 Karen Rothmyer, "Mediawatch," *Mother Jones*, November/December 1992, 18–19.

41 John H. Hinderaker & Scott W. Johnson, "George Bush's Tax Return," *National Review*, May 30, 1994, 40–42; Donald Bartlett and James Steele, *America: Who Really Pays the Taxes?* (New York: Simon & Schuster, 1994).

42 Barbara Ehrenreich, "Helping the Rich Stay That Way," *Time*, April 18, 1994, 86.

43 Ed Rubinstein, "Reaganomics Revisited," *National Review*, February 3, 1992, 14.

44 Lawrence Kudlow, "Middle-Class Tax Hike," *National Review*, June 13, 1994, 25–26.

45 Gloria Borger, "Talking Straight to the Middle Class," *U.S. News & World Report*, January 10, 1994, 43.

46 Michael Duffy, "The 12-Minute Makeover," *Time*, December 26, 1994, 108–9.
47 Kenneth T. Walsh, "Rival Suitors," *U.S. News & World Report*, February 6, 1995, 28–30.
48 "Rival Suitors."
49 "Middle-Class Blues," *National Review*, November 7, 1994, 14–15.
50 John B. Judis, "Off Center," *New Republic*, October 16, 1995, 4–56; Seymour Martin Lipset, *Political Man: The Social Bases of Politics* (New York: Doubleday and Company, 1960).
51 Joe Klein, "Stalking the Radical Middle," *Newsweek*, September 25, 1995, 32–36; Gordon S. Black and Benjamin D. Black, *The Politics of American Discontent: How a New Party Can Make Democracy Work Again* (Hoboken, NJ: Wiley, 1994).
52 Michael Lind, "The Radical Center or the Moderate Middle," *New York Times Magazine*, December 3, 1995, 72–73.
53 Marc Levinson, "Hey, You're Doing Great," *Newsweek*, January 30, 1995, 42.
54 Joe Klein, "Where the Anger Went," *Newsweek*, November 4, 1996, 33.
55 Richard Parker, "Centrism, Populist Style," *The Nation*, October 7, 1996, 19–21.
56 Ramesh Ponnuru, "The Potemkin Presidency," *National Review*, September 2, 1996, 38–40.
57 Joseph S. Coyle, "How to Beat the Squeeze on the Middle Class," *Money*, May 1995, 106–12.
58 Louise Lief and Mary Brophy Marcus, "Kids at Risk," *U.S. News & World Report*, April 28, 1997, 66–68.
59 Charles J. Whalen, "The Age of Anxiety," *USA Today Magazine*, September 1996, 14–16.
60 Lynn H. Ehrle, "The Myth of the Middle Class," *Humanist*, November/December 1996, 17–20.
61 Paul Krugman, "The Spiral of Inequality," *Mother Jones*, November/December 1996, 44–49.
62 "The Spiral of Inequality."
63 Andrew Hacker, "Meet the Median Family," *Time*, January 29, 1996, 41–3.
64 "Meet the Median Family."
65 David Leonhardt, "Two-Tier Marketing," *BusinessWeek*, March 17, 1997, 82–90.
66 "Two-Tier Marketing."
67 Stephen Moore, "Is the Rising Tide Lifting All Boats?" *USA Today Magazine*, May 1998, 29.
68 "Is the Rising Tide Lifting All Boats?"
69 Aaron Bernstein, "A Sinking Tide Does Not Lower All Boats," *BusinessWeek*, September 14, 1998, 194.
70 Juliet B. Schor, *The Overspent American: Upscaling, Downshifting, and the New Consumer* (New York: Basic Books, 1998).
71 Richard Lowry, "Nonjudgment Day," *National Review*, April 6, 1998, 30–34; Alan Wolfe, *One Nation After All: What Middle-Class Americans Think About God, Country, Family, Racism, Welfare, Immigration, Homosexuality, Work, The Right, The Left, and Each Other* (New York: Viking Adult, 1998).
72 John Horn, "Mise-en-cents," *The Nation*, April 5–12, 1999, 48–50.
73 Elizabeth Austin, "Why Homer's My Hero," *The Washington Monthly*, October 2000, 32.
74 *The Overspent American.*

6

THE PERFECT STORM

It would be a disaster of epic proportions. It would be the perfect storm.

TV meteorologist in the 2000 movie *The Perfect Storm*

In March 2011, thousands of people rallied to protest against the way they were being treated by the government. Guards tried to hold back the angry mob, which was determined to occupy the building where elected officials were meeting. Social media had served as a vehicle for the shouting crowd to organize the uprising that was a result of what the protestors genuinely believed was government oppression and even tyranny. Money, not surprisingly, was at the root of it all, the demonstrators' frustrations over steadily dropping income reaching boiling point.[1]

The event described above was not part of the "Arab Spring," of course, but took place in Madison, Wisconsin, a city known more for cheddar cheese and brewpubs than civil unrest. But after the governor of the state passed a bill limiting the bargaining rights for government employees, the people had had enough. Most of the protestors were middle class, a group convinced it had "been on the losing end of almost every economic trend in America in the past 30 years," as Bill Wolpin of *American City and County* described it. Massive job losses, plummeting home values, and shrinking retirement nest eggs were all part of this most recent recession, and the prospect of losing the right to bargain with the government (and possibly lose some or all of a pension) was too much to bear. Watching big banks get bailed out by the government when they had been largely responsible for triggering the financial meltdown only added fuel to the fire. The American middle class, at least this small slice of it, was mad as hell and was not going to take it anymore.[2]

America's Forgotten Majority

The very embodiment of the "establishment" a half-century ago, the American middle class was increasingly feeling outside of it as the group's economic and social status continued to fall. The middle class of today is in many other ways strikingly different than the one that flourished in the postwar years. More blacks and Hispanics were making up the middle class as they moved up economically (the fruits of the civil rights movement), and the wave of immigrants over the past few decades was making the group younger. Rather than being a fixed body of people or one with a defined set of demographics, the middle class was thus a constantly shifting target. In addition to this morphing aspect, there remained no agreement regarding what level of income qualified an American to be judged middle class. Some believed it was the middle 20 percent quintile, while others felt it was the middle three quintiles, or 60 percent of Americans, while still others made a case for the middle 40 percent of households. (The definition of what constituted being "lower class," i.e., "poor," or "upper class," i.e., "rich," was similarly disputed.) Because level of education was strongly tied to income, a reasonable argument could be made that being middle class was simply a matter of whether one had a college degree. Class in America continued to be hazy and ambiguous, with no consensus regarding its composition or its boundaries.[3]

Although it was perfectly obvious that there were major gaps among Americans along social and economic lines, the nebulous nature of class made them less apparent. "The middle class, in current American parlance, is such an elastic concept that it actually includes *all* classes," noted Rob Long of *National Review* in 2000, both poor folks and rich ones firmly believing they belonged to the group. There was, however, one group of Americans that did not want to be recognized as middle class. Because they enjoyed their "higher" socio-economic status, members of the upper middle class preferred to distance themselves from those who they deemed as less sophisticated. "Upper middlers are the Restoration Hardware shoppers and the grilled-salmon-with-mango-salsa eaters," Long thought, seeing them as the "Merlot people."[4] Other nicknames for the upper middle class were floated as the turn-of-the-century bubble increased the segment's numbers. "Affluents" was sometimes used, as was "overclass." David Brooks called them "Bourgeois Bohemians" or just "Bobos" in his *Bobos in Paradise*, while *Money* labeled them the "ultra" middle class. The magazine considered a household income between $150,000 and $250,000 as the economic range of "ultras," which about 4 percent of Americans enjoyed. (The 1 percent of American households earning more than $250,000 was determined to be "rich.") As Long made clear, Ultras were notable for their discretionary income and eagerness to spend it. A good number of them had caught what Robert Frank called "luxury fever," emulating the rich by buying designer brands in every product category imaginable.[5]

Still, the concept of class remained so vague in the United States that most of its citizens could not tell you who composed the largest one. Most Americans would say the middle class was the largest, and that they were part of it. Politicians and the media typically reinforced this idea to the point where it was generally believed that the United States was simply a "middle-class nation." The truth, however, at least according to two new books published in 2000, was that the working class represented the majority in America. Ruy Teixeira and Joel Rogers' *America's Forgotten Majority* and Michael Zweig's *The Working Class Majority* each made a compelling case that more Americans were working class than middle class, something that many of us would have a tough time believing (or liking). Both books posited that the 1980s and 1990s had been kind to a college-educated managerial/professional class, while a much larger working class had struggled and lost ground over that same period of time. Calling everybody middle class obscured that fact, the authors argued, part of Americans' confusion about and even denial of class. It was true that acknowledging the mere existence of a working class here was somewhat distasteful, as it conveyed that we had a social hierarchy like that of the 19th century or those in Europe. And if we had a working class, it meant we had a managerial/professional class and an ownership class, something smacking of Marxist anti-capitalistic ideology and a divisive society. Even presidential candidate Al Gore's focus on "working families" rubbed some the wrong way, the term prompting critics to claim he was engaging in "class warfare." Ralph Nader had long openly acknowledged class politics, but it was rare for a major candidate to build a campaign strategy around any group outside the safe and friendly confines of the American middle class.[6]

The bitter truth was that class definitely existed in the United States, and there were great differences among Americans both socially and economically. Tremendous variations were common within the middle class alone. Not only were the lifestyles of the working (or lower middle) class and the managerial/professional (or upper middle) class typically dissimilar, but even those in the exact middle of the middle class could find themselves in very different economic situations. This became vividly apparent in the *New York Times'* 2002 look at seven families around the country who all earned the national median income of $54,400. Not just how but where one lived made a huge difference in the kind of house and car one owned and whether it was possible to save money or afford the occasional splurge. Whether families had taken advantage of the stock market bubble of the late 1990s also mattered a great deal. With a mortgage payment of just $425 on their three-bedroom house, for example, a Louisiana family making that amount felt "well off," while a family from the Bronx dreamed of having enough money to buy a home of their own. Likewise, a family of farmers in Wisconsin had hundreds of thousands of dollars of debt from agricultural loans, while a family from Manhattan who had done well with their investments had socked away $100,000. The clever exercise illustrated that the common label "middle class" obfuscated the great disparity in Americans' standards of living, even among those making the exact amount of money.[7]

Because of the growing diversity of the middle class, finding high concentrations of "average" Americans was becoming a more challenging pursuit. For most marketers, it was important to know which areas of the country had the highest number and highest percentage of members of the middle class. For the time being, the middle class remained the sweet spot for many products and services, a giant market of consumers that often accounted for the majority of a company's sales revenue. Marketers now generally considered those households with an annual income between $45,000 and $75,000 to be middle class. There were twenty-six million such households in the United States in the early 2000s (about a quarter of the total number), and marketers actively sought to reach them with advertising and promotion for their brands. "Will it play in Peoria?" was thus not just a rhetorical question for most businesses. Marketers really did want to know where "average" American consumers tended to live in order to make best use of their budgets and to test products. Peoria, Illinois would actually not be a bad choice; the city ranked thirty-third on the country's list of percentage of middle-class households. The best choice would be to head directly to Wisconsin, as five of the ten metro areas with the highest percentage of middle-class households were located in that state. Sheboygan, Appleton-Oshkosh-Neenah, Wausau, Green Bay, and Janesville-Beloit were as average as they came, in terms of income anyway, with York (Pennsylvania), Elkhart-Goshen (Indiana), Lancaster (Pennsylvania), Cedar Rapids (Iowa), and Sioux Falls (South Dakota) rounding out the list.[8]

Perhaps even more so than marketers, politicians were keen on appealing to the middle class. Because using the term "middle class" was like shooting with a shotgun, i.e., difficult to miss one's target, presidential candidates again used it liberally for the 2004 campaign. An economic recovery had already begun, but that did not stop the Kerry-Edwards campaign from referring to average earners' financial struggles as a "middle-class squeeze." Kerry had begun his campaign talking about topics like energy independence and global warming, but quickly found that issues central to middle-class concerns—job insecurity and the costs of health care, local taxes, and college tuition—resonated much stronger with voters.[9] Independents liked the Democrats' populist message steeped in the premise that the Bush administration was favoring the rich over the middle class and poor, while the Republicans dismissed it as a "glass-half-empty" perspective.[10]

Like marketers and politicians, charities relied heavily on connecting with the middle class. Families with household incomes of less than $100,000 contributed about 60 percent of charity dollars, according to the Center of Philanthropy at Indiana University, a statistic that indicated it was the middle class rather than the upper class that collectively gave more money away to worthy causes. As well, there were extraordinary stories of frugal people who had somehow accumulated small fortunes and gave them away to causes they felt strongly about. A Pittsburgh shoe shiner had recently donated more than $90,000 to a local hospital, for example, while a Minneapolis handyman gave over a million dollars to New York City after 9/11. Average earners who received a sudden windfall, such as by winning a lottery, were also known to give it away, uncomfortable with the idea of being considered wealthy. Contrary to public opinion, not everybody wanted to be a millionaire, the appeal of remaining middle class stronger for some than becoming one of the privileged few.[11]

A Largely Hidden Problem

Most of the middle class, however, would rather have large sums of money given to them than give them away. Television glorified wealth, of course, with the two most popular shows in 2000 (*Who Wants to Be a Millionaire?* and *Survivor*) each designed around a big cash prize for winners. Smart, middle-class people were increasingly asking themselves why they were not rich like the dot-commer or investment banker down the block. Financial advice books also suggested that wealth was not just a desired state but an entirely normal one. (The title alone of Suze Orman's *The Courage to Be Rich* implied that it was cowardly to not be rich.) "Our thinking has become so distorted that being comfortably middle-class now feels like the next step to actual poverty," observed Elizabeth Austin in *The Washington Monthly*, many Americans now viewing an average $50,000 annual household income as chump change. Much of the most prosperous civilization in the history of the world felt poor, a clear sign there was something wrong with our values. The new upper middle class had raised the stakes in measuring status, turning consumption into a fine art that many wanted to master but few really could because of a lack of resources (or simply taste). Envy, dissatisfaction, and discontent were pervasive, especially among baby boomers who once considered class privilege a social pathology. "It's hard to find any hint that regular middle-class life might be pleasant, honorable, or desirable," Austin concluded, our obsession with money bad for individuals and the nation as a whole.[12]

Robert H. Frank agreed that the media's veneration of wealth made many middle-class Americans feel destitute. "In the midst of the longest sustained economic boom in history, many American families are experiencing an unprecedented sense of impoverishment," he wrote for the *New York Times* in 2000, the simple awareness of the tremendous wealth some possessed lowering others' own self-worth. Rapidly escalating consumption, especially that being enjoyed by the thousands of new dot-com millionaires and a few billionaires, was making average earners want to spend more. Savings were significantly down and credit card debt was at historically high levels, a fair reflection of the (futile) effort to try to mimic the lifestyles of the rich. The cards may have been stacked against the middle class in terms of taxes and other economic factors, but many with average incomes were doing themselves no favors by choosing to spend money rather than save it.[13]

The concentration of wealth in the early 21st century was eerily reminiscent of the polarized class dynamics of a century earlier, raising some interesting questions. Did the emergence of another Gilded Age suggest that the flourishing of the middle class in mid-century America was a cultural anomaly, i.e., a rare or even unique event produced by a series of economic and social forces unlikely to occur again? Paul Krugman of the *New York Times* thought so after looking at economic data going back almost a hundred years. "The middle-class America of my youth [the 1950s and 1960s] is best thought of not as the normal state of our society, but as an interregnum between the Gilded Ages," he wrote in 2002, the New Deal and war having flattened the nation's collective wealth (a process Claudia Goldin and Robert Margo called the "Great Compression"). As the income gap began expanding in the 1970s, the middle class began shrinking, effectively returning us to our pre-Depression class hierarchy. The implication was that Americans' current expectations for a vast and strong middle class were based on an exception rather than a rule and were thus unrealistic. Perhaps the United States was not as different from other nations as we liked to believe, our mythology of "classlessness" purely an illusion. If so, pining for the days when the lifestyles of the well to do and the less well off were not very different was naïve and futile, as there was no chance the postwar American Way of Life was about to return a half-century later.[14]

Michael Lind saw things somewhat differently. "The United States has always been an economic paradise for the middle class," he wrote in *The Atlantic* in 2004, the government playing an active role in its creation and perpetuation. Since the nation became a nation, widespread material prosperity was as essential to American life as civil liberties or political democracy, Lind argued, the chance to make more money as important as any other reason for immigrants to come here. For over two centuries, the United States had been a hospitable home for a middle class, he explained, as opportunist Americans moved from the farm to the factory to the corporation in great numbers. This is what distinguished us from Europeans, Lind felt, our middle class dwarfing their small bourgeois class sandwiched between the large peasant and elite aristocratic classes. However, Lind broke away from this traditional view by suggesting that the emergence of our mass middle class was not a natural result of capitalism, believing instead that it was a product of "government-sponsored social engineering." Whether it was the availability of cheap farmland and building of railroads in the early 19th century, protectionist tariffs and limitations on immigration in the late 19th and early 20th centuries, or the New Deal whose effects extended until the 1960s, the federal government vigorously served the interests of a middle class. Like most, Lind saw the pendulum begin to swing in the 1970s and accelerate through the 1980s and 1990s, as manufacturing shifted abroad. Goods became cheaper to buy but money became more difficult to acquire as jobs went overseas and our service economy developed. The government had lost control of its massive social engineering project, the system no longer rigged for the middle class.[15]

In their *The Two-Income Trap: Why Middle-Class Mothers and Fathers Are Going Broke*, Elizabeth Warren and her daughter Amelia Warren Tyagi also pinpointed the 1970s as when the discretionary income of middle-class families began to go in reverse. Two-earner families now had less money to spend than a one-earner family a few decades ago, they concluded after analyzing the data, a result of continually rising fixed costs, i.e., mortgage payments, car loans, health insurance, childcare, and taxes.[16] "Whether looking for housing, tax breaks, health care, child care, luxury cars, white-collar jobs, or countless other elements, services, and products seemingly essential to American life," Mark Mitchell agreed in *Independent School*, "the middle class just cannot catch a break."[17] If pretax income was a fair measure of economic status, in fact, one could argue there was no middle class in America anymore. In 2005, 300,000 Americans (the top 1 percent of income earners) made almost as much money as the remaining 150 million American earners, meaning the nation consisted of a tiny upper class and a huge underclass.[18]

That the middle class could not seem to catch a break was not lost on television executives. New reality shows like *Three Wishes*, *Extreme Makeover: Home Edition*, and *The Miracle Workers* were offering precisely those products and services "essential to American life" as prizes to average folks who could not afford them. Giving away college tuition, a bigger house, even a necessary surgical procedure to those in need had become a formula for high ratings (and viewers' tears). Oprah Winfrey was now giving away new cars and other big-ticket items to deserving audience members, this too capitalizing on the actual reality of downward mobility. Such shows "target a timely anxiety: the middle class's fear of failing," James Poniewozik of *Time* believed, with no coincidence that the goodies given away were the pillars of economic and social mobility. "In this moment of crisis, these series swing into place like a virtual social net," Poniewozik explained, as television networks did for a select few what the government was failing to do for the many.[19]

Magically solving a few Americans' problems may have made good television, but the economic challenges of the middle class were mostly unseen. "It's a largely hidden problem, this quiet erosion of the middle class," Barbara Ehrenreich and Tamara Draut observed in *The Nation* in 2006, thinking the downwardly mobile did not get as much attention as the poor. Downsizing (or right-sizing or smart-sizing, as it was sometimes called) was decimating the middle class. Some who once held managerial positions in IT, marketing, or engineering were driving cabs or doing janitorial work, while others with college degrees were working retail just to pay the bills. Having borrowed thousands, sometimes tens of thousands of dollars to get their degree, those who had been laid off frequently found themselves in serious debt. Fourteen thousand white-collar workers had recently been laid off from Ford alone, making one wonder if they would ever have jobs as good as the ones they had just lost. Being unemployed left a gap on one's résumé, making them "untouchable" to some companies. In his *The Disposable American*, Louis Uchitelle described how being downsized was not only disastrous financially but emotionally as well. After a couple of years of being unemployed or working for minimum wage, some doubted they could ever hold a managerial job again because their confidence was so shattered. "This is the new world of the middle class," Ehrenreich and Draut wrote, "haunted by debt, stalked by layoffs, pinched by vanishing pensions and health benefits, and forced into ever more contingent forms of work as 'real' jobs give way to benefit-free contract work." The middle class was not really in the "middle," they believed, but hovering slightly above the working poor, making class in America decidedly bottom heavy.[20]

Much like the people who lived in them, neighborhoods in cities across America were either going up or going down, depending upon economic circumstances. Overall, there were fewer urban middle-class neighborhoods in 2000 than there were in 1970, according to a study published by the Brookings Institution in 2006. Fifty-eight percent of metropolitan neighborhoods were defined as middle class in 1970, while just 41 percent were three decades later. Neighborhoods were, in other words, stratifying, a physical reflection of the changes going on within America's class system. Some were becoming more expensive and exclusive, while others were becoming more run-down and crime-ridden. If Americans were more likely to be rich or poor, so were the places they lived, something that made perfect sense. New York City and Los Angeles were the cities most divided by class, not surprisingly. Bedford-Stuyvesant was a very long way from the Upper East Side, economically speaking, and South Central equally distant from Beverly Hills.[21] Only 16 percent of New Yorkers were middle class, in fact, and 17 percent of Los Angelenos. The nation's suburbs too were losing the middle class, the Brookings Institution found. Of the dozen suburban communities studied, the middle-class population dropped from 64 percent to 44 percent between 1970 and 2000, with high-income and low-income families making up the difference. America was becoming an "Upstairs, Downstairs" society, such studies suggested, the middle class possibly going up to the top floor but more likely heading down to the bottom one.[22]

Positively American

The significant concern over class in America was all the more interesting given that we were popularly believed to be a classless nation. For a country that supposedly did not have strong class distinctions, i.e., where upward of 90 percent of citizens claimed to belong to the same (middle) class, in other words, we sure spent a lot of time talking about the subject. This was most apparent to those from other countries. Clive Crook, an ex-patriot from England, for example, found Americans' obsession with class highly ironic given that the subject was now rarely discussed in his native country. Most Americans would agree that social class was integral to the British way of life and political process but, in fact, this was an outdated stereotype. It was American politicians (and voters), not their British counterparts, who were preoccupied with matters of class, something Crook found surprising and strange. Crook also considered the nearly universal adoration of the American middle class odd, as in England being called "middle class" was rather insulting, a euphemism for being self-satisfied and self-righteous. Here the bourgeois value of hard work was held in high regard as the principal means of economic mobility while across the pond it was deemed as, well, bourgeois.[23]

Although the Brits tended not to use the term "middle class" because of its negative connotations, a leading newspaper there did employ one that was similar to its American equivalent. The *Daily Telegraph* had recently begun using the term the "coping classes," which it defined as people who were "overburdened by tax, crippled by mortgage repayments, and struggling to meet the demands of young people and elderly parents." Like the term "middle class" in the States, "coping classes" could be interpreted as a huge swath of people, and thus served as a way for the newspaper to demonstrate empathy for a large number of readers. Like the American middle class, the British coping classes were experiencing harder times as a recession worsened and as food prices rose. British politicians had yet to adopt the term, but it appeared that things overseas were not as different as Crook made them out to be.[24]

Charles Schumer, the Democratic U.S. senator from New York, was exactly the type of politician whose rhetoric Crook found so odd relative to that of British elected officials. Schumer was one of the loudest spokespersons for the American middle class, using the group to define his political platform and backing it up through his voting record. Schumer summed up his views in his 2007 book *Positively American: Winning Back the Middle-Class Majority One Family at a Time*, explaining how Washington has been less than supportive of middle-class families and offering ways in which it could do better (such as by making college tuition tax deductible). As some other writers have done, Schumer used a fictional family, the Baileys, to represent the American middle class, describing them as possibly "a straighter version" of the Griffins on the Fox animated sitcom *The Family Guy*. "They need help and nobody's talking to them," Schumer said in an interview, thinking the government should modestly tax junk food advertising to pay for other ads that informed viewers how unhealthy the products were. (Apparently the Baileys were as portly as Peter Griffin.) Schumer also believed that property taxes should be reduced by half, this another means of getting the middle class back on its feet.[25]

Schumer was hardly the only politician to suggest that Washington had let down the middle class. In their 2006 essay for *Blueprint Magazine*, "Saving the American Dream," Senator Hillary Rodham Clinton, Senator Tom Carper, and Governor Tom Vilsack showed how the middle class and our core mythology of the American Dream were indelibly connected through the 20th century. The "basic bargain" of the Dream—that all Americans should have the chance to make the most out of our potential—"built the greatest middle class the world has ever known," the three (all Democrats) co-wrote. In the first few years of the new century, however, that bargain had been broken, replaced by an economic philosophy that everyone would ultimately gain by favoring the wealthy. This new direction surely was not benefitting the middle class, the trio explained, with rising costs and falling incomes more of a recipe for an American nightmare than an American Dream. "These trends aren't just a burden for middle-class families," Clinton, Carper, and Vilsack wrote, but "undermine our way of life because middle-class strength and growth have been the backbone of America." Like Schumer, the three had a set of ideas regarding how Washington could mend its ways and give the middle class the attention it deserved. They had recently formed something called the American Dream Initiative, "an opportunity agenda for the middle class and all who aspire to join it." All of the initiative's measures were designed to give Americans the opportunities they deserved, a means of reinstituting the "basic bargain" of the American Dream.[26]

Businesspeople, journalists, and academics also pointed out how the decline of the American middle class was a serious blow to our national identity. In his "last page" editorials in *U.S. News & World Report*, Mort Zuckerman continued to voice his concerns about the state of the American middle class. Zuckerman, a Canadian-born billionaire and owner of a media empire including that magazine, was a champion for the American Dream, having achieved it himself as a naturalized citizen. "Our nation's core bargain with the middle class is disintegrating," he wrote on Christmas Day 2006, a typical remark in support of the group he felt was being left behind as wealthy people like he got richer. Zuckerman's concern for the middle class appeared genuine as he empathized with Americans' anxieties over job security, health insurance, and retirement plans. For Zuckerman and others, the deterioration of the middle class was clearly an un-American phenomenon, something that was contrary to our basic values and history. That the median income of the middle class was not rising in the current economic expansion was especially frustrating to Zuckerman, as things would no doubt get a lot worse when the next recession came along. (It did the very next year.) Insecurity over the possible loss of a job or the appearance of a major health issue was crushing Americans' natural inclination to take risks, this also antithetical to the country's distinctiveness. An America consisting largely of families living in constant fear of bankruptcy was not the country Zuckerman recognized, and he urged policy makers to make housing, education, health care, and childcare more affordable to the middle class.[27]

Lou Dobbs had also become a one-man army for the middle class, making a strong case in his 2006 bestseller *War on the Middle Class* that the government, corporations, and special interest groups were all working against the interests of the largest group of people in the country. Dobbs' book was based on research for his show on CNN, *Lou Dobbs Tonight*, on which he covered stories about health care and job outsourcing under the title "The Middle-Class Squeeze." After reporting the failures of America's education system, the segment was re-titled "Assault on the Middle Class." Dobbs soon realized that even "assault" was too mild a word for what was taking place, however, renaming the segment

"War on the Middle Class." His show and book cast the members of the middle class as victims of powerful and greedy forces (including the mainstream media), believing it did not stand much of a chance of surviving the war if present trends continued. Not just liberals but many conservatives thought Dobbs was too extreme in his views (the Bush administration would not grant him interviews), but the man was saying what a lot of middle-class Americans felt but could not articulate.[28]

Two other recently published books—Yale political scientist Jacob Hacker's *The Great Risk Shift* and union leader Andy Stern's *A Country That Works*—preached a similar kind of economic populism, and offered ideas on how the middle class could win the war being waged against them. Income disparity was a common theme in all these books, their authors maintaining that the still growing divide between an under class and upper class was hurting those in the middle.[29] No one had completely lost hope for the middle class, however, and some saw light at the end of the tunnel. The emerging green economy could provide thousands of jobs for Americans of all class levels, the more optimistic believed, leading to the Green Jobs Act that was passed by the House in 2007. Renewable energy, energy-efficient vehicles, and green buildings were just some of the opportunities waiting around the corner as America and much of the world embraced "sustainability" in all its forms. "Across every industry, new job possibilities are emerging for those with the skills to bridge the divide between the old, fossil-fuel-based economy and the new, energy-efficient one," exclaimed Brita Belli of *E Magazine* in 2007, thinking, "everything's coming up green." "Green-collar" jobs could go a long way toward rebuilding a crumbling middle class, Belli and quite a few others felt, a 21st century version of the blue-collar jobs that were instrumental in vastly expanding the group in the last century.[30]

A Vexing Contradiction

Until everything came up green, however, it appeared that the middle class would fall further and further behind the wealthiest Americans. For the middle class, however, did it really matter some asked that a "super-rich" class had emerged in America? Class polarization was probably not ideal, but did the good fortune of one group necessarily negatively impact another? Barbara Ehrenreich certainly thought so, coming up with a few solid reasons how the concentration of wealth to a limited few was directly impacting the lives of the many. First, much of the wealth on the top was built on the work at the bottom, she argued, the owners and managers of businesses the beneficiaries of cheap labor. (Wal-Mart was the worst violator of this classic industrial-era model.) Second, the ability for what she termed an "overclass" to pay any price for housing and education made costs higher for everyone, forcing the middle class to settle for less. (Exorbitant tuitions at elite colleges continued to steer qualified students from average income families to state universities or community colleges.) Finally, wealth and politics were two peas in a pod, Ehrenreich reminded readers of *The Progressive*, their cozy relationship leading to the creation of economic policies favoring the rich and disfavoring anyone who was not. (The failure of universal health insurance to get passed by Congress was a prime example.) Ehrenreich clearly did not subscribe to the aphorism "a rising tide lifts all boats," thinking that the lifting of a few boats (or yachts) was keeping the majority of the fleet down.[31]

That the middle class was "losing its place at the table," as a U.S. senator had recently put it, was all the more surprising given the number and range of powerful people who claimed to be on its side. Well-known media people such as Dobbs, most politicians (including President Bush), and the occasional celebrity (like Rosie O'Donnell) had all made public statements in support of the middle class, especially with regard to the nation's income inequality. Empathy for the middle class crossed party lines, with not just liberals but many conservatives unhappy about how the rich were getting richer and the poor appeared to be making no headway. Like the old joke about the weather, everybody was complaining about the state of the middle class but nobody seemed to be doing anything about it. Besides the fact that speaking up for the middle class was simply a popular thing to do, one explanation for the "all talk, no action" was that from a broad, historical perspective, it could be argued that those with average incomes were doing quite well. Economists had research showing that class mobility had not changed much through the years, and that all income groups had made some gains over the long term. In addition, more Americans than ever (70 percent) now owned their homes, and two-thirds of high school graduates were going on to college (versus one-half in 1970). Was the American middle class really "vanishing," as so many believed, or, in a historical sense, prospering?[32]

Northwestern University economist Robert J. Gordon believed the latter. There was no doubt that income inequality was increasing, Gordon reported, but his research showed that the middle class had enjoyed steadily improving standards of living over the last couple of decades. "Anybody who thinks things are getting worse should go to Best Buy and notice the type of people who go [there]," he said in 2006, believing the way that the government calculated the cost of living was part of the problem. Real income was understated, he and other economists were sure, meaning things were not as bad for the middle class as politicians and the media made them out to be. "You have to wonder who's buying all those flat-screen TVs, serving precooked rotisserie chicken for dinner or organizing their closets with Elfa systems," agreed Virginia Postrel of *Forbes*, thinking much of the fretting about the middle class was symptomatic of "the American standard of whining."[33] Brian Kantz, writing for the *National Catholic Reporter*, echoed this view, thinking the "crisis" of the middle class was mostly media hype. If the middle class felt poorer, it was only because it wanted or felt it needed more stuff than it used to. Two or three cars rather than one, a bigger house, a computer, Internet, and cable were now part of a typical middle-class lifestyle, meaning it was necessary to make more money than in the past.

Compared to most people around the world, the American middle class was positively rich, its "crisis" nothing more than how to keep up its pricey standard of living.[34]

Anecdotal evidence could be found for such a contrarian's viewpoint. Restaurants that Americans with household incomes of $60,000 or less regularly frequented had recently lost customers, a good example of how the middle class was having to cut back. Casual dining places like Applebee's, Outback Steak House, Ruby Tuesdays, TGI Fridays, and the Cheesecake Factory were all reporting flat or negative sales, while business at fast food chains like McDonald's, Burger King, and Taco Bell was very good. "The triple whammy of gas prices, housing-market collapse and the credit crunch [is] the perfect storm," said a Los Angeles advertising executive whose agency was losing the Sizzler account. Other casual dining chains were moving their business to new ad agencies, but the problem was less about advertising, more about the economy. Consumers were without a doubt strapped for cash, quite literally losing their place at the table. But was it such a tragedy that the middle class had to eat a Big Mac or Whopper instead of Applebee's Chicken Fajita Rollup or TGI Friday's Pulled Pork Sandwich?[35]

The plight of the middle class ran deeper than missing a few meals at one's favorite restaurant chain, however. An ambitious study published by the Pew Research Center in 2008 reported that 56 percent of Americans believed they either had not moved ahead or had fallen behind in the past five years, a finding Pew considered "the most downbeat short-term assessment of personal progress in nearly half a century." The Pew study (in which a whopping 91 percent of respondents said they were somewhere in the middle class) also found that 80 percent of Americans found it difficult to maintain "middle-class lifestyles" compared to 67 percent in 1986. Robert J. Samuelson felt something deeper resided under the numbers, however. "Middle-class families value predictability, order and security, and these reassuring qualities have eroded," he wrote for *Newsweek*, the possibility that one could lose everything the real source of anxiety. While Americans had become generally more prosperous, they felt more vulnerable, in other words, perhaps because they now had more to lose. "The prevalence of middle-class ambitions and values subjects us to a vexing contradiction," Samuelson observed, our expectations for higher living standards making us feel more insecure and fearful when they are threatened.[36]

A Turning Point

Successful politicians recognized the anxiety the middle class felt, and capitalized on it every chance they could. Some of those in the political sphere were even taking the time and effort to determine who was fighting hardest for the middle class. A Washington, DC-based organization called the Drum Major Institute for Public Policy (DMI), for example, rated congressional members based on their voting record on ten issues related specifically to the interests of the American middle class. In 2008, 34 senators and 199 representatives earned an "A" grade, while one-third of all representatives and almost 40 percent of all senators received an "F." Virtually all politicians claimed to be looking out for the middle class but, if DMI's scorecard was accurate, a good number of them were not living up to their promises. The three top presidential candidates that election year all happened to be U.S. senators, allowing for a fair comparison of their respective commitment to the middle class. Senators Barack Obama and Hillary Clinton each earned a grade of "A+," but Senator McCain received an "incomplete" as he was absent for most of the graded votes. McCain was, in fact, the only senator to receive such a grade. Even Tim Johnson, a senator from South Dakota who suffered a serious brain hemorrhage and missed about nine months of work, voted on more of the specified issues than McCain.[37]

Charles Schumer's commitment to the middle class had only intensified over the decade he was in office. As chairman of the Democratic Senatorial Campaign Committee, Schumer was helping other Senate candidates around the country get elected or re-elected through what he referred to as the "Schumer Method." Based around the interests of the middle class, the Schumer Method was a way for the senator to spread his gospel throughout the Democratic Party. Schumer insured that the party was staying true to its brand, something he felt Democrats had not done well since the "Reagan Revolution." The middle class was not the poor or the working class, Schumer continually reminded fellow Democrats, an important distinction when forging policy. Schumer was also determined to convince the "liberal-elite" that trying to help the middle class was a good thing, i.e., that the poor should not be the sole recipient of government assistance programs. If his method worked as well as he thought it could, Schumer believed a new Democratic era that bonded the government to the middle class could last for a generation or longer.[38]

Schumer's message appeared to be on target, but there were few signs that the middle class was making any progress. The mortgage crisis only intensified the effects of the recession, putting more American families into debt. "America's middle class is at a turning point," said Elizabeth Warren, who was now overseeing the Federal Reserve, thinking the country was getting dangerously close to a two-class economy. "The outcome of this recession will either be a significantly strengthened middle class—which has less debt and a stronger safety net, both on its own and through new government regulation—or the middle class we once knew will disappear," she warned. The United States may soon consist of "a substantial upper class that's financially secure and then a very large underclass that lives paycheck to paycheck," she believed, a society precisely like that of many developing nations. Avoiding such a scary scenario depended in part on government policy, the ex-Harvard law professor maintained, but national and individual financial security also rested on consumers paying off their credit card debt and car loans as soon as possible.[39]

A president seemingly dedicated to the interests of the middle class represented a major sign of hope for those Americans "losing their place at the table." That an

African American could become president helped make matters of class (versus those of race) a national priority, this itself perhaps good news for a struggling middle class. "However inspirational the story of his ascent, Barack Obama will be judged largely by whether he can rebuild a ladder of upward mobility for the rest of America, too," wrote Joel Kotkin for *Newsweek* in 2009, the president inheriting a climate of growing inequality as he came into office.[40] President Obama included a middle-class tax cut in the 2008 economic stimulus bill (with Schumer's help), and mentioned the middle class no less than twenty times in a September 2009 speech to the AFL-CIO. Because of his working-class background, Vice President Joe Biden served as the president's ambassador on middle-class issues. Biden oversaw the administration's Middle Class Task Force, whose mission was to "restore the link between economic growth and middle-class income." With health care reform the administration's top priority, however, the task force had yet to take on any major initiative, much less tackle the colossal job of figuring out how to shrink the income divide.[41]

Like President Clinton, who appeared to become fully committed to the interests of the middle class in the midpoint of his first term as a re-election tactic, President Obama began to more aggressively appeal to average earners after some time in office. Consistent with political pundits who argued that the Democratic Party needed to shift to the economic center and cut its New Deal and Great Society roots tied to the working class and poor, Obama swung even closer to the middle class in early 2010. The recession and foreclosures had of course hit the middle class hard, bringing them closer to the kind of disenfranchised Americans that Obama had targeted during his campaign and first year in office. The president's 2010 State of the Union speech was filled with references to saving for college, retirement, and childcare, all hot buttons for those at both the upper and lower ends of the middle class. By not addressing such concerns, Obama risked losing disenchanted middle-income voters to the Republican Party and the emerging Tea Party movement. Not coincidently, the Commerce Department had just reported that 92 percent of Americans now thought of themselves as being middle class, all the more reason to propose policies that would make their lives better. No official definition of "middle class" still existed, making it easy for the administration to expand its parameters for political purposes.[42]

Waking Up from the American Dream

A parade of new statistics backed up President Obama's intensified commitment to the American middle class. The income divide was not getting any smaller, bad news to those who believed it was strongly linked to the health of the middle class. By 2011, the top 1 percent of American households held 34.3 percent of total private wealth, more than the bottom 90 percent.[43] Five percent of Americans accounted for 37 percent of all consumer purchases, meaning those who made the most money also not surprisingly spent the most money.[44] Not only were the rich accounting for a continually rising share of total income, wealth, and spending but the non-rich were losing share. Two out of five Americans who considered themselves middle class said they were struggling to remain so, according to a 2010 ABC World News poll, the most recent recession (of five since 1980) and persistent job losses (25 of the last 26 months) explaining the statistic.[45] According to 2010 U.S. Census figures, the annual income of middle-class families had dropped more than $2,500 over the past decade, a reversal of gains made between the late 1960s and late 1990s. Continually rising income was a, perhaps the, defining trait of middle-class life in America in the second half of the 20th century, something that could not be said to be true in the first decade of the 21st century. A decline in savings along with lower house values further diminished the "nest egg" of the middle class, making paying for college for a child or planning for retirement much more problematic.[46]

Given the recent housing bust and long-term loss of manufacturing jobs, it was surprising to some that the middle class had not completely disappeared. "The remarkable thing about the American middle class is that we still have one," James K. Galbraith observed in *Mother Jones* in 2010, thinking teachers and civil service workers were the last men and women of the once enormous group standing. Social Security and Medicare represented the final line of defense for the middle class and, predictably enough, these were now in danger of being cut. "The same forces that went after the unions in the 1980s, that relentlessly pushed free-trade agreements while manufacturing jobs evaporated, and that destroyed housing values in the 2000s [are] on the prowl again," Galbraith wrote, not having to say it was certain Republicans who represented these villainous forces.[47] In his book *Pinched,* Don Peck echoed Galbraith's concern that the middle class was all but extinct. Income inequality typically flattened out during a recession, but that did not hold true between 2007 and 2009, when the highest earners pulled further ahead of everyone else. Since then, the wealthy have recovered nicely, while the middle class has struggled mightily to get back to its already tenuous position. Millions of white-collar and blue-collar jobs disappeared in the "Great Recession," perhaps never to return. Pay rose for top earners and wages dropped among the less educated during the recession, another blow to the middle class.[48]

Jacob Hacker, who had shown in *The Great Risk Shift* how income disparity was hurting the middle class most, continued his argument in *Winner-Take-All-Politics.* As the book's subtitle ("How Washington Made the Rich Richer—and Turned Its Back on the Middle Class") suggested, Hacker and co-author Paul Pierson made the case that it was politicians (versus technology or globalization, say) who were most at fault for causing such great economic inequality in the United States. If the government could be credited for facilitating the creation of a great middle class in the 1930s, 1940s, and 1950s through tax and other policies, it was equally responsible for bringing it down in the 1980s, 1990s, and 2000s. (The 1960s and 1970s could be seen as transition decades.) Again, the rich and super-rich surged ahead of everyone else these last few decades, the numbers showed, direct beneficiaries of business-friendly lobbying and legislation. Both parties could be blamed for this transformation of the American political land-scape. "If Republicans have been the perpetrators, Democrats have been the enablers," Peter Steinfels of *Commentary* wrote in his review of the book, each party catering to conservative interests in its own way. The result of this political maneuvering completely contradicted the American mythologies of classlessness and social mobility. Contrary to popular belief, we were now the most eco-nomically unequal nation in the developed world, the authors boldly concluded, our class structure based on income distribution not all that different from a banana republic.[49]

Other countries are also proving that the collapse of the middle class is not a global phenomenon. In the "BRICS" (Brazil, Russia, India, and China), per capita income is booming, meaning the middle classes of those countries are expanding rapidly. Some of this is certainly at the expense of the United States, as American jobs shift overseas because of labor costs. Other countries are now not just gobbling up American manufacturing jobs but ones in many service areas as digital technology further makes geography less relevant. (Even some American government jobs have been outsourced to foreigners.)[50] Education and infra-structure are also improving in these countries, as they go through a boom period not unlike the one America experienced in the postwar years. "America, in my view, is not toast, but I think its middle class will spend some hard time in the toaster oven," quipped Andrew Feinberg of *Kiplinger's Personal Finance*, thinking the quality of life for most of us would decline in the foreseeable future.[51]

If there is any silver lining to the expansion of the middle class in the BRICS for the United States, it is that consumers in these countries have more money to spend, likely increasing the global demand for American-made products.[52] Among "developing nations," in fact, Brazil's retail sector is growing faster than any other country in the world, according to A.T. Kearney's 2012 Global Retail Development Index, with China and India placed third and fifth respectively on the list. A growing middle class in each country, complemented by high consump-tion rates and per capita spending, large urban (and relatively young) populations, and political and financial stability, is a perfect recipe for marketers wishing to expand their presence around the world.[53]

Most important, perhaps, Americans themselves across racial, income, and political lines believe the middle class is shrinking. Two-thirds of those asked in an October 2011 Hill Poll said the middle class was getting smaller (14 percent said it was growing and another 14 percent believed it was staying the same size), most of them blaming greater income inequality for the contraction.[54] Recent Census data confirms Americans' instincts are right. "If a broad and prosperous middle class is the key to a healthy America, the United States is ill," Nigel Holmes wrote in *American History* a couple of months later after looking at five decades of income statistics. The percentage of households in the middle three quintiles of income has shrunk significantly since 1967 while, not surprisingly, the top quintile ($100,000 or more, adjusted for inflation) has ballooned. Other studies indicate that the bottom quintile of earners remain in a state of denial regarding their class status. Forty-one percent of Americans with family incomes of less than $20,000 claimed they were middle class, one recent study reported, the demarcations of class in this country as vague as ever.[55]

Meanwhile, however, downward mobility in America shows no sign of letting up. One-third of Americans raised in the middle class now fall out of the group as adults, a 2011 Pew study called "Downward Mobility from the Middle Class: Waking Up from the American Dream" found.[56] Median household income adjusted for inflation continued to drop in 2011, and more Americans than ever (fifty million) have no health insurance. "The fading fortunes of the middle class are probably the top factor fueling vast dissatisfaction with government and a pervasive sense of national decline," wrote Rick Newman of USNews.com in September of that year, the common feeling that one was falling behind more than imaginary.[57] Some could not help but wonder how the collapse of the American middle class occurred, and if it was permanent. "The puzzle is why so little has been done in the last 40 years to help deal with the subversion of the economic power of the middle class," former secretary of labor Robert Reich wrote that same month, thinking the government could have done a lot more to create "problem solvers and innovators" through all levels of education. A higher minimum wage, different tax structure, and making Medicare available to all Americans were other things the government could and should have done to preserve the middle class, Reich believed. Instead, administrations aligned themselves with Big Business in the name of free markets, ignoring the consequences to average earners. "Reviving the middle class requires that we reverse the nation's decades-long trend toward widening inequality," he stated, thinking it was not too late to level the playing field.[58]

The Defining Issue of Our Time

Rhetorically, at least, politicians continue to be firmly committed to reviving the middle class, although how that can and should be achieved remains highly divisive. In his 2012 State of the Union address, President Obama defined economic fairness as "the defining issue of our time," citing the case of Debbie Bosanek, Warren Buffett's secretary, as a prime example of the country's rigged system. Bosanek paid a higher tax rate than the billionaire, a fact even Buffett publicly acknowledged was absurd.[59] Reversing income inequality through tax reform, offering financial incentives for American manufacturers, and investing in education and transportation would go a long way toward restoring fairness to the system, the president confidently stated, and ultimately build a stronger middle class. Republicans had serious doubts about such a plan, however, seeing the private sector as much more capable of benefitting middle-class (and all other) Americans than any steps the government could take. Economists were themselves divided on the subject, reminding both parties that larger forces at work—globalization, technology, the decline of unions, and the growth of single-parent households, to name just a few—had been squeezing the middle class for decades. Anything resembling the "Great Compression" of the postwar years was unlikely at best, making greater polarization perhaps inevitable.[60]

The run-up to the 2012 presidential election was, as in most campaigns of the past half-century, heavily centered around the interests of the middle class even with both candidates coming from typically elitist backgrounds (academically for Obama and financially for Republican candidate Mitt Romney, despite the latter's two Harvard degrees).[61] After the recent financial crisis and recession, the American middle class could use a lot of help if it is indeed going to be "revived." Between 2007 and 2010, the media household lost almost 40 percent of its wealth, according to the Federal Reserve, with middle-class families taking the biggest hit as usual. As in the past, the poor had less to lose during this particularly bad economic stretch (and benefitted from government stimulus programs), while the rich found ways to keep their heads above water. In fact, the wealthiest 10 percent of Americans gained 2 percent in net worth during the financial crisis (they owned more crash-proof bonds), a clear sign that the nation's playing field was hardly even.[62]

Obama stayed on message throughout the campaign, seeing higher taxes for the wealthy as the best way to pay for improvements in the nation's infrastructure. Romney envisioned drastic spending cuts and lower taxes as the better route to creating a better future for the American middle class, a classic expression of the basic two-party model predicated on what the role of the government should be. The political debate over if and how to resuscitate an ailing middle class was symptomatic of our never-ending difficulty in dealing with matters of class in general. Steps to remedy income inequalities or even acknowledging class distinctions were, for some Republicans, "class warfare," a politically-motivated maneuver that was more divisive than unifying. Part of the problem was that there was still no agreement on who was a middle-class American and who was not. The government still used quintiles to measure the distribution of household income distribution (those in the three middle sections earned between $20,000 and $100,000 in 2009), but even that rough gauge ignored how many people were in the house. A childless couple making $50,000 was quite a bit more "middle class" than a couple with the same income but six children, in other words. Using education as a determining measure of middle-class status was not much better. Which household was more middle class: a one-income ($40,000) family headed by someone who was college-educated, or a two-income family ($60,000) in which neither breadwinner went to college? Race, ethnicity, and gender further complicated the issue, as did geography because of greatly different costs of living, especially in housing.[63]

Francis Fukuyama (who had deservedly received much attention when he announced in 1989 that it was "the end of history" when the Soviet Union was collapsing) recently made the case that the decline of the middle class in the United States and the rest of the world poses a major threat to liberal, free-market democracy. It was, rather than a particular politician's policies, the modern, global economy that was the real danger, today's inequalities of wealth way out of balance. Globalization, abetted by technology, was well on the way to making it impossible for many to achieve middle-class status, a process that had begun in the 1970s but accelerated rapidly with the digitalization of markets.[64] Joe Biden, Obama's point man for the middle class, believes "American innovation" distinguishes us from other countries, a view that had better be correct if the United States stands a chance of competing with the likes of India and China in the decades ahead. "I'm here to tell you the United States is better positioned than any other country in the world to be the world's leading economic power of the 21st Century as it was in the 20th," the vice president said in March 2012, seeing the nation's universities as "idea factories" that would continue to churn out new members of the American middle class.[65]

Given what many college graduates were currently doing or, more accurately, not doing, Biden's optimism did not seem warranted. In fact, the grandchildren of those who survived a great depression and a world war to ultimately prosper were comparing their bleak situation to that of "the greatest generation." In a 2012 Pew survey, more than half of 18- to 24-year-olds reported they were living with their parents or had recently done so, not a surprise given that the unemployment rate for young adults was the highest it has been since the government began keeping track in 1948. Being jobless early in one's career is a terrible path to gaining entry into the middle class, history has shown, another economic boom like "the greatest generation" rode during the postwar years highly unlikely. Temporary jobs, low pay, and perpetual job searching is the norm for today's twentysomethings, a bad omen for the future of the American middle class. Another primary symbol of middle-class status—owning a car—is also becoming more rare among "millennials," the cost of insurance and gas just too high to afford one.[66]

Things are not much better for a good number of that generation's middle-class parents. Amazingly, given the high unemployment rate in this country, many companies are going abroad to recruit skilled factory workers like machinists, tool and die makers, and computer-controlled machine programmers and operators. "These are good quality middle-class jobs that Americans should be training for," said Gardner Carrick of the Manufacturing Institute, dismayed to see "the backbone of manufacturing" going to foreigners. American skilled factory workers are literally a dying breed, and their numbers will get even smaller as more of them retire. This kind of "insourcing" (versus outsourcing, which can be understood because of the economics involved) is making things tougher for the middle class than they need to be, as there is no reason why Americans cannot learn how to qualify for these kinds of jobs.[67]

Even those fully employed and making a solid middle-class income are too often finding themselves in the red. Middle-income consumers are flocking to agencies offering debt-reduction plans, their credit card debt typically almost half of what they earn in a full year. At one such credit counseling firm, Atlanta-based CredAbility, the average client earned $54,000 and owed $24,000, a clear violation of the cardinal rule to not spend more money than one has or can reasonably pay off over time. Interestingly, this segment of the middle class, most of them not just employed but homeowners, found it more difficult to get out of debt than lower-income people. "They have become used to driving new cars and getting the latest cell phone," explained a CredAbility executive, their lifestyle and "status anxiety" responsible for their money troubles. Poorer people understood the concept of having to cut back, in other words, while these average earners (the median income in the United States remains around $50,000) did not. It is hard to have sympathy for this portion of the middle class, needless to say, their predicament (in which debt-reduction agencies negotiate lower interest rates with credit card companies) purely of their own making.[68]

The troubles of the American middle class, most of them beyond the group's control but some not so, has become a theme to which many of us can relate. The theme frequently shows up in our popular culture, not surprisingly, with movies, television shows, and pop music all addressing in multiple ways the tough times that average Americans are experiencing. The revival of *Death of a Salesman* on Broadway in 2012 was a telling sign of the times, I believe, as it is difficult to think of another story that better expresses the tragedy of the middle class, or at least one member of it. *Death of a Salesman* was, for Lee Siegel of the *New York Times*, "the most devastating portrait of punctured middle-class dreams in our national literature," making it entirely understandable how it was again a hit on Broadway more than sixty years after its debut.[69]

Siegel, however, wondered if the play should have been revived at all given, as he put it, "the American middle class—as a social reality and a set of admirable values—has nearly ceased to exist." Much indeed had changed for the middle class and the nation since the show opened in 1949. Tickets now cost $111 to $840, ten times what they cost for the original run ($1.80 to $4.80) after adjusting for inflation. It was unlikely that many members of the audience of the revival were middle class, Siegel pointed out, something probably not true in 1949. The top tax rate in 1949 was a whopping 82 percent while in 2012 it was 28 percent, this too a telling indicator of how things had changed for the better for the rich and not so for the middle class. Even the traditional value of hard work had seriously eroded, Siegel believed, making it unlikely that audiences today would identify with Willy Loman's plight as they had at mid-century. "Even what's left of the middle class disdains a middle-class life," he caustically observed, thinking, "Everyone, rich, poor and in between, wants infinite pleasure and fabulous riches."[70]

Siegel nicely captured one of the key paradoxes of class in America: the nearly universal desire to be recognized as middle class while, at the same time, enjoying a lifestyle that far exceeded one that an average income could afford. Americans appear to be inspired by characters on television and in movies who hold middle-class jobs but somehow are able to live in fabulous apartments or houses, a good example of how we as a people like to have our cake and eat it too. The reality is, of course, much different. "Almost everyone—even affluent professionals and entrepreneurs—wants to identify with the middle class, but increasingly, the genuine middle is a tough place to be," Peter Morici, a University of Maryland economist, wrote for the *Chicago Tribune*. With a contracting economy and to-the-victors-go-the-spoils national ethos, it should not be surprising that it is difficult to even find a true middle class, much less save it.[71] In his *The Servant Economy*, economist Jeff Faux made the (Marxian) case that the nation's elite was purposely squeezing the middle class as a kind of social control. A dubious claim, but there is no doubt at this point that the cultural elite has distanced itself as far away as possible from the middle class and that our society is a deeply divided one.[72] The future of the American middle class is more uncertain than ever, but time remains for us to heed Euripides's wise call that "it is the middle that saves the country."

Notes

1 Bill Wolpin, "A Middle Class at War with Itself," *American City and County*, March 2011, 6.
2 "A Middle Class at War with Itself."
3 Alison Stein Wellner, "The Money in the Middle," *American Demographics*, April 2000, 56–64.
4 Rob Long, "The Upper Middle," *National Review*, November 6, 2000, 24–25.
5 Jon Gertner, "What is Wealth?", *Money*, December 2000, 94; David Brooks, *Bobos in Paradise: The New Upper Class and How They Got There* (New York: Simon & Schuster, 2000).
6 Jack Metzgar, "Muddle in the Middle, or The Class Act in Politics," *The Nation*, October 30, 2000, 25; Ruy Teixeira and Joel Rogers, *America's Forgotten Majority: Why the White Working Class Still Matters* (New York: Basic Books, 2000); Michael Zweig, *The Working Class Majority: America's Best Kept Secret* (Ithaca, NY: Cornell University Press, 2000).
7 Camille Sweeney, "The Middle of the Middle Class," *New York Times Magazine*, June 9, 2002, SM74–81.
8 "The Middle to Upper-Middle Class," *American Demographics*, December 2002–January 2003, 38–39.
9 Lee Walczak and Richard S. Dunham, "Running on Middle-Class Relief," *BusinessWeek*, February 9, 2004, 35–36.
10 Jyoti Thottam, "How Real Is the 'Squeeze'?", *Time*, July 19, 2004, 41.
11 Lauren Gard, "Ordinary People, Extraordinary Gifts," *BusinessWeek*, November 29, 2004, 94.
12 Elizabeth Austin, "Why Homer's My Hero," *The Washington Monthly*, October 2000, 30; Suze Orman, *The Courage to Be Rich: Creating a Life of Material and Spiritual Abundance* (New York: Riverhead, 1999).
13 Robert H. Frank, "Why Living in a Rich Society Makes Us Feel Poor," *New York Times Magazine*, October 15, 2000, SM62.
14 Paul Krugman, "For Richer," *New York Times Magazine*, October 20, 2002, SM62+.
15 Michael Lind, "Are We Still a Middle-Class Nation?" *The Atlantic*, January/February 2004, 120–28.

16 "Are We Still a Middle-Class Nation?"; Elizabeth Warren and Amelia Warren Tyagi, *The Two-Income Trap: Why Middle-Class Mothers and Fathers Are Going Broke* (New York: Basic Books, 2003).

17 Mark Mitchell, "Is the Middle-Class Squeeze for Real?", *Independent School*, Winter 2006, 76–82.

18 Mortimer B. Zuckerman, "Uneasy in the Middle," *U.S. News & World Report*, June 11, 2007, 72.

19 James Poniewozik, "When You Wish Upon TV," *Time*, June 13, 2005, 48–50.

20 Barbara Ehrenreich and Tamara Draut, "Downsized but Not Out," *The Nation*, November 6, 2006, 4–5; Louis Uchitelle, *The Disposable American: Layoffs and Their Consequences* (New York: Knopf, 2006).

21 "The Middle Class Once Happened Here," *The Atlantic*, September 2006, 48.

22 Bill Wolpin, "Upstairs, Downstairs," *American City and County*, August 2006, 6.

23 Clive Crook, "The Phantom Menace," *The Atlantic*, April 2007, 40–41.

24 Peter Wilby, "The Not-So-Good-Any-More-Life," *The New Statesman*, April 21, 2008, 16.

25 "It's the Middle Class, Stupid," *People*, February 26, 2007, 55; Chuck Schumer, *Positively American: Winning Back the Middle-Class Majority One Family at a Time* (Emmaus, PA: Rodale Books, 2007).

26 "Saving the American Dream," *Blueprint Magazine*, July 22, 2006.

27 Mortimer B. Zuckerman, "America's High Anxiety," *U.S. News & World Report*, December 25, 2006, 100.

28 Raymond L. Fischer, "Marginalizing the Middle Class," *USA Today Magazine*, July 2007, 74–75; Lou Dobbs, *War on the Middle Class: How the Government, Big Business, and Special Interest Groups Are Waging War on the American Dream and How to Fight Back* (New York: Viking, 2006).

29 Amity Shlaes, "The Politics of Middle-Class Anxiety," *Commentary*, March 2007, 24; Jacob S. Hacker, *The Great Risk Shift: The Assault on American Jobs, Families, Health Care, and Retirement—And How You Can Fight Back* (New York: Oxford University Press, 2006); Andy Stern, *A Country That Works: Getting America Back on Track* (New York: Free Press, 2006).

30 Brita Belli, "Welcome to Green-Collar America," *E Magazine*, November/December 2007, 27–31.

31 Barbara Ehrenreich, "The Bloated Overclass," *The Progressive*, August 2007, 16.

32 Nick Gillespie, "America's No. 1 Endangered Species," *Reason*, April 2007, 18.

33 Virginia Postrel, "The American Standard of Whining," *Forbes*, September 4, 2006, 118.

34 Brian Kantz, "What 'Crisis' of the Middle Class?", *National Catholic Reporter*, July 1, 2005, 22.

35 Emily Bryson, "Sliding Economy Takes a Toll on Casual Dining," *Advertising Age*, October 15, 2007, 8.

36 Robert J. Samuelson, "The End of Entitlement," *Newsweek*, May 26, 2008, 39.

37 "Congress Squeezing Middle Class," *USA Today (Magazine)*, May 2008, 6–7.

38 Joshua Green, "The Man in the Middle," *The Atlantic*, January/February 2009, 74–79.

39 Kimberly Palmer, "The Fate of the Middle Class," *U.S. News & World Report*, March 2009, 52.

40 Joel Kotkin, "The End of Upward Mobility?", *Newsweek*, January 26, 2009, 64.

41 John Maggs, "Middle Class Still Squeezed," *National Journal*, September 19, 2009, 12.

42 John Maggs, "How Obama Lost (and Found) the Middle Class," *National Journal*, January 30, 2010, 3.

43 Mark Engler, "The Hole in America's Middle," *New Internationalist*, January/February 2011, 52.

44 Robert B. Reich, "The Limping Middle Class," *New York Times*, September 4, 2011, 6.

45 Bill Wolpin, "In the Middle of the American Dream," *American City and County*, March 2010, 6.

46 Ron Klain, "Middle-Class Americans Suffer in Silence, for Now," *Bloomberg News*, September 20, 2011.

47 James K. Galbraith, "Attack on the Middle Class!!," *Mother Jones*, November/December 2010, 26–29.

48 Don Peck, *Pinched: How the Great Recession Has Narrowed Our Futures & What We Can Do About It* (New York: Crown, 2011).

49 Peter Steinfels, "The Great Reversal," *Commentary*, March 11, 2011, 20–22; Jacob S. Hacker and Paul Pierson, *Winner-Take-All-Politics: How Washington Made the Rich Richer—and Turned Its Back on the Middle Class* (New York: Simon & Schuster, 2010).

50 Tim Ferguson, "Those Middle-Class Job Blues," Forbes.com, July 20, 2011, 45.

51 Andrew Feinberg, "Is America Toast?" *Kiplinger's Personal Finance*, July 2011, 41.

52 Gillian Tett, "The Rise of the Middle Class—Just Not Ours," *Atlantic*, July/August 2011, 63.

53 Richard Woodward, "World: Brazil Tops Retail Expansion Table," just-style.com, June 14, 2012.

54 "Hill Poll: Inequality Fears Grow," *The Hill*, October 31, 2011, 1.

55 Nigel Holmes, "Middle-Class Squeeze," *American History*, December 2011, 15.

56 Henry J. Reske, "Pew Study: One-Third of Middle Class Fall in Status," *Newsmax*, September 7, 2011.

57 Rick Newman, "How to Escape the Middle-Class Squeeze," USNews.com, September 13, 2011.

58 "The Limping Middle Class."

59 Linda Feldmann, "In State of the Union Address, Obama Tries Out for Hero of Middle Class," *Christian Science Monitor*, January 25, 2012, 17.

60 Zachary A. Goldfarb, "Middling Prospects," *Washington Post*, January 31, 2012, A11.

61 Paul Begala, "Elitists for President," *Newsweek*, April 23, 2012, 21.

62 Tim Mullany, "Families' Wealth Dives 39% in 3 Years," *USA Today*, June 12, 2012, A1.

63 Bill Steiden, "Middle Classification," *Atlanta Journal-Constitution*, January 29, 2012, A4.

64 David Ignatius, "A Middle Class Imperiled," *Washington Post*, January 5, 2012, A17.

65 James Q. Lynch, "Biden: No One Can Match American Innovation," *The Cedar Rapids Gazette*, March 2, 2012.

66 Jean Hopfensperger, "Changed: The Middle Class Redefined," *Minneapolis Star Tribune*, May 5, 2012, A1.

67 Michael Kling, "CNNMoney: American Manufacturers Importing Workers," *Newsmax*, March 6, 2012.

68 Ann Carrns, "Debt Help for Middle Class," *New York Times*, February 4, 2012, B4.

69 Lee Siegel, "Death of a Salesman's Dreams [Op-Ed]," *New York Times*, May 3, 2012, A31.

70 "Death of a Salesman's Dreams [Op-Ed]."

71 Peter Morici, "Saving the Middle Class," *Chicago Tribune*, January 4, 2012, 21.

72 Jeff Faux, *The Servant Economy: Where America's Elite is Sending the Middle Class* (Hoboken, NJ: Wiley, 2012).

CONCLUSION

It is entirely reasonable, I believe, to make the case that the collapse of the middle class and concurrent breakdown of the American Dream is the biggest story of the nation's history over the last half-century. It is tempting to think that the current crisis of the American middle class is something new and unique, but history suggests otherwise. Since the mid-1960s, in fact, the middle class has been in a kind of crisis mode, although how it has played out has varied significantly based on the prevailing social, economic, and political climate. The state of the middle class can be seen as the country's "sensitive spot," almost all of us worried about the group's relative health and its prognosis for the future. Although we naturally view the ailing of the middle class as an undesirable and dangerous condition, in some ways it has served as a uniting force that has brought us closer as a people. Our nearly universal concern for the fate of the middle class has functioned as one of our very few common denominators, in other words, something that has helped bind us together.

The American middle class can be seen as having to confront a series of cataclysmic events since the group's zenith in the early 1960s. In the mid-sixties and through the remainder of that decade, social and cultural forces tore apart the middle class, leaving the huge group much smaller and weaker. Significant numbers of young people, women, African Americans, white ethnics, and gays effectively abandoned the traditional middle class dominated by the WASP patriarchy, finding greater meaning and purpose in smaller, tighter-knit communities with different, often conflicting philosophies and lifestyles. With a host of sizable and politicized sub-cultures now operating alongside and sometimes competing with the mainstream, the middle class no longer held the power and influence it did a decade earlier. The middle class became the target of critical attacks and was put in a defensive position, its values questioned by groups with alternative perspectives and ways of life. Youth culture's protest of the Vietnam War, women's and gays' fight for equal rights, and the racial and ethnic pride movements can all be seen as causes that chipped away at the "consensus" led by the white, male middle class.

Already reeling from these powerful cultural and social forces, the middle class faced serious economic challenges in the 1970s. A bad recession combined with double-digit inflation threw the postwar economic engine in reverse, inflicting further damage on an already wounded middle class. Having survived that test, the middle class now had to face 1980s "Reaganomics," economic policies that served to push the group into an "upper" or "lower" segment. Cloven in half, the middle class was forced to operate in a much more competitive cultural climate during this decade, with members of the group finding themselves either moving up or down. For the last two decades and change, the middle class has done everything it could to simply survive. The gap in income and wealth between the rich and everybody else that began to spread in the late 1960s became a gulf over this period of time, more bad news for the middle class. Incredible concentrations of wealth among the top 1 percent and 5 percent of the population effectively drove the middle class further back in the nation's economic and social strata, creating what can be considered a small but powerful upper class and a large, weak under class.

Tumbling the numbers clearly reveals the economic decline of the American middle class since the late 1960s. In its "5 Charts on the State of the Middle Class" released in October 2012, the Center for American Progress (a liberal think-tank) showed how the group went backward according to a variety of income-based metrics. The share of the nation's income going to the middle 60 percent of households dropped from 52 percent in 1968 to 46½ percent; 8 percent fewer households today are earning middle-class incomes than in 1970; the typical American family in 1989 had a debt load equal to 58 percent of annual income, while in 2010 debt averaged 154 percent of annual income; median household income has declined over the past decade, this after a two-decade period of no growth. Compounding these reversals has been the double-whammy of what it takes to maintain a middle-class lifestyle; the cost of many things, particularly housing and a college education, has risen precipitously over the years.[1] Median wealth fell a whopping 40 percent between 2007 and 2010, according to a recent report from the Federal Reserve, a direct result of this decrease in money coming in and increase in money going out.[2] The American middle class was "fewer, poorer, and gloomier," claimed a much publicized Pew Research report from August 2012, its numbers showing that the 2000s had been the last of four consecutive decades in which the group lost ground.[3]

Many conservatives, it need be said, pooh-pooh all this depressing number crunching, seeing things quite differently. Scott Winship of the Brookings Institution, for example, has argued that the principal reason that the middle class has "shrank" is that Americans have grown richer over time, meaning the price of admission to belong to the group has risen (a good thing).[4] It is also important to keep in mind that by global standards, today's America's middle class is very wealthy. To be part of the richest 1 percent on a global scale requires an annual income of just $34,000, according to World Bank economist Branko Milanovic, meaning middle-class Americans actually belong to the world's upper-upper class.[5]

The story of the black middle class is perhaps a happier one but has a much different and more complicated set of cultural dynamics. While the white middle class was running its gauntlet of challenges, many African Americans were making significant economic and social progress. The blossoming of the black middle class can be seen as coming a generation later than that of the white middle class as some of the country's institutional racism began to erode. However, the intersection of class and race—America's two most highly charged subjects—emerged as a primary site of conflict as the black middle class "moved up" between the 1960s and 1980s. Because the rise of the black middle class coincided with the civil rights movement, a host of issues related to racial identity became central in the African American community. Did blacks have a separate class system or did they belong to the country's (white-dominated) one? Were blacks who achieved middle-class status morally obligated to help "less fortunate" African Americans and ethically responsible to play a visible role in the struggle for equal rights? Middle-class blacks were roundly criticized for adopting lifestyles that mimicked those of their white counterparts, and the mainstream media condemned for focusing on African Americans who had "made it." Members of the black middle class may be enjoying the fruits of their achievements, more militant African Americans loudly expressed, but they would never realize true power or be accepted by the white community. Indeed, many of those within the black middle class felt ambiguous about their new status, their "twoness" magnified as they straddled different worlds defined by race. Despite the progress made, African Americans today still trail whites (and Hispanics) in achieving middle-class status, a 2012 Brookings Institution report showed, our national field hardly level when it comes to race.[6]

In addition to adding to our understanding of the relationship between race and class, the cultural history of the American middle class over the last half-century helps put the current crisis of the group in much needed perspective. Despite all the gnashing of teeth that the middle class is on the brink of extinction, we know that is not likely true as we have heard that same claim many times before. The middle class has survived other crises, so it is reasonable to conclude that it will survive this one and those to come. Likewise, it would be silly to think the American Dream is going to completely disappear, it too an enduring dimension of our national identity. Fears that both the middle class and the American Dream are in great jeopardy seem to be built into our cultural DNA, perhaps reflecting our repressed suspicions that we are not as democratic a nation as we pretend to be. Vast inequalities in income and wealth and "downward mobility" threaten our idea of what it means to be an American, explaining why calls to address and correct these "anomalies" have been a fixture these last fifty years. Income divide and class polarity have risen exponentially in recent years but little action has been taken to reverse the trend, leaving what is left of the middle class in a precarious, vulnerable position today. Some look back to the postwar era as the "normal" state of affairs, and wonder why the middle class cannot again enjoy the prosperity it did during those years.

The truth, however, is that the flourishing of the middle class during the postwar years was the anomaly. A unique set of forces came together in the 1950s to create a brief, shining moment favoring average earners, these forces very unlikely to ever coalesce again. Unfortunately, we tend to look at the postwar consensus grounded in "classlessness" as the rule rather than the exception, the yardstick by which to measure contemporary affairs. This is a no-win situation, and not very helpful to solve the very real problems of the middle class. Rather than lament about what we have lost, we need to agree what we have to gain by helping the middle class recover much of what it has lost over the last half-century. Some of the greatest minds in history have observed how important a middle class is to any society, inspiration that should serve as a guiding principle for our elected officials. Both political leaders and those in Big Business have a vested interest in tilting the system toward the wealthy, however, something that needs to be corrected if we are serious about putting the middle class in the "middle" once again.

Our lack of ability to deal with (or even acknowledge) matters of class compounds the problem. Our denial of class in America explains why upward of 90 percent of us claim to be middle class despite clear evidence to the contrary. It also explains why we cannot even adequately define "middle class" despite many attempts to do so. Americans of virtually all income groups continue to define themselves as middle class in part because there is still no official meaning to the term (unlike "poor," of which the U.S. Department of Health and Human Services has at least a crude formula).[7] Non-income-based markers of middle-class status (e.g., having a steady job, putting away money for retirement, owning a home, or sending one's kids to college) are useful but subjective measures that further blur the boundaries of class. There will likely always be a tension associated with the middle class and class in general here in the United States, it is safe to say, as major social and economic disparities violate our creed of egalitarianism. (Race remains problematic in this country, of course, but at least that issue is grounded in our inherent pluralism.) The pervasive belief that we are a "middle-class society," all of us falling somewhere within the same group, is simply false. In short, our current understanding of and approach to class is not a good foundation for social change, making attempts to do more for the middle class than praise the group in political speeches all the more challenging.

Yet there is hope for those wishing for a larger, more financially secure American middle class. Economic policies can be changed, after all, and politicians who are serious about representing the middle class elected. The title of James Carville and Stan Greenberg's 2012 book—*It's the Middle Class, Stupid!*—says it all, yet both Democrats and Republicans have not done nearly enough to protect a group that can be said to have become an endangered species.[8] "Republicans went crazy, Democrats became useless, and the middle class got shafted," posited Mike Lofgren in his *The Party is Over* of the same year, believing neither party has stood up for those with average incomes.[9] The middle class has been woefully passive for far too long, and needs to be much more proactive about charting its own destiny rather than waiting for change to happen. A "Middle Class Party" is bubbling up in Connecticut, in fact, such a thing is precisely what is needed to make the middle class more than a talking point for those running for office. "The Middle Class Party will represent middle class Americans on taxes, jobs, foreign trade and aid, military spending, social security, Medicare, social programs, governmental budgets, civil rights, etc.," explains the originator of the idea, the Berlin, Connecticut Property Owners Association.[10]

While certainly grassroots, efforts like this one can perhaps have the makings of something very big. (A "Middle Class Party" actually flourished briefly in the Netherlands in the early 20th century.) Despite all the rhetoric, neither Democrats nor Republicans are truly committed to the interests of the middle class, making the formation of such a party one possible way progress can be made. Similarly, an "American Dream Movement" is in the works. A number of activist organizations, including "Rebuild the Dream," are part of this movement "fighting back against the attack on ordinary Americans."[11] With the possible exception of the much broader counterculture of the late 1960s, nothing like this kind of populist movement has been attempted, reason enough to think the tide may be turning for the American middle class. By borrowing some of the philosophy and methods of the Tea Party and Occupy Wall Street (OWS) movement, a "Middle Class Party" or "American Dream Movement" can perhaps reverse the one-way direction of the American middle class over the last half-century.

Indeed, the rise of the Tea Party and OWS movement is cause to be bullish on the American middle class despite the mountains of historical evidence suggesting otherwise. Unions, for example, have recently embraced some of the ideology and language of OWS, finding the movement's commitment to direct action, democratic decision-making, and rank-and-file militancy helpful to their cause.[12] The protests in Wisconsin prove that the middle class can be mobilized toward OWS-style campaigns when its interests are at stake, an effort that can be expanded on a national scale. Rather than a left wing or right wing group, a centrist or, better yet, party-free movement offers the greatest chance for the American middle class to reverse the trend of the last half-century. Aligning somehow with the growing middle classes in the BRICS would also make a lot of sense for Americans as the world becomes increasingly flat. "The alternative narrative is out there, waiting to be born," wrote Francis Fukuyama in his 2012 essay "The Future of History: Can Liberal Democracy Survive the Decline of the Middle Class?," believing the world will be a significantly better place for a robust middle class.[13]

Notes

1 John Stodder, "Middle Class: This Campaign Is for You," *Long Island Business News*, October 16, 2012.
2 Paul Begala, "Middle Class, R.I.P.," *Newsweek*, June 25, 2012, 20.
3 "The Lost Decade of the Middle Class," pewresearch.org, August 22, 2012.
4 Scott Winship, "What 'Lost Decade'?: The Pew Research Council Invents a Middle-Class Decline," *National Review*, October 1, 2012, 38.
5 Charles Kenny, "We're All the 1%," *Foreign Policy*, March–April 2012, 24.
6 Rosa Ramirez, "Why Do Blacks Trail in Benchmarks Leading to Middle Class?," Nationaljournal.com, September 21, 2012.
7 Steve Thorngate, "Defining the Middle," *Christian Century*, October 31, 2012.
8 James Carville and Stan Greenberg, *It's the Middle Class, Stupid!* (New York: Blue Rider Press, 2012).
9 Mike Lofgren, *The Party is Over: How Republicans Went Crazy, Democrats Became Useless, and the Middle Class Got Shafted* (New York: Viking, 2012).
10 "The Middle Class Party of America is Forming in Connecticut," www.theyoungturks.com, May 4, 2011.
11 www.rebuildthedream.com.
12 Steve Early, "A Lesson for Labor from Occupy Wall Stree4," *Synthesis/Regeneration*, Spring 2012, 31.
13 Francis Fukuyama, "The Future of History: Can Liberal Democracy Survive the Decline of the Middle Class?," *Foreign Affairs*, January–February 2012, 53–61.

SELECTED BIBLIOGRAPHY

Adams, James Truslow. *The Epic of America*. New York: Little, Brown, and Company, 1931.

Baltzell, E. Digby. *Philadelphia Gentlemen: The Making of a National Upper Class*. New York: Free Press, 1958.

Baritz, Loren. *The Good Life: The Meaning of Success for the American Middle Class*. New York: Alfred A. Knopf, 1989.

Bartlett, Donald and James Steele. *America: What Went Wrong?* Kansas City, MO: Andrews McMeel, 1992.

———. *America: Who Really Pays the Taxes?* New York: Simon & Schuster, 1994.

Beckert, Sven and Julia B. Rosenbaum. *The American Bourgeoisie: Distinction and Identity in the Nineteenth Century*. New York: Palgrave Macmillan, 2010.

Bendix, Reinhard and Seymour Martin Lipset. *Class, Status, and Power: A Reader in Social Stratification*. New York: Free Press, 1953.

Billingsley, Andrew. *Black Families in White America*. New York: Prentice-Hall, 1968.

Black, Gordon S. and Benjamin D. Black. *The Politics of American Discontent: How a New Party Can Make Democracy Work Again*. Hoboken, NJ: Wiley, 1994.

Bledstein, Burton J. and Robert D. Johnston, eds. *The Middling Sorts: Explorations in the History of the American Middle Class*. New York: Routledge, 2001.

Blumin, Stuart M. *The Emergence of the Middle Class: Social Experience in the American City, 1760–1900*. New York: Cambridge University Press, 1989.

Brooks, David. *Bobos in Paradise: The New Upper Class and How They Got There*. New York: Simon & Schuster, 2000.

Bruce-Briggs, B., ed. *The New Class?* New Brunswick, NJ: Transaction Books, 1979.

Carville, James and Stan Greenberg. *It's the Middle Class, Stupid!*. New York: Blue Rider Press, 2012.

Centers, Richard. *The Psychology of Social Classes*. Princeton, NJ: Princeton University Press, 1949.

Coles, Robert. *The Middle Americans: Proud and Uncertain*. New York: Little, Brown, 1971.

Davis, Allison, Burleigh B. Gardner, and Mary R. Gardner. *Deep South: A Social Anthropological Study of Caste and Class*. Chicago: University of Chicago Press, 1941.

Dobbs, Lou. *War on the Middle Class: How the Government, Big Business, and Special Interest Groups Are Waging War on the American Dream and How to Fight Back*. New York: Viking, 2006.

Dollard, John. *Caste and Class in a Southern Town*. New Haven, CT: Yale University Press, 1937.

Drake, St. Clair and Horace R. Cayton. *Black Metropolis: A Study of Negro Life in a Northern City*. New York: Harcourt, Brace and Company, 1945.

Dubois, W.E.B. *The Philadelphia Negro: A Social Study*. New York: Schocken Books, 1899.

Ehrenreich, Barbara. *Fear of Falling: The Inner Life of the Middle Class*. New York: Pantheon Books, 1989.

Faux, Jeff. *The Servant Economy: Where America's Elite is Sending the Middle Class*. Hoboken, NJ: Wiley, 2012.

Frazier, E. Franklin. *Negro Youth at the Crossways: Their Personality Development in the Middle States*. Washington, DC: American Council on Education, 1940.

——. *Black Bourgeoisie: The Rise of a New Middle Class in the United States*. Glencoe, IL: Free Press, 1957.

Galbraith, John Kenneth. *The Affluent Society*. Boston: Houghton Mifflin, 1958.

Gans, Herbert J. *The Levittowners: How People Live and Work in Suburbia*. New York: Pantheon, 1967.

——. *Middle American Individualism: The Future of Liberal Democracy*. New York: Free Press, 1988.

Grier, Dr. William and Dr. Price Cobbs. *Black Rage*. New York: Basic Books, 1968.

Hacker, Andrew. *Politics and the Corporation*. New York: Fund for the Republic, 1958.

Hacker, Jacob S. *The Great Risk Shift: The Assault on American Jobs, Families, Health Care, and Retirement—And How You Can Fight Back*. New York: Oxford University Press, 2006.

Hacker, Andrew and Paul Pierson. *Winner-Take-All-Politics: How Washington Made the Rich Richer—and Turned Its Back on the Middle Class*. New York: Simon & Schuster, 2010.

Harrington, Michael. *Toward a Democratic Left: A Radical Program for a New Majority*. New York: Macmillan, 1968.

Johnston, Robert D. *The Radical Middle Class: Populist Democracy and the Question of Capitalism in Progressive Era Portland, Oregon*. Princeton, NJ: Princeton University Press, 2003.

Jones, Landon. *Great Expectations: America and the Baby Boom Generation*. New York: Coward McCann, 1980.

Katznelson, Ira. *When Affirmative Action Was White: An Untold History of Racial Inequality in Twentieth-Century America*. New York: W.W. Norton, 2005.

Kronenberger, Louis. *Company Manners: A Cultural Inquiry Into American Life*. New York: Bobbs-Merrill, 1954.

Kruse, Kevin M. *White Flight: Atlanta and the Making of Modern Conservatism*. Princeton, NJ: Princeton University Press, 2005.

Landry, Bart. *The New Black Middle Class*. Berkeley: University of California Press, 1987.

Levy, Frank. *Dollars and Dreams: Changing American Income Distribution*. New York: W.W. Norton, 1988.

Lipset, Seymour Martin. *Political Man: The Social Bases of Politics*. New York: Doubleday and Company, 1960.

Lofgren, Mike. *The Party is Over: How Republicans Went Crazy, Democrats Became Useless, and the Middle Class Got Shafted*. New York: Viking, 2012.

Lynd, Robert S. and Helen Merrell Lynd. *Middletown: A Study in Contemporary American Culture*. New York: Harcourt, Brace and Company, 1929.

Lynes, Russell. *The Taste-Makers*. New York: Harper, 1954.

Marquand, John P. *Point of No Return*. Boston: Little Brown, 1949.

Merton, Robert K. *Social Theory and Social Structure*. New York: Free Press, 1949.

Miller, Arthur. *Death of a Salesman*. New York: Viking Press, 1949.

Mills, C. Wright. *The New Men of Power*. New York: Harcourt, Brace and Co., 1948.

——. *White Collar: The American Middle Classes*. New York: Oxford University Press, 1951.

Moskowitz, Marina. *Standard of Living: The Measure of the Middle Class in Modern America*. Baltimore, MD: The Johns Hopkins University Press, 2004.

Murray, Charles. *Coming Apart: The State of White America, 1960–2010.* New York: Crown Forum, 2012.

Myrdal, Gunnar. *An American Dilemma: The Negro Problem and Modern Democracy.* New York: Harper & Brothers, 1944.

Newman, Katherine S. *Falling from Grace: The Experience of Downward Mobility in the American Middle Class.* New York: Free Press, 1988.

Ofari, Earl. *Myth of Black Capitalism.* New York: Monthly Review Press, 1970.

Orman, Suze. *The Courage to Be Rich: Creating a Life of Material and Spiritual Abundance.* New York: Riverhead, 1999.

Packard, Vance. *The Status Seekers: An Exploration of Class Behavior That Affects You, Your Community, Your Future.* New York: David McKay, 1959.

Papadimitriou, Dimitri B. and Edward N. Wolff, eds. *Poverty and Prosperity in the USA in the Late Twentieth Century.* New York: Palgrave Macmillan, 1993.

Parker, Richard. *The Myth of the Middle Class.* New York: Harper Collins, 1972.

Peale, Norman Vincent. *The Art of Living.* New York: Abingdon Press, 1937.

——. *A Guide to Confident Living.* New York: Prentice-Hall, 1948.

——. *The Power of Positive Thinking.* New York: Fawcett Crest, 1952.

Peck, Don. *Pinched: How the Great Recession Has Narrowed Our Futures & What We Can Do About It.* New York: Crown, 2011.

Phillips, Kevin. *The Politics of Rich and Poor: Wealth and the American Electorate in the Reagan Aftermath.* New York: Random House, 1990.

——. *Boiling Point: Democrats, Republicans, and the Decline of Middle-Class Prosperity.* New York: Random House, 1993.

Reissman, Leonard. *Class in American Society.* Glencoe, IL: Free Press, 1959.

Riesman, David. *The Lonely Crowd.* New Haven, CT: Yale University Press, 1950.

Rose, Stephen J. *The American Profile Poster.* New York: Pantheon, 1986.

Ryan, Mary P. *Cradle of the Middle Class: The Family in Oneida County, New York, 1790–1865.* New York: Cambridge University Press, 1983.

Sachs, Jeffrey D. *The Price of Civilization: Reawakening American Virtue and Prosperity.* New York: Random House, 2011.

Samuel, Lawrence R. *The American Dream: A Cultural History.* Syracuse, NY: Syracuse University Press, 2012.

Scammon, Richard M. and Ben Wattenberg. *The Real Majority: An Extraordinary Examination of the American Electorate.* New York: Coward-McCann, 1970.

Schor, Julia B. *The Overspent American: Upscaling, Downshifting, and the New Consumer.* New York: Basic Books, 1998.

Schumer, Chuck. *Positively American: Winning Back the Middle-Class Majority One Family at a Time.* Emmaus, PA: Rodale Books, 2007.

Sennett, Richard and Jonathan Cobb. *Hidden Injuries of Class.* New York: Knopf, 1972.

Sorokin, Pitirim. *Social Mobility.* New York: Harper & Brothers, 1927.

Stern, Andy. *A Country That Works: Getting America Back on Track.* New York: Free Press, 2006.

Strobel, Frederick R. *Upward Dreams, Downward Mobility: The Economic Decline of the American Middle Class.* Savage, MD: Rowman & Littlefield, 1993.

Sugrue, Thomas. *The Origins of the Urban Crisis: Race and Inequality in Postwar Detroit.* Princeton, NJ: Princeton University Press, 1996.

Sullivan, Teresa, Elizabeth Warren, and Jay Lawrence. *The Fragile Middle Class: Americans in Debt.* New Haven, CT: Yale University Press, 2000.

Teixeira, Ruy and Joel Rogers. *America's Forgotten Majority: Why the White Working Class Still Matters.* New York: Basic Books, 2000.

Thurow, Lester C. *Zero-Sum Solution: Building a World-Class American Economy.* New York: Simon & Schuster, 1985.

Uchitelle, Louis. *The Disposable American: Layoffs and Their Consequences.* New York: Knopf, 2006.

Walkowitz, Daniel J. *Social Workers and the Politics of Middle-Class Identity*. Chapel Hill: University of North Carolina Press, 1999.

Warner, W. Lloyd and Paul S. Lunt. *The Social Life of a Modern Community*. New Haven, CT: Yale University Press (Yankee City Series), 1941.

Warner, W. Lloyd, Marchia Meeker, and Kenneth Eells. *Social Class in America: A Manual of Procedure for the Measurement of Social Status*. Chicago: Science Research Associates, 1949.

Warren, Elizabeth and Amelia Warren Tyagi. *The Two-Income Trap: Why Middle-Class Mothers and Fathers Are Going Broke*. New York: Basic Books, 2003.

Wattenberg, Ben. *The Real America: A Surprising Examination of the State of the Union*. New York: Doubleday, 1974.

——. *In Search of the Real America: A Challenge to the Chaos of Failure and Guilt*. New York: G.P. Putnam, 1978.

Weems Jr., Robert E. *Desegregating the Dollar: African American Consumerism in the Twentieth Century*. New York: NYU Press, 1998.

Whyte, William H. *The Organization Man*. New York: Simon & Schuster, 1956.

Withers, Carl (West, James, pseudonym). *Plainville, USA*. New York: Columbia University Press, 1945.

Wolfe, Alan. *One Nation After All: What Middle-Class Americans Think About God, Country, Family, Racism, Welfare, Immigration, Homosexuality, Work, The Right, The Left, and Each Other*. New York: Viking Adult, 1998.

Zweig, Michael. *The Working Class Majority: America's Best Kept Secret*. Ithaca, NY: Cornell University Press, 2000.

INDEX

8/19/14

3/20/19
6 ✓
2/19/20

8/15/14